Martialling Peace

Series Editors: Victoria M. Basham and Sarah Bulmer

The Critical Military Studies series welcomes original thinking on the ways in which military power works within different societies and geopolitical arenas

Militaries are central to the production and dissemination of force globally but the enduring legacies of military intervention are increasingly apparent at the societal and personal bodily levels as well, demonstrating that violence and war-making function on multiple scales. At the same time, the notion that violence is as an appropriate response to wider social and political problems transcends militaries: from private security, to seemingly 'non-military' settings such as fitness training and schooling, the legitimisation and normalisation of authoritarianism and military power occurs in various sites. This series seeks original, high-quality manuscripts and edited volumes that engage with such questions of how militaries, militarism and militarisation assemble and disassemble worlds touched and shaped by violence in these multiple ways. It will showcase innovative and interdisciplinary work that engages critically with the operation and effects of military power and provokes original questions for researchers and students alike.

Available Titles:

Resisting Militarism: Direct Action and the Politics of Subversion
Chris Rossdale

Making War on Bodies: Militarisation, Aesthetics and Embodiment in International Politics
Catherine Baker

Disordered Violence: How Gender, Race and Heteronormativity Structure Terrorism
Caron Gentry

Sex and the Nazi Soldier: Violent, Commercial and Consensual Contacts during the War in the Soviet Union, 1941–1945
Regina Mühlhäuser (translated by Jessica Spengler)

The Military-Peace Complex: Gender and Materiality in Afghanistan
Hannah Partis-Jennings

Politics of Impunity: Torture, The Armed Forces and the Failure of Transitional Justice in Brazil
Henrique Tavares Furtado

Conscientious Objection in Turkey: A Socio-legal Analysis of the Right to Refuse Military Service
Demet Çaltekin

Poetic Prosthetics: Trauma and Language in Contemporary Veteran Writing
Ron Ben-Tovim

The Gendered and Colonial Lives of Gurkhas in Private Security: From Military to Market
Amanda Chisholm

Martialling Peace: How the Peacekeeper Myth Legitimises Warfare
Nicole Wegner

Forthcoming:

Beyond the Wire: The Cultural Politics of Veteran Narratives
Nick Caddick

War and Militarisation: The British, Canadian abd Dutch Invasion of Southern Afghanistan
Paul Dixon

Inhabiting No-Man's-Land: Army Wives, Gender and Militarisation
Alexandra Hyde

Mobilising China's One-Child Generation: Education, Nationalism and Youth Militarisation in the PRC
Orna Naftali

Martialling Peace

How the Peacekeeping Myth Legitimises Warfare

NICOLE WEGNER

EDINBURGH
University Press

Edinburgh University Press is one of the leading university presses in the UK. We publish academic books and journals in our selected subject areas across the humanities and social sciences, combining cutting-edge scholarship with high editorial and production values to produce academic works of lasting importance. For more information visit our website: edinburghuniversitypress.com

Edinburgh University Press Ltd
13 Infirmary Street, Edinburgh, EH1 1LT

First published in hardback by Edinburgh University Press 2023

Typeset in 10.5/13 ITC Giovanni Std by
IDSUK (DataConnection) Ltd
A CIP record for this book is available from the British Library

ISBN 978-1-4744-9283-6 (hardback)
ISBN 978-1-4744-9284-3 (paperback)
ISBN 978-1-4744-9285-0 (webready PDF)
ISBN 978-1-4744-9286-7 (epub)

CONTENTS

DEDICATION AND ACKNOWLEDGEMENTS

This book is dedicated to the critical scholars and feminist 'giants' who have come before me and whose work makes mine possible. For some of these scholars, I am deeply grateful to call you my colleagues and friends.

The book was composed during a postdoctoral fellowship at the University of Sydney. I want to thank my partner, Matt, who agreed to uproot our life to move across the world for my fellowship, and who has believed in this project, these ideas, and my potential, long before the research had even taken shape. I love you. I am also thankful for many colleagues in the Department of Government and International Relations who offered advice and support throughout the process, in the form of feedback at colloquium presentations and regular check-in conversations (in particular, Susan Park and Sarah Phillips). I am so appreciative to have met and worked with Megan MacKenzie, who was a fervent supporter from the start, helped the book find the right 'home' with Edinburgh University Press (EUP), provided feedback through the drafting, and modelled the kind of academic I strive to be. She's the absolute best. I have benefited immensely from the mentorship and friendship of Laura Shepherd, whose 'white board planning sessions' helped the book to take shape, and to my dear friend Cait Hamilton who listened to me complain endlessly about the direction and argumentations I just couldn't figure out. These ideas also benefited from thoughtful feedback and cheerleading from Liane Hartnett and Roxani Krystalli. This book is the product of a beautiful and generous network of feminist friends; their emotional and material care made the writing possible and taught me much about what peace can be. I wish to thank the series editors, Victoria Basham and Sarah Bulmer, and the supportive editorial team at EUP who compassionately helped the book's development during a global pandemic. All content errors and oversights remain, of course, my own.

Finally, as the book will delve into, this work was completed during my years on various Indigenous territories (lands of the Erie, Neutral, Huron-Wendat, Haundenosaunee, Mississaugas, Nehiyawak, Nahkawininwak, Nakota, Dakota, Lakota, Denesuline, and Gadigal nations) and is possible because of the extraordinary privileges – the 'peace' – I was afforded as a settler on these lands. This book in indebted to those relations and seeks to address their asymmetries.

Introduction
Martialling Peace: How the Peacekeeping Myth Legitimises Warfare

This is a not a book about peacekeeping practices. This is a book about storytelling, fantasies, and the ways that people connect emotionally to myths about peacekeeping. This book considers the mythologised images, stories, and tropes about peacekeeping that have been used to justify military deployments. It examines the politics of military force deployed in the name of peace.

Peacekeeping as an international practice is imbued with a great deal of moral legitimacy. This perceived legitimacy stems from the belief that peacekeeping is how we might use militaries in a helpful, benign, and productive way. For 'middle power' countries with smaller military capacity, peacekeeping has been positioned as a practical, useful and niche mechanism to create change in international politics. Internationally, there is a dominant sense that peacekeeping is a public 'good' used to create peace and stability in the face of global violence. The peacekeeper – impartial, disciplined and restrained in their lethal capacity – is a powerful trope. The dominant association of peacekeeping with neutrality, consent, and non-violence broadly encompasses what I refer to as the peacekeeping myth. The myth is intentionally one-dimensional and operates to depoliticise peacekeeping as practice. It prevents us from asking critical questions about military violence as the peacekeeping myth presumes lethal military force is required to create peace. In short, then, this book details how the peacekeeping myth, as a discursive process, (re)creates a narrow vision of peace, one that is heavily martialised.

Peacekeeping mythology contains the assumption the military is required to secure the semblances of peace that exist across space and time. This myth obscures our ability to think critically about using military force. The fantasy of the neutral, benign and helpful peacekeeper is deeply implicit in the reproduction of ideological militarism, and in turn, the legitimisation of warfare and the deployment of lethal force by international militaries. Following Enloe (2000), I see peacekeeping mythology as reproductive of cultural and social processes where society imagines military needs and militaristic presumptions to be valuable and normal. The peacekeeping myth reproduces militarism.

Militarism, described as 'the social and inter-national relations of the preparation for, and conduct of, organised political violence' (Stavrianakis and Selby 2012: 3), is an ideological framework that demonstrates the relationship between coercive and violent state practices and social relations that uphold and legitimise these practices. I use militarism as an analytical scaffold throughout this book, following Chris Rossdale's framing of militarism that understands how as researchers we must 'situate violent acts within a social context, recognize the co-constitution of war and society, and draw an account of racism, patriarchy, capitalism and imperialism' (Rossdale 2019b: 4). Militarism is a 'social system of values and practices which promote and underpin the use of military approaches to a vast range of situations' (Rossdale 2019b: 67), including the peculiarity I tackle in this book, which is the deployment of military force to ensure some form of 'peace'. Militarism, therefore, is not only a driving force for the perpetuation of war, but militarist logics influence many of the practices, assumptions and logics associated with global peace and peacekeeping.

Militarism might popularly be imagined as brash or overt shows of military power or ability, exemplified by US 'military appreciation half-time shows' with ultra-masculine warriors and state-of-the art equipment or Russian military parade spectacles of machine-gun toting soldiers singing the national anthem. Yet critical scholarship has demonstrated that militarism is much more nebulous than overt celebration of military power: the promotion and preparation for war is not an isolated top-down state process, but is deeply entwined with everyday militarisms, or common-sense beliefs and everyday practices that obscure the politics of organising, funding and deploying armed forces (Bernazzoli and Flint 2009; Basham 2016, 2018; Decker et al. 2016; Dyvik and Greenwood 2016; Gray 2016; Kershner and Harding 2019; Beier and Tabak 2020; Partis-Jennings 2020; Welland 2021; Wegner 2021b). As Cohn and Ruddick (2004: 406) explain,

> The practice of war entails far more than the killing and destroying of armed combat itself. It requires . . . creating a culture in which wars are seen as morally legitimate, even alluring; and shaping and fostering the masculinities and femininities which undergird acquiescence to war.

The celebration of peacekeeping as a legitimate deployment of military force is expressed through the unproblematised acceptance of militarism. Diverting national funding to peace operations, exalting the deaths of soldiers killed while trying to 'secure peace', celebrating peacekeeping history in self-congratulatory nationalism, or justifying the asymmetrical use of militarised coercion against 'disorderly' unarmed civilians are all instances of martial violence legitimised or obscured through peacekeeping's militarist logics.

Peacekeeping has been presented as the 'softer', more humanitarian-focused use of militaries in managing global conflict (Duncanson 2013). The mythology of peacekeeping covertly sanctions ideological militarism and, in turn, helps to perpetuate armed violence. The valorisation of peacekeeping as a desirable function for militaries reinscribes the belief that the military is an essential institution for states to create change in global politics. Peacekeeping scholarship and practice assume the inevitability of violence. 'Softer' solutions to global conflict – from policing to international peacekeeping – reproduce a demand for inter/national military funding, training and deployment. In the case of Canada to be explored in chapters to follow, militarism is not simply about glorifying war, but involves the specific national projects and rhetoric whereby military (peacekeeping) history, activities and objectives are *celebrated* forms of state achievements and international power and authority.

The aim of this book is to demonstrate how peacekeeping mythology, promoted through gendered, racialised and colonialist nationalist discourses, perpetuates militarist ideology that legitimises militarised violence. It will do so by showing how popular conceptions of 'peace' are heavily martialised and how *peace has become martialled* to justify the use of coercive force by the Canadian military in interventions overseas and at home. The mythologisation of peacekeeping (and its corresponding desires for martial peace) matter for anyone concerned with understanding how war systems and their attendant forms of violence are maintained and reproduced in contemporary politics.

Methods

This project has relied on discourse analysis as the mechanism for studying this subject. The term 'discourse' is an analytical category that describes a multitude of meaning-making resources (Fairclough et al. 2011). Discourses operate as systems of signification: 'things do not mean (the material world does not convey meaning); rather, people construct the meaning of things, using sign systems (predominantly, but not exclusively linguistic)' (Milliken 1999: 229). For Foucault, discourse can be understood as 'practices that systemically form the objects of which they speak' (1972: 49). Therefore, discourses do not exist out in the world; rather they are 'structures that are actualized in their regular use by people in discursively ordered relationships' (Shapiro 1989: 11). Following Shepherd (2006), discourses as systems of meaning-making encompass narratives, texts and images that 'fix' meaning, however temporarily, and enable us to make sense of the world. Analysing discourse requires an analysis of narratives or stories that comprise the larger system of discourse that sustains and renders plausible certain perspectives, while excluding other perspectives. The mythologisation of peacekeeping, therefore, is a discursive process that helps to make sense of military mandate or identity, but one that is embedded in a broader discourse about the *naturalness* or necessity of militarised political violence globally.

Discourse analysis is a tool for examining social practices and political orders that are generally accepted as 'natural'. These practices are commonly perceived as truths, or common sense. Discourse analysis uses a variety of techniques to destabilise these 'truths', to show the socially constructed foundations and practices that sustain them as common sense. Discourse analysis is useful for studying the assumptions that are present in mythologies by exploring the broader discourse through which these narratives make sense. It is not the goal to expose a grand truth that has been obscured, but rather to understand that there are a multitude of competing narratives, ideas and perspectives present in all discourse, and that only certain perspectives become dominant and (re)produced. The objective of discourse analysis 'is not to establish the "right story" but to render ambiguous predominant interpretations of state practices and demonstrate the inherently political nature of official discourses' (Milliken 1999: 243). It therefore is not the intention to deconstruct or (un)package narratives to reveal previously masked truths, but rather to show the contingency of claims made and to reveal that all discourse is (re)created in a highly political fashion. This is applied specifically to discourses about peace, peacekeeping and order.

Case Study and Empirical Materials

The entrenched notion of Canada as a 'peacekeeper par excellence' (Jockel 1994) and the stubborn association of Canadian foreign policy with peacekeeping makes Canada a ripe case study for examining the reproduction of the peacekeeping myth. While there is ample literature that seeks to dismantle the peacekeeper myth due to its assumed falsities, this book explores Canada as a case study of how mythologies intersect with the politics of militarism globally. It will also examine the particular puzzle of why the peacekeeper mythology resolutely endured throughout the combat-dominant period of the war in Afghanistan and alongside the asymmetrical use of martial force to dispel Indigenous land protests in Canada over many decades.

In the analysis to follow, I draw upon a wide array of empirical data, including texts from government officials, the Canadian Forces, and a large sample of media publications (digital and print). For government sources, I used publicly available information, specifically media briefings and speeches accessed through the Department of National Defence (DND) webpage, the Prime Minister's Office, Foreign Affairs and International Trade. I also relied upon text from the Government of Canada's Canada in Afghanistan webpage (now archived). I extensively used the April 2006 House of Commons proceedings, as there was lengthy debate about the role of the Canadian Forces in Afghanistan during this session. The Parliament of Canada's Independent Panel on Canada's Future Role in Afghanistan's final report (2008), *Canadian Forces in Afghanistan: Report of the Standing Committee on National Defence* (Standing Committee on National Defence 2007), and the Government of Canada's Canada's *Engagement in Afghanistan* quarterly reports (available June 2008–July 2011) were also used in this analysis. I closely examine the Canadian Forces' 2006 'Fight' advertising campaign (Department of National Defence) and in addition to using the video advertisements as a primary source, I also analysed two research studies prepared for DND: Environics Research Group's *Advertising Post-Test: Prepared for DND* (2007) and Decima Research Group's *Key Findings of Qualitative Research for the Canadian Forces Recruitment Advertising Campaign 'Fight'* (2007). I drew upon photographic materials from the Department of Defence's Combat Cam (available at http://www.combatcamera.forces.gc.ca/site/index-eng.asp), where photos from deployed photographers on various missions document activities of the Canadian Armed Forces (CAF) and make photo packs publicly available for download. For Chapter 5's examination of martial force used within Canada, I relied upon the *Citizens' Forum on Canada's Future* (Privy Council Office 1991) and the Ipperwash Report (Linden 2007) as 'official' documents and media supplementation from *APTN News*, *Al Jazeera* and *The Tyee*.

To supplement the 'official' discourse in Chapter 4, I examine how the peacekeeper mythology was articulated in media discourse. The media outlets that these texts were accessed from include *Calgary Herald*; *Canada AM*; *The Canadian Press*; *CBC News*; *CTV News*; *Edmonton Journal*; *The Globe and Mail*; *Guelph Mercury*; *Hamilton Spectator*; *Maclean's*; *Montreal Gazette*; *National Post*; *Ottawa Citizen*; *Saskatoon Star Phoenix*; *The Toronto*

Star; The Tyee; Vancouver Province; Vancouver Sun; Victoria Times Colonist; Waterloo Region Record; Western Morning News; Windsor Star; Winnipeg Free Press. The analysis did not contain francophone-directed media outlets, and outside of the 'national' sources (*Globe and Mail, National Post, CBC News, CTV News*), there is a heavy bias for Canadian Western and Central news outlets.

I also draw upon narratives from popular media coverage, usually authored by journalists and published for a broad audience. Texts included Chris Wattie's *Contact Charlie: The Canadian Army, the Taliban, and the Battle That Saved Afghanistan* (2008); Bernd Horn's *No Lack of Courage: Operation Medusa, Afghanistan* (2010); Christie Blatchford's *Fifteen Days: Stories of Bravery, Friendship, Life and Death from Inside the New Canadian Army* (2008); Kevin Patterson and Jane Warren's *Outside the Wire: The War in Afghanistan in the Words of Its Participants* (2008), Pete Fisher's *Highway of Heroes: True Patriot Love* (2011); Kathy Stinson's *Highway of Heroes* (2010); Christie Blatchford's *Helpless: Caledonia's Nightmare of Fear and Anarchy and How the Law Failed All of Us* (2011). These stories centred on embedded journalists' perceptions of militarised activities in Afghanistan and militarised police deployments domestically.

Another integral discursive site of meaning-making of the peacekeeper myth is academic, and spans several subdisciplinary bodies of literature, including feminist international relations (IR), Canadian foreign policy studies, peace and conflict studies, critical military studies, and middle power theorisations in international relations, which will be discussed in greater detail over the chapters to follow. Dominant reproductions and destabilising narratives about the peacekeeper myth have occurred throughout many academic debates, and, as Chapter 1 details, alongside other dominant myths in international relations.

Chapter Structure

The manuscript is structured around the core argument that the peacekeeper myth is a key framework to understand how war-like relations and warfare are legitimised. I demonstrate this by considering how peace has been martialled to justify violence, which can help illustrate how peace is used to justify war. By focusing on Canada as a case study, I show the salience and adaptability of the peacekeeper myth by exploring how this myth was both challenged and condoned by (non-peacekeeping) military activities conducted by the Canadian Forces during and following the Afghanistan war, and how the myth's malleability has extended to other martialled institutions such as police forces like the Royal Canadian

Mounted Police, the Ontario Provincial Police and the Sûreté du Québec. The peacekeeper myth therefore builds upon emerging literature in critical military studies that seeks to theorise the continuum between militarised state violence in international and domestic settings and problematise the militarist logics that inform these various practices.

Chapter 1 considers the visions of peace implicit in discourses about global peacekeeping. Building upon literatures that conceptualise militarism, militarisation and martial politics, this chapter outlines how the peacekeeping myth relates to existing frameworks and puts forward a concept to bridge existing work in critical military studies and peace studies: martial peace. I explain how martial peace is not novel, rather another way to understand disciplinary preoccupation with negative peace and a heuristic to explain how martial politics (or the long-standing and overlooked violence within liberal societies) is upheld through the association of peace with orderliness.

Chapter 2 offers an overview of the political functions of myths and maps the peacekeeper myth throughout United Nations (UN) doctrine and academic theorisations about UN peacekeeping in international relations. I consider how the distinctions between traditional peacekeeping (associated with consent, neutrality and non-violence) and second- or third-generation peacekeeping (exemplified by UN missions post-1970 that involve significantly more robust mandates) have imbued discourses about peacekeeping with the understanding that it is distinct from other forms of militarised violence, including peacemaking, counterinsurgency and warfare. The reproduction of peacekeeping and warfighting has stood to imbue peacekeeping with moral legitimacy, based on assumptions that the intent of peacekeeping is what makes its use of force justifiable.

Chapter 3 considers how peacekeeping mythologies vary across time and space, particularly across national contexts. This chapter introduces the cultural specificities of the Canadian peacekeeping myth and demonstrates how this mythology has been reinforced through academic theorisation, popular culture and political memorialisation. I consider how four key values have been associated with the Canadian peacekeeping mythology – paternal helpfulness, altruism, non-violence and innocence – and suggest that the power of the peacekeeper mythology lies in the emotional resonance of these characteristics believed to reflect unique Canadian ethico-political values.

Chapter 4 explores how the Canadian peacekeeping myth was manoeuvred in discourses about Canada's role in the war in Afghanistan between 2001 and 2014. I show efforts by elites to 'shed' the peacekeeping myth, believed by many in defence circles to be a feminising image that did little to protect Canada's reputation and national security from racialised threats in the global 'war on terror'. Despite efforts to rebrand and re-masculinise Canada's foreign policy image, the peace-keeping myth's potency and desirability by Canadians influenced official rhetoric to pivot back towards elements of the peacekeeping myth: helpfulness, altruism, non-violence and innocence. Considering official branding discourse during the war in Afghanistan, this chapter shows how elites were able to legitimise explicitly non-peacekeeping activities in Afghanistan by aligning these activities with symbolism of the peace-keeping myth.

Chapter 5 considers how the peacekeeping myth, and assumptions about 'peace' and order in Canada, has been negotiated alongside the use of militarised force against Indigenous populations. Drawing upon Alison Howell's (2018) martial politics frameworks, I consider how the extensive reproduction of the Canadian peacekeeping myth detailed in Chapter 3 occurred alongside decades of militarised police actions against Indigenous land rights activists in Canada. Seeking to illustrate the connections between global peacekeeping and domestic police 'peace-keeping', this chapter considers what is really at stake in the cel-ebration of Canadian peacekeeping mythology: a distraction from Can-ada's colonial and imperialist history through the promotion of 'peace' as centred on orderliness for settler populations.

I conclude by making the case for why the peacekeeping myth should matter for scholars concerned about how military power operates, the extension of war and war-like relations across many levels of global life, and the ways that military violence is 'remembered, memorialized, consumed, and inscribed with meaning' (Basham et al. 2015: 2). Mar-tial peace plays a central role in how liberal orders can obscure their attendant violences. This matters for scholars of militarism, as I not only challenge contemporary understandings of what constitutes 'warfare' and 'peace' but propose that the very narrow construction of these terms elides colonial and imperial violence.

I also consider how the peacekeeper myth, and emotional attach-ments to these narratives, build upon Tiina Vaittinen's critique of the focus of peace scholarship, where the research gaze 'tends to be aimed a locality distinct from our own doorsteps: a poor country, a community in an armed conflict or recovering thereof' (2019: 98). I echo Vaittinen's call that 'it is crucial to pay attention to what is going on at our own door-steps [as] they often appear as mere beneficiaries of the violent structures of global capitalism' (2019: 98), rather than active participants in the global injustices we seek to rescue others from. For Canadians, the nar-ratives of Canada's positive self-image as a peacekeeper (Howell 2005) help to obscure ongoing colonial and imperial relations that the Canadian state is suspended within, benefits from, and actively reproduces through mythologies about peace and peacekeeping.

Yet, I am one of those Canadians, and the peacekeeping myth has served to protect my own complicity in colonial violence, upheld throughout various privileged parts of my personal and professional life. As an IR scholar and settler Canadian, therefore, this work is deeply personal. It is my humble attempt to not simply talk about, or 'reveal', the ways that colonial and imperial violence have been enabled by common understandings of peace, but actively challenge the 'peaceful' political structures that I have benefited from, at the expense of injustice and violence for many others. As I'll explain throughout the book, what is at stake in this analysis is not simply an anti-militarist agenda (although I certainly identify as an anti-militarist feminist). What is at stake is challenging what is commonly understood to fall into the realms of 'warfare' and 'peace', and how academic research based on these narrow definitions is complicit in eliding colonial and imperial violence. But it is also about challenging the mechanisms – both material and discursive – that perpetuate the status quo. Dear reader, I consider my own research complicit in this project and it is my humble desire that this book begins to crack open the assumptions that perpetuate colonial, racist and gendered violence that is upheld in dominant visions of peace.

CHAPTER 1

Putting the 'Peace' in Peacekeeping: Martial Peace, Martial Politics and the Objects of Our Peacekeeping Desires

The practice of peacekeeping has been legitimised by its association with a normatively desirable outcome: peace. Daniel Levine has written that peacekeeping is 'distinguished from other forms of warfare by its *object* rather than its *nature*' (Levine 2014: 193, emphasis added). It is therefore important that we consider the object of peacekeeping – peace – that is promoted in the mythologisation of the construct.

I first offer a brief exploration of scholarly approaches to peace and the ways in which these ideas have been embedded within, and are influential of, contemporary understandings of 'peacekeeping'. I then explore how, far from an objective observable condition, 'peace' is a normatively loaded political concept, particularly in the ways it is employed in aspirations for global peacekeeping. I proceed to illustrate why these imaginations about peace and peacekeeping are important for understanding militarism, and, as the book promises, the legitimisation of warfare. While extensive interdisciplinary scholarship examines the links between militarism and war (Cockburn 2009; Sjoberg and Via 2010; Stavrianakis and Selby 2012; Bacevich 2013; Basham 2013; Mabee 2016), my work instead focuses on the intersections between militarism and peace. Drawing upon Allison Howell's framework of martial politics, I explain how peacekeeping discourses evoke a particular vision of peace – martial peace – that legitimises military deployments for the desired goal of peace. I conclude the chapter by signalling why martial peace is problematic and what we need to know about this vision of peace to understand about the politics of the peacekeeper myth.

Visions of Peace

The UN Charter makes forty-five references to peace, yet the term is not actually defined; former Secretary General Boutros-Boutros-Ghali described the concept as 'easy to grasp' (Otto 2020: 26). I disagree, and an overview of peace scholarship confirms my opinion. IR and peace studies have evolved disciplinarily as systematised areas for the study of war and how to end it, with the latter discipline embracing the normative goal of finding peace. The *Journal of Peace Research*'s founding editor, Johan Galtung, argued that peace 'is among the most consensual' values (Regan 2014: 347). Yet peace itself does not have a clear definition or conceptualisation, despite the vast literatures devoted to exploring it. As the editorial of the inaugural issue of the *Journal of Conflict Resolution* (1957) notes, 'we are all interested in peace but we too often abuse the term "peace"' (Regan 2014: 346).

While there are long-standing efforts to define peace (Boulding 1978; Galtung 1985; Rapoport 1992; Boulding 2000; Richmond 2003, 2008; Mueller 2007; Gleditsch et al. 2014), despite extensive scholarship, peace is still under-theorised.[1] Many approaches can be criticised as methodologically state-centric in focus and epistemologically reductive of peace as an absence of war or conflict.[2] State-centric approaches to an understanding of peace theorise it as an absence of inter-state war, such as 'democratic peace' (Russet and Oneal 2001), 'territorial peace' (Gibler 2012) and 'capitalist peace' (Schneider and Gleditsch 2010). In scholarship examining non-state-centric theorisation of peace, 'negative peace' approaches have dominated, looking at 'precarious peace' (George 2000), 'adversarial peace' (Bengtsson 2000), 'conditional peace' (George 2000) and 'cold peace' (Miller 2001). While working outside statist frameworks, these latter approaches primarily define peace as the absence of violent physical conflict (Diehl 2016).

Emerging approaches that seek to broaden the study of peace outside state-centric conceptualisations include new scholarship on 'networked peace' (Richmond 2019), 'everyday peace' (Mac Ginty 2014), or 'good enough peace' (Richmond 2014). Some of these studies that see peace as 'aspirational' (Klem 2018) have built upon critical peace scholarship inspired by Johan Galtung's (1971) distinctions between positive peace and negative peace. Negative peace, or the absence of physical conflict, is contrasted with positive peace, defined as the absence of structural violence, whereby social structures maximise human flourishing and prevent injury (Seyle 2019). Efforts to assess conditions of positive peace, such as the Davenport scale (Davenport et al. 2018; see also Wallensteen 2015), or the Global Peace Index (Institute for Peace and Economics 2022) have been small advancements, but the normative ambitions of these taxonomies are unclear. Even in peace-focused academic journals, the primary attention of peace scholars' research has been paid to negative peace (Gleditsch et al. 2014). Peace is also less studied than conflict, as recently illustrated by Diehl's (2016) assessment of conference papers on the International Studies Association's 2015 schedule, where peace-focused research accounted for only 19 per cent of presentations.

The result has been the reconstitution of the conflict/peace dichotomy. Jean Bethke Elshtain referred to peace as an 'ontologically suspicious concept' (1995), often conflated with 'security' and positioned in opposition to 'war' (Blanchard 2003: 1299). Even in scholarship that seeks to expand understandings of peace, 'peace' is often positioned in opposition to war and conflict. These approaches fail to recognise the ways that peace and conflict are not irreconcilable, but are often interlinked spectres (Cockburn 2004; see also Ruddick 2003). Feminist peace research[3] has built upon post-colonial peace theory by Mahatma Gandhi and Frantz Fanon that considers the intersections of structural, cultural and psychological violence to assess the various ways that conflict and violence permeate peacetime but also how war and conflict can be shot through with moments of peace (Singh and Poddar 2021; see also Enloe 2004; Nordstrom 2004; Confortini 2006; Wibben et al. 2019; Krystalli 2021). Despite this, even gender-sensitive and feminist peace scholarship has yet to find consensus about what peace is, or how we 'keep' it.

There is ongoing need to envision pathways to meaningful peace (MacKenzie and Wegner 2021). This book seeks to problematise visions of peace in peacekeeping discourses, and the normative foundations of these concepts. I build upon feminist conceptualisations of desire (Molloy 1995; Otto 2020) to understand how discourses about peace and peacekeeping have come to name, order and represent a 'social and physical reality whose effects simultaneously enable and constrain a set of options for practical action in the world' (Molloy 1995: 238). A driving question behind my research is: *Why is peacekeeping so desirable and what politics does it uphold?* I am interested in how this discourse has been mobilised, inspired by Laura Shepherd's provocation about the discursive power of 'peace'. As Shepherd remarks,

> peace is inherently A Good Thing, and no one can be 'against' peace. A feminist curiosity reminds us to resist the closure implied in any discourse of peace, remembering that it is always important to ask on whose behalf peace is being sought or claimed and with what effects. (Shepherd 2014: 107)

My work, therefore, aligns with other scholarship critical of liberal peace approaches, work that has opened pathways for studying peace with post-structuralist concerns about discourse, knowledge, power, identity and othering (Richmond 2008: 441) Following Bart Klem, who theorises peace as *an aspiration* rather than condition, this project seeks to 'scrutinise the agendas propagated under the banner of peace: which beliefs are reified, and which power relations are served' (Klem 2018: 236). I do so through an exploration of peacekeeping discourse and the ways in which peacekeeping has been mythologised (see Chapter 2). As the book will illustrate, discourses of peacekeeping uphold a 'teleological perspective with peace as its equivocal telos' (Klem 2018: 235). Violence and warfare are waged in the name of peace, despite a lack of political or academic consensus about the 'peace' we seek to 'keep'. Peace, therefore, rather than being a temporal condition which militarism and militarisation impedes, is in fact an aspirational discourse that reproduces militarist ideology and its attendant practices. This book considers how discourses and practices of 'peace' uphold militarist ideology. Patricia Molloy (1995: 235–6) argued that a feminist reconceptualisation of peace requires a cultural critique of militarism and a deconstruction of the type of strategic thinking that informs the discourse within which we live, act and form our subjectivities.

Militarism, Militarisation, Martial Politics and Martial Peace

The central claim of this book – that peacekeeping legitimises warfare largely due to the aspirational symbolism and normative exaltation associated with 'peace' – therefore requires we investigate what kind of peace is envisioned in these discourses and how it upholds militarism. The peacekeeping myth hinges its legitimisation of military force on a particular type of peace that I call *martial peace*. Akin to Galtung's articulation of 'negative' peace, martial peace as the referent of peacekeeping discourse is envisioned alongside broader ontological and epistemological assumptions in IR theory.

Martial peace, I argue, is the vision of peace used to justify international peacekeeping as well as domestic peacekeeping and policing. Martial peace is the discursive mobilisation of peace to justify martial violence. Martial peace is a form of negative peace because it implies that 'peace' can only be ensured by the presence of militarised force. Martial peace is the vision of peace purported by those who scoff at disarmament or police abolition because it is assumed in these visions that peace is not possible without militarised force to secure it. Martial peace, in its discursive constructions, also assumes that peace is always at risk of collapse because otherwise 'un-peaceful', unruly or disobedient targets are lurking in the shadows to disrupt it. Martial peace is the order enforced on 'unliberal' populations by militarised forces: a vision, a ruse, a discursive justification for using illiberal violence to prop up liberal democratic politics.

Martial peace is significant, not because it is conceptually novel or notably distinct from other forms of negative peace theorised in peace studies, but because it heuristically illustrates the reproduction of militarist ideology in discourses about peace. I will discuss and outline martial peace after a brief discussion of how the concept is situated within the larger body of scholarship that examines militarism, militarisation and martial politics, explored largely through the burgeoning interdisciplinary area of critical military studies (CMS).

Critical military studies, distinct from military sociology,[4] focuses on elements and consequences of military power by exploring the ways in which social practices and political contestations influence military practices, processes and geographies (Basham et al. 2015: 2). CMS challenges the notion that there is a concrete boundary between 'military' and 'civilian' spheres of relations and uses critical IR approaches to analytically consider (and in some work, normatively challenge), the fluid and unbounded ways that that military ideology is crafted across a diverse range of spaces and temporalities, including in spheres previously understood to be 'civilian'.

CMS has therefore considered the broad and fluid circulations of military ideas in society through the lens of militarism. In international relations broadly, there has been ambiguity and disagreement on what militarism is. Anna Stavrianakis and Jan Selby (2012) offer five possible models of militarism: ideological, behavioural, institutional, sociological, and the propagation of military personnel and equipment. Sociological perspectives, including that of Shaw (1991), seek to study how military values influence social structures, often drawing from Mann's (1987) definition as 'a set of attitudes and social practices which regards war and the preparation for war as a normal and desirable social activity' (cited in Eastwood 2018: 35). Stavrianakis and Selby themselves define militarism as 'the social and international relations of the preparation for, and conduct of, organized political violence' (Stavrianakis and Selby 2012: 2).

Throughout this book, I define militarism akin to Cynthia Enloe's definition that sees it as 'a complex package of ideas that, together, foster military values in both military and civilian affairs [which] justifies military priorities and military influences in cultural, economic, and political affairs' (2007: 11). Militarism, therefore, can be understood as ideology, often associated with the 'glorification of war' (Higate and Henry 2009, 134). Like James Eastwood (2018), I reject the notion that conceptualising militarism as ideology somehow ignores the social relations upon which these ideas are fostered and reproduced as 'ideology is reducible neither to the beliefs those subjects hold nor to the material practices that insatiate those beliefs. Rather, ideology is a structural relationship between social practices and the individuals who participate in them, which works by producing those individuals as subjects' (33) and, in turn, positions that ideology as desirable, even as this may occur unconsciously (48). In this sense, militarism involves the ideological legitimation of violence (Eastwood 2018: 48), a system by which power operates to 'take the political out of the ideological . . . and appear to be natural and unalterable' (Åhäll 2016: 161).

Militarism is not simply about glorifying war. Militarism involves *justifying* military action through narratives that legitimise the deployment of the military and *reproducing* discursive environments whereby criticising military activities is rendered taboo (Wegner 2021b). It can be an 'ambivalent, involuntary or unconscious phenomenon that manifests itself in a variety of ways' (Eastwood 2018: 48). The peacekeeping myth, to be explored in the following chapters, and the illusion of martial peace that it upholds, therefore services to both justify and legitimise deployment of the military in the name of peace and reproduce discursive environments about peacekeeping whereby is it taboo to criticise these forms of military deployments. Militarism as a concept helps to elucidate the social relations that make organised political violence possible (Rossdale 2019b: 3–5)

The conceptualisation of militarism as ideology also helps to distinguish it from militarisation. Militarisation, a topic of great interest in feminist international relations scholarship, is related to, yet distinct from, militarism as ideology. Catherine Lutz (2002) described militarisation as:

> Simultaneously a discursive process, involving a shift in general societal beliefs and values in ways necessary to legitimate the use of force, the organization of large standing armies and their leaders, and the higher taxes or tribute used to pay for them . . . [it] is intimately connected not only to the obvious increase in the size of armies and resurgence of militant nationalism . . . but also to . . . the shaping of national histories in ways that glorify and legitimate military action. (2002: 723)

Whereas militarism is the logics – the 'common sense' – about military force as necessary, just or 'good', militarisation is the consequences of these logics, the ways they are reproduced in sociopolitical environments that result in subjects who 'desire military power' (Shepherd 2018: 210). Feminists, like Enloe (2007), note that militarisation is not simply the acquisition of military approaches, technologies or deployments, but also about how civilians are and become militarised. This process stems from militarism and results in the normalisation of the idea of war (Åhäll 2016), whereby people and things become controlled by the military or 'depend[s] for [their] well-being on militaristic ideas' (Enloe 2000: 3).

One critique of militarisation has been the concern that scholarship has used militarisation to detail how these civilian spaces become 'militarised', with Alison Howell warning that these frameworks suggest the existence of an uncontaminated 'peaceful domain of "normal" or "civilian" politics unsullied by military intrusion' (2018: 118). Howell argues that many analyses of militarisation do not account for the way that liberal democratic societies are always already constituted by war-like relations, particularly in the force used against racialised, Indigenous, disabled, gendered and classed populations deemed to be threatening. She instead offers martial politics as an alternative framework that recognises the indivisibility of war/peace, military/civilian and national/social security (118) in liberal democratic societies where martial politics is 'the liberal norm, not the exception' (121).

While Howell's critiques have spurred new and important conversations, militarisation is not incompatible with martial politics. Militarisation can still be valuable analytically, particularly when we recognise that militarisation (or calls for demilitarisation) is 'not an absolute or totalizing process' (Eichler in Mackenzie et al. 2020: 826–7), and that drawing upon militarisation analytically need not ignore the 'entanglements and co-extensiveness of military and civilian spheres' (827). Militarisation, can therefore, be understood as an 'always-incomplete social (re)production of desiring subjects' (Haigh 2020: 23), and one that reorders relations in different ways across different temporal and spatial dimensions. Militarisation conceptually provides a framework for understanding the innumerable constellations of military power in socio-political life, including the effects of these power configurations on vulnerable and historically marginalised communities, which Howell astutely has called 'martial politics'.

The analytical frameworks of militarisation and martial politics are not incompatible, and I draw from Howell's articulations to demonstrate the relationship between martial politics (the 'normal' affairs in liberal societies whereby war-like relations between the state and marginalised communities are long-standing), militarism (the ideological or 'common sense' assumptions that legitimise and justify both war and war-like relations), and peace. As I will outline below, understanding how peace become martialised – martial peace – is key to understanding how simplistic representations of militarism with formal or organised war fail to recognise the ways that militarism ideologically is so ubiquitous that it also permeates contemporary understandings of peace.

Martial politics, and the emerging scholarly focus on martiality, is attentive to how liberal violence has been normalised (Basham 2013), including the ways this happens outside statist wars and within liberal societies (Millar 2021). Katharine Millar emphasises that while not all violence is martial, there is a preoccupation with militarism and accounts of martial violence with the state, soldiering and war (2021: 4). I argue we can better understand militarism when we decentre it from 'traditional' associations with soldiering, combat and war, and consider how discourses of peace, peacekeeping and policing are also reproductive of militarist logics, which are key facets in global imperial and colonial violences. As Nivi Manchanda and Chris Rossdale explain, militarism informs the processes whereby 'liberal capitalist society is structured by warlike relations *and* [also] the strategies through which these relations are concealed, obscured or naturalized' (2021: 8). Discourses of peace and peacekeeping are strategies by which martial politics and militarist logics are upheld and obscured. The peacekeeping myth and its political consequences (outlined in the chapters to follow) are not simply the legitimisation of warfare (as this book's title suggests) but also the obfuscation of violence more broadly conceived, including colonial violence.

Within these discourses, we must also be attentive to how liberal violence (and its accompaniment by militarisation) intersects with race in liberal governance (Hall 2021). Manchanda and Rossdale consider how racism and coloniality are not simply the consequences of militarism, but 'are in fact integral to its functioning' (2021). They argue that 'policing [may b]e a more integral concept for contemporary militarism than war' (2020: 12), as 'global martial politics [are] concerned with a series of technologies and practices directed towards producing and maintaining capitalist order, pacifying unruly, disobedient and criminalized subjects' (12–13). This applies to the relationship between militarism and peacekeeping as well. International peacekeeping was partly derived from imperial policing, 'a spectre peacekeeping has tried and partly failed to avoid' (Richmond 2014: 509). Peacekeeping and policing rely on similar tactics and on similar modes of legitimation.

Yet what I wish to contribute to these emerging conversations is that policing and peacekeeping are not simply done in the name of security, but done in the name of peace. Peace has been discursively *martialled* to legitimise the use of liberal violence in international peacekeeping and policing. Peacekeeping has been described as 'a major contribution to the twentieth century project of peace in the sense of providing a tool through which a preliminary, negative peace could be consolidated' (Richmond 2014: 509). As Chapter 2 will detail, peacekeeping has become mythologised as a mechanism whereby violence is used to enforce peace. And that vision of 'peace' is one rooted in colonialist ontologies whereby racialised violence is obscured and the reordering of martial politics happens through discourses of peace.

The relationship between martial politics and martial peace, therefore, is that martial politics are legitimised through discourses about peace and visions of martial peace. If martial politics are the 'normal politics' whereby violence is enacted on racialised, Indigenous, disabled, queer populations deemed a threat to civil order, martial peace is the narrow and partial vision of civil order that these imaginaries deem peaceful. If martial politics are the 'war-like relations' inherent in liberal democracies, then martial peace is the discursive legitimisation of these relations through narratives that demand negative peace, even at the expense of justice or reconciliation. Martial peace isn't a condition, it's a discursive imaginary. Martial peace is a nostalgically incomplete vision of liberal relations in global societies that obscures (or outright ignores) martial politics and its attendance violences.

The relationship between martial politics and martial peace is highly racialised, since the status quo is one where patriarchy, white supremacy and capitalism structure daily life (hooks 1995). The suppression of black activism in the United States through police interventions (Manchanda and Rossdale 2021), or, as Chapter 5 outlines, the suppression of Indigenous activism in Canada, is justified as violence that upholds the peace and order required in liberal democracies. In the case of international 'peacekeeping', or the misconstruing of this concept during the war in Afghanistan as discussed in Chapter 4, the need for peace and order has also been used to justify martial violence. Militarised interventions, even when cloaked in the language of humanitarianism, uphold white supremacy because they uphold desires about how the world should look, and those visions preserve colonialism and the ongoing exploitation of brown and black bodies globally (Bouka 2021). Martial peace is the vision that justifies such intervention, and therefore a critical investigation of peacekeeping and the martial peace that it purports to keep is required.

Martialling Peace through Peacekeeping Myths

While, discursively and intellectually, peacekeeping has been positioned as distinct from, or antithetical to, war and other forms of militarised violence, the 'peace' in discourses about peacekeeping has been a vision of negative peace. I suggest that this vision of peace can be called 'martial peace'. Peace, in these discourses, has been *martialled* to legitimise military violence and warfare: peacekeeping becomes positioned as the morally unimpeachable alternative to war. And, as Chapter 2 will illustrate, martial politics and martial violence are justified through discourses of (martial) peace and myths about peacekeeping. The mythologisation of peacekeeping in political discourse is one mechanism whereby martial peace has been celebrated and where martial politics have been obscured.

The peacekeeper myth relies upon normative imaginaries of peacekeeping as a form of ethical violence, sustained by the assumption that their intention of 'peace' justifies their martial and coercive means. Peacekeeping myths exist in a discursive environment where war is imagined as inevitable, military violence is justified as utilitarian, and peace is alarmingly under-developed as a theoretical and operational concept. As peace scholar Oliver Richmond has explained, 'The goal of ending violence (both overt and structural) while avoiding the use of violence (both overt and structural) is a critical goal for [the] world' (Richmond 2014: 515). Yet visions of martial peace assume that militarised force is required to keep or enforce peace. What is too often unnoticed is the ways 'peacekeeping, peacebuilding, and state building are clearly vital to maintaining the current order' (Richmond 2014: 517) and how discourses of peace play a central role in the legitimisation of these projects.

We must, therefore, consider how visions of (martial) peace, as mythologised and romanticised in discourses of peacekeeping, play a key role in justifying military deployments and warfare. Chapter 2 will introduce the framework of myth to illustrate how the mythologisation of peacekeeping within discourses about UN peacekeeping contributes to the justification of war and violence. The peacekeeping myth and the vision of peace it claims to uphold matters for anyone concerned about ongoing corporeal, material, ecological, colonial, and gendered and sexualised violence that is widespread in international relations. The power afforded to military institutions, their political influence over a variety of policy areas, and the unconscious ways that this power is obscured through discourse and practice is an important element in upholding existing global hierarchies and violence.

Notes

1. It is worth noting that a similar line of investigation has been explored in (critical) war studies, where 'disciplines can be thought of as centring on

core ontological problematics – areas of contestation over the nature of their subject – which then served as enabling conditions for various traditions of inquiry within those disciplines' (Barkawi and Brighton 2011: 134). Discussions about a lack of sustained investigation into what war is (ontologically) show that a preponderance of empirical research has left gaps in theoretical explorations of war (Burke 2007; Barkawi and Brighton 2019). In peace and conflict studies and IR, similar shortcomings exist.

2. Rebuttals to this critique include the concern that 'if peace is defined as a situation where all forms of structural violence are fully addressed, it becomes utopian and loses its empirical traction' (Klem 2018: 235). Large-n studies require 'crisp categories' (Klem 2018: 235), hence the interdisciplinary focus on negative peace conceptually.

3. Feminist peace scholars have critiqued peace as not-war, particularly in the liberal visions put forward by Immanuel Kant in his essay 'Perpetual Peace': his vision for peace assumes it can only exist among 'like kinds and equals only', resulting in the need to eliminate or deny difference, rather than envision possibilities for peace in an asymmetrical and infinitely different world body (Molloy 1995: 235).

4. Military sociology is focused mainly on the assumption that there is a divide between 'civilian' spheres of political life and 'military' spheres responsible for securing the consent for military pursuits of organised violence, including theory on how these two spheres interact (Huntington 1957; Janowitz 1971).

CHAPTER 2

Myths, Peacekeeping and the Peacekeeping Myth

While Chapter 1 considered the narrow vision of negative peace – martial peace – associated with peacekeeping, this chapter takes a closer look at peacekeeping itself and the ways that discourses about peacekeeping have resulted in the peacekeeper myth: the belief that peacekeeping is a moral, softer, more legitimate means of using militarised force in the world. The peacekeeper myth is a powerful one; it has enabled international interventions in the name of peace to become legitimatised and widely practised, a puzzling phenomenon of increased militarised interventions in a political world where sovereignty is presumed to be central (Barnett 2005).

The mythologisation of peacekeeping has contributed to processes of militarisation, such as the demand and purchase of military technologies and the perpetuation of foreign policy strategies that utilise military force to create peace. It has also led to problematic activities adjacent to keeping of 'peace' by military personnel, such as sexual exploitation of women and girls by peacekeepers (Notar 2006; Ndulo 2009) that have resulted in 'UN Babies' or Peacekeeper-fathered children (Lee and Bartels 2020), the torture of children (Razack 2004), fraud (Lederer 2020), and the failure of peacekeepers to protect civilians from mass atrocities (such as in Rwanda in 1994 and Srebrenica in 1995). The peacekeeper myth distracts us from asking what kind of 'peace' military occupations uphold, and therefore also obscures the martial politics that peacekeeping missions may reinforce. The peacekeeper myth is distracting, therefore, allowing us to imagine militarised coercion in romanticised ways while avoiding looking closely at the attendant violent practices associated with the deployment of militarised forces.

The peacekeeper myth, however, is also productive. It reproduces ideological militarism as a commonsensical element of international politics. It positions militaries as forces for good (Duncanson 2009, 2013), rather than a 'destructive form of riot control' (Greener 2013: 636), potentially lethal tools for political control. The peacekeeper myth reproduces the idea that military force can be used in ethical and justifiable ways. The peacekeeper myth and ideological militarism co-constitute each other. Both militarism and the peacekeeper myth are circulated discursively to reproduce one another, making the myth appear straightforward, commonsensical and apolitical; these meanings transform into 'just the way things are or the ways things ought to be' (Weber 2014: 6). This has the effect of obscuring the politics of peacekeeping and of legitimising military activities conducted in the name of peace.

Myths can be used to imagine cohesion in a group collective with otherwise limited shared histories, territories, languages or religion. Myths also can be used to distract, to shame, to silence or to wield acquiescence. Myths can therefore be both productive and destructive. The peacekeeping myth is no different; political actors have used the peacekeeping myth to shame, to distract, and to foster acquiescence of, if not direct support for, military violence. At the heart of the peacekeeping myth is the power to enable and disable certain politics surrounding military violence. The power of the peacekeeper myth lies in its paradoxical ability to legitimise violence in the name of peace. The peacekeeper myth smooths over what should be obvious tensions regarding the use of military force and militarised violence to 'wage' peace both internationally and domestically, which I discuss in Chapters 4 and 5 respectively.

In the next section, I offer a conceptualisation of what myths are, and introduce the approach I take to study and explore myths. I then investigate how peacekeeping has been conceptualised as distinct from other forms of militarised intervention and how the discursive distinctions between 'traditional peacekeeping' and other forms of military interventions have resulted in the mythologisation of peacekeeping..

Myths and Mythologies in International Relations

What they are

Myths are widely believed narratives that function to cast particular political and ideological commitments as apolitical truths. They are deeply embedded in, and shape, our perspectives of the world and how we think the world works. Myths 'send explicit messages about appropriate, ideal, acceptable, and legitimate behaviours, identities, and practices' (MacKenzie 2015: 9). Myths are culturally created, and they are distinctly political: they can enable and they can obscure.

Myths are stories so dominant or compelling that we take them to be truths. Roland Barthes (1972) called myths 'depoliticized speech' as they remove the storytelling involved in myth creation from political critique and instead cast mythologised stories as 'natural'. They have also been defined as a 'narrative created and believed by a group of people that diverts attention away from a puzzling part of their reality' (Yanow 1992: 191). Myths function to explain, but they can also obscure or distract. Myths – dominant stories within discourse – are enmeshed in a web of discursive power where some meanings are reproduced, and others are discarded. Myths, therefore, 'are not simply "believed" but believed in a particular way that elides their own implication in relations of power and instead constitutes them not only as "true" but as *natural*' (Millar 2016: 179). Studying myths requires us to break apart naturalised, seemingly true concepts to expose the ways that these concepts are both incomplete and yet also highly politicised.

I am interested in the peacekeeping myth because it assumes that peace can be created through military threat or enforcement and is entirely premised on the assumption that *this is a good thing*. It seems nearly impossible to critique peacekeeping as a practice: who, after all, would want peace to not be kept? However, it is important and necessary to interrogate the peacekeeping myth by critically investigating the beliefs about peacekeeping taken as common-sense truths. These include, for example, the belief that peacekeeping is antithetical to warfare, and the belief that peacekeeping is the 'softer', more legitimate use of militarised force globally. In doing so we can 'refocus our attention on how cultural configurations of power and ideology make . . . [these] stories *appear* to be true' (Weber 2014: 7, emphasis in original), but also to understand the ways that war and its attendant violences are made possible through discursive legitimisation.

It is important to remember that myths cannot 'do' things by themselves, but they can be (and are) mobilised and used to perpetuate particular 'truths' about the world and how we should behave in it. It is in this way that myths and ideologies are co-constitutive[1] and deeply political, even as they appear to be apolitical or common sense. The peacekeeper myth, therefore, relates to other ideological 'common senses' dominant in Western international relations that give meanings, purpose and identities to individuals, collectives and states.[2] Militarist ideology is largely reproduced through realist theory in international relations that presupposes that conflict is inevitable and that states can best protect political interests through military coercion. This presupposition infuses the peacekeeping myth not just as plausible, but as naturalised.

There are two interdependent components of myths: their sources (how they become mythologised) and their performative effects (or political consequences) (Bliesemann de Guevara 2016: 17). Myths develop through narrative and storytelling in ways that evoke emotional and cognitive resonance with the individuals who believe them. The reproduction of these stories, and the resonance of the stories with other myths, ideologies or knowledge paradigms, turn the stories from widely used narratives into myths where the story feels natural. The performative effects of the myth, in turn, also stand to reinforce the emotional resonance of the stories and give impetus to the continued reproduction of the myth.

The significance of national myths

One common use of myths is in the creation of nationalist storytelling (Bell 2003: 66). Duncan Bell reminds us that there are not singular or irreducible national narratives or an essentialist 'national identity'; however, there are certainly 'nationalist myths' that, as a story, 'simplifies, dramatises and selectively narrates the story of a nation's past and its place in the world, its historical eschatology; a story that elucidates its contemporary meaning through (re) constructing its past' (Bell 2003: 75). Bell coined the term 'national mythscape' to describe the 'discursive realm, constituted by and through temporary and spatial dimensions, in which the myths of the nation are forced, transmitted, reconstructed and negotiated constantly' (75).

Once a national mythscape is developed, it requires constant upkeep, including a historical and spatial context from which ongoing and future manifestations may be made legible. The (re)production of national myths is an ongoing project – one that is not simply the result of top down rhetoric (for example, government decrees) but also informed by bottom-up beliefs and activities (for example, cultural norms and practices). For example, the American myth of Manifest Destiny is part of the American national mythscape. The mythologisation of westward expansion in the United States has romanticised colonial acquisition of Indigenous-controlled territories on the west coast of the continent. Manifest Destiny conceptually defines and empowers American identity, in not-so-covertly racialised fashion (Weinberg 1935; Brauer 1999). The term, coined by John O'Sullivan, editor of two prominent media outlets, was used to invoke the perceived right of America to annex Texas.[3] Yet, Manifest Destiny did not become a myth just because O'Sullivan's newspapers and subsequent media outlets published the idea widely. The myth of Manifest Destiny was also reinforced by government policies such as the 1862 Homesteaders Act (which allowed homesteaders to claim 160 acres of land free if they lived and worked on it for five years) and the Pacific Railway Act of 1862 (BBC Bitsize, n.d.). As myth requires upkeep and ongoing cultural investment to continue to hold sway, Manifest Destiny as a myth is also reproduced in cultural practices, such as celebrations on Columbus Day and American Thanksgiving that romanticise colonial history and perpetuate notions of white entitlement to Indigenous land (Shear 2019).

Consider also, the Australian national mythscape and the Anzac (Australian and New Zealand Army Corps) mythology. The Anzac myth positions Australia's 'birth' as a nation during the First World War, imagined as solidifying Australian international identity through Australia's military sacrifices during the Gallipoli campaign in Turkey (Searle 1965). Notions of mateship and larkenism, token values of Australian-ness, stem from this myth (Donoghue and Tranter 2015) While this is a common mythscape reproduced through prime ministerial addresses (Bromfield 2018), it is also reproduced through material investments such as the iconic Anzac Bridge in Sydney, or the Australian War Museum, slated to have a AU$500 million expansion in 2020. It also is reproduced through social practices such as the public holiday Anzac Day (Brown 2014), where many Australians participate in early morning parade pageantry before flocking to the pub to play 2-up, a gambling tradition of returned First World War veterans. First World War romanticisation is central to the Australian national mythscape, defining what it means to be Australian through the creation of values associated with the Anzac 'digger' myth (Lake et al. 2010) and repurposed often by politicians who seek to mobilise militarised Australian nationhood for political gain (Bromfield and Page 2020).

The national mythscape concerns a state's place in the world, its role in the world, and the perceived identities of its citizens that marks the nation as distinct from others. The peacekeeper myth, while broader than a national myth, is indeed embedded in national mythologies, an examination that later chapters in this book will undertake. The peacekeeper myth is therefore not only about what the practice of peacekeeping is assumed to be, but also about the perceived values of nations that undertake this practice. The peacekeeper myth exists across national contexts in varying ways, but its various manifestations are often used to reinforce nationalist identity. Mythologised peacekeeping involves stories about who 'we' are as a nation, who 'they' are as other nations, and what type of individual and collective morality 'we' have when we agree to partake in international peacekeeping.

How to study myths

The study of myths can be divided into two approaches: studying 'myth as fiction' and studying 'myth as symbolic' (MacKenzie 2015: 9). The first approach is often a structural or positivist interpretation of myth. Structural interpretations of myths might aim to 'reveal' some sort of wrong consciousness about the story. The second approach is studying 'myth as symbolic' (MacKenzie 2015: 9). This approach is relatively under-examined in IR and is the direction I take in this book. Categorising myths as symbolic means that the analyst cares less about the historical 'accuracies' of the myth, and instead seeks to consider what the myth symbolises or how the myth functions politically. Studying myths as symbolic requires critical examination of the effects of the myth, recognising that much of social life is organised through mythology and therefore there is no inherent 'truth' in which we may get to by unravelling the myth-as-fiction.

I investigate 'myths as symbolic' using a post-structural approach. Post-structural analyses focus on how meanings are constituted through forms of *representation*, including language and imagery. Post-structuralism considers how particular meaning-making constructions (for example, myths) enable certain practices and politics and exclude others. Meaning-making happens through discourse, whereby the words, images and emotions we use and associate with particular concepts define our political reality (Hall 1997; Åhäll 2015). Discourse fixes meaning *temporarily*, enabling people to make sense of their worlds within particular moments (Shepherd 2008: 215). Therefore, the goal of post-structural analyses is to re-politicise representations that appear to be natural, fixed or timeless (in this case, the peace-keeper myth), by examining how certain ideas, words and images are included or excluded in our conceptualisations. These conceptualisations are always culturally based (Åhäll 2015: 34) and therefore are not universal; they manifest in a variety of nuanced ways across national and cultural contexts.

As myths serve to provide significance and meaning to social and political life they are reproduced through narrative(s) and other semiotic signifiers (including imagery). Yet, myth is 'not a single narrative . . . but a process of continual work on a basic narrative pattern that changes according to the circumstances' (Bottici and Challand, cited in Bliesemann de Guevara 2016: 318). In the chapters that follow, I will tease out the cultural specificities of the peacekeeper myth as well as the ways this narrative pattern has adapted to changing geopolitical and spatial shifts in global politics.

How Peacekeeping Becomes Mythologised

As I note above, the peacekeeping myth is *the belief that peacekeeping is an apolitical, softer, less violent, morally legitimate use of military force*. This is exemplified in a description by Daniel Levine who explains: 'Peacekeeping is not simply a variety of war . . . peacekeepers are military personnel put to a different purpose' (Levine 2014: 194).

Peacekeeping is seen as a legitimate and 'good' use of military force and resources. I argue, however, that any use of militarised force results in problematic activities *and* outcomes regardless of whether the aims are 'peacekeeping' or 'war-making'. Peacekeeping therefore requires sustained critical investigation. It can lend itself to bolstering militarisation activities and processes, including the financing, development and use of military technologies and military techniques. It may also result in martial practices such as the deployment of lethal violence, exacerbation of environmental destruction, unintended and intentional civilian harm, and the promotion of asymmetrical political interests on a global scale.

Feminists have long been critical of representations of peacekeeping as a non-violent, de-militarised practice in international politics. There has been a documented racist, homophobic, misogynist military culture in many peacekeeping units (Razack 2004; Whitworth 2004; Reeves 2012). Peacekeepers have participated in the sexual exploitation of civilians (Higate 2007; Gunnarsson 2015; Karim and Beardsley 2016). There has also been criticism of the paradox of lethally trained military agents conducting purportedly humanitarian objectives (Cockburn and Zarkov 2002; Mazurana et al. 2005; Rubinstein 2008; Higate and Henry 2009). Despite this, the assumed moralism of the peacekeeper myth lives on, resilient and adaptable in modern political contexts.

This book does not directly follow feminist critiques of peacekeeping by 'myth-busting' peacekeeping to reveal historical insidious components of the practice. Feminists before me have identified an unease with peacekeeping as a celebrated alternative to military force (Whitworth 2004). My investigation of this myth, instead, is an exploration of its development, evolution and political power to enable and mobilise militarism as a naturalised component of international politics. The peacekeeper myth requires the romanticisation of peacekeeping as something morally superior to organised warfare, thereby legitimising military force as apolitical when done in the name of peace. What I am interested in is *how* peacekeeping has become mythologised in such a way that it is understood unidimensionally according to certain values, and, in turn, how this myth is used to valorise military violence (specifically by Western democratic nations) by positioning the use of military violence as both politically legitimate and necessary to enforce peace and stability.

The mythologisation of peacekeeping occurs in two broad ways: peacekeeping as mediated knowledge and peacekeeping as a catch-all phrase. First, peacekeeping activities are mediated to the public. Many civilians know very little about the mechanics, processes and in-theatre activities of military deployments or the procedural practices of global governance institutions. Civilian audiences receive information about their militaries' overseas deployments through mediated representations: speeches made by government leaders and politicians, perhaps, as well as media coverage that, in Western democratic states increasingly since the Gulf War, allows citizens mediated visual insight to conflict. Much of this information is curated through journalistic narrative and also limited by government restrictions on what information can be released to ensure mission security. The result is that on-the-ground perspectives are often neatly presented through controlled messaging. As will be outlined in the examination of a Canadian case study, the cultural specificities of the peacekeeper myth have evolved from a mediated representation of what is involved in international peace operations, one that Chapter 3 illustrates is highly sanitised imagery.

Second, peacekeeping has become a vague catch-all term. 'Peace-keeping' is an umbrella term that is often applied somewhat carelessly to a variety of historical and contemporary practices by both United Nations-organised initiatives and regional organisation military deployments such as NATO-led missions. While peacekeeping is one of several options in the spectrum of peace support efforts of the United Nations that includes peacemaking, peace enforcement, peace-keeping and post-conflict peacebuilding (United Nations n.d.. p. 9), these areas have overlapping mandates and, in the case of 'traditional peacekeeping', have evolved significantly since their early formations post-Second World War (United Nations Peacekeeping Operations 2008). In addition to the lack of clarity in UN doctrine about what 'peacekeeping' constitutes, there is also a variance in scholarly taxonomies of peacekeeping.[4]

The mythologisation of peacekeeping, therefore, has occurred both through diverse interpretation of its conceptual roots in United Nations doctrine and practices, as well as through the mediation of peacekeeping as a particular practice (non-violent, helpful, altruistic and innocent), evoked in discourse by many individual states to signal these perceived elements of their 'identities'.

Peacekeeping and the Lack of Conceptual Clarity

So, what *is* peacekeeping? At the heart of the peacekeeping myth is a very traditional conceptualisation of peacekeeping: that lightly armed troops are deployed with the consent of all warring parties, do not use force outside of self-defence or immediate protection of civilians, and remain impartial to the political desires of warring factions, instead only abiding by the requirements of the mission mandate. Indeed, part of the power of the myth is its obfuscation of the distinctions between kinds of peace operations, as I explore in Chapters 3 and 4. In some cases, like the Canadian case study that I explore, the myth is actually *reinforced* through individual and collective unwillingness to consider these distinctions and instead home in on the emotional, self-referential, feelgood elements of the myth.

The United Nations' Charter does not explicitly mention 'peacekeeping' even though articles of the Charter are used to enforce this type of co-ordinated military activity. Chapter VI of the Charter outlines 'diplomatic strategies', and Chapter VII outlines 'coercive measures' including sanctions and the use of force to stop aggression (Howard and Dayal 2018). Former UN Secretary Dag Hammarskjöld famously described peacekeeping as 'Chapter Six-and-a-Half' (cited in Howard and Dayal 2018). While there are no formal international agreements that outline required conduct of peacekeeping interventions, the United Nations has three doctrines associated with peacekeeping: *limited force* that is restricted to self-defence or upholding the mission mandate, *consent* of warring parties prior to deployment, and *impartiality* of peacekeepers in the implementation of agreements (United Nations Peacekeeping n.d.a.). This 'holy trinity' (Levine 2014) has informed the perceived legitimacy of UN peacekeeping, even while these terms themselves are often vague.

UN Peacekeeping practices began with unarmed observers in two missions established in Palestine (UNTSO, 1948) and Kashmir (UNMOGIP, 1949), but the first deployment of lightly armed troops was to Egypt in UNEF-1 in 1956 to monitor the military withdrawal of France, Britain and Israel from the Suez region. Peacekeeping has evolved significantly since then, shifting in practice and mandate. Early missions had mandates with significant limits on force (only to be used in selfdefence), which have been adapted in response to peacekeeping missions' inability to prevent mass atrocities (such as UNAMIR in Rwanda and UNPROFOR in the former Yugoslavia). Contemporary missions, following the Brahimi Report (United Nations 2000), now permit force deployment beyond self-defence, including protection of civilians and upholding the mission mandate. What peacekeeping 'looks like' on the ground varies according to the mission mandate. Missions do not share identical mandates, particularly as UN peace operations have evolved since 1948. 'Peacekeeping' is therefore a fluid term that has been used to describe activities that extend beyond the ceasefire monitoring by lightly armed troops in UNEF-I.[5] Further complicating the fluid nuances or historical evolution in/of 'peacekeeping'[6] is additional distinctions between peacekeeping, peace enforcement and peacemaking. It is to this that I turn now.[7]

Peacekeeping, Peacemaking, Peace Enforcement

The literature on 'peacekeeping' tends to make a broad distinction between peacekeeping, peace enforcement and peacemaking. By way of definition, UN peace operations are often distinguished by their purpose or mandate. The purpose of 'peacekeeping' is the implementation of peace accords (Howard and Dayal 2018: 74). The United Nations Department of Peacekeeping Operations (DPKO) describes peacekeeping as 'a technique designed to preserve the peace, however fragile, where fighting has been halted, and to assist in implementing agreement achieved by the peacemakers . . . to help lay the foundation for sustainable peace' (UN DPKO 2008: 18). Peacekeeping, therefore, assumes that there is some type of agreement in place that peacekeepers will uphold and enforce as third parties to a conflict. The agreement may be formal or informal, even 'partial', providing the 'situation can be meaningfully interpreted in terms of parties seeking a peaceful resolution to the conflict, even if there is no stable peace yet' (Levine 2014: 7).

The 'holy trinity' of UN peacekeeping mandates relates to the three tenets of restrained force, impartiality and consent. Prior to 1992, peacekeeping mission mandates were organised ad hoc, but all contained stipulations about the *restraint on force*, often restricted to self-defence or non-initiation. The 'third party' status of peacekeeping forces reflects their perceived *impartiality*/neutrality from local politics. Finally, the required *consent* of involved factions imbues peacekeeping with perceived legitimacy, rationalised by the fact that the presence of external martial forces is desired by all parties.

In contrast, 'peace enforcement operations' are intended to protect civilians and convince non-complying parties to sign peace accords by using compellent force (Howard and Dayal 2018). The DPKO identifies 'peace enforcement' as 'the use of military and other measures to enforce the will of the UN Security Council' (United Nations Peacekeeping n.d.b: 10–11). Peacekeeping missions are distinguishable from peace enforcement missions, whereas in the former, personnel are only permitted to use force at the 'tactical' and not 'strategic' level (Levine 2014: 7) – or, put differently, force to interfere with the *acts* of groups but not enough force to defeat or destroy the groups themselves (2013: 136)

Peacemaking is a third form of UN peace operation. The DPKO distinguishes 'peacemaking' – diplomatic efforts to resolve a conflict in progress – from post-conflict 'peacebuilding', which are strategies to enhance state capacities to prevent future violence. Peacemakers might include diplomatic envoys, governments, regional organisations, or the United Nations, but may also be unofficial groups that strive to utilise diplomatic, non-martial solutions to reach an agreement (United Nations Peacekeeping Operations 2008).

While nuanced terminology for UN peace operations therefore exists, in practice there is often a great deal of overlap – or, at times, misuse – of terms that contain the phrase 'peace' to describe international military interventions. The UN 'toolkit' for peace is filled with many options, but the semantics which all utilise 'peace' as a referent goal for these diverse activities makes the nuances unclear. From a simple perspective, one might assume that the goal of all these activities is 'peace', and that the methods and approaches to accomplish this broad goal vary.

As discussed in Chapter 1, the 'peace' envisioned in these operations is often a very narrow vision of peace. Sandra Whitworth explains that the mandates of UN peacekeeping missions are the result of negotiations both within the Security Council and between belligerents in a conflict; mandates 'identify who is to be saved and who is to be left to die' (2004: 33) in their establishment of *how* order and normalcy are to be accomplished through peacekeeping. Despite the presentation of 'traditional peacekeeping missions' like UNEF-1 as 'neutral', all peacekeeping missions contain political priorities and bias because inherent to the peace and order being 'kept' are structural politics that are protected.

More Concepts: Classical versus Muscular Approaches to Peacekeeping

The United Nations is not the only one to propose a taxonomy of peace operations; researchers, too, have sought to identify different kinds of peace missions (Diehl et al. 1998; Demurenko and Nikitin 1997; Bellamy et al. 2010). There is, however, a challenge inherent in the various taxonomies and typologies of peace missions. As Alex Bellamy (2004) notes, there are often fundamental disagreements about the *purpose* of peacekeeping activities – whether the goal is to build global peace through liberal democratic political apparatus or whether it should simply be concerned with facilitating conflict between states. He notes that most of these approaches fail to critically assess what type of world order UN member states are perpetuating by uncritically focusing on the minute details of peace operations without a view to the political nature of peace operations themselves.

The *purpose* of peacekeeping missions is also ambiguous. Peacekeeping missions, then, might be designed to constrain or contain hostilities (Greig and Diehl 2005; Gilligan and Sergenti 2007), or they might strive to prevent the recurrence of war following a ceasefire (Fortna 2008; Howard 2008). Alternatively, they might limit 'peacekeeping' to consent-based missions authorised to use force only in self-defence (such as Bellamy and William's 'traditional peacekeeping' model). The problem is, though, that the concept of 'peacekeeping' associated with the peacekeeping myth does not account for these nuances in peace operations.

While peacekeeping as a UN practice does have regulations that distinguish it from more robust military interventions, like Chapter VII-sanctioned peace enforcement missions, there is scholarly literature documenting the blurred distinctions between latter-generation (1990s to present) multidimensional peacekeeping with peace enforcement. The distinction between traditional peacekeeping and latter-generation peacekeeping – called 'second'- or 'third'-generation peacekeeping, Cold War peacekeeping (Richmond 2014), prickly peacekeeping (James 1995: 264), strategic peacekeeping (Gow 1995: 78–9) or assertive peacekeeping (Pugh 1996: 208) – often refer to missions of the late 1990s and 2000s that are perceived to fall into the 'grey area' between traditional peacekeeping and Chapter VII mandated peace enforcement. These 'grey area' missions of 'muscular' or 'robust' peacekeeping are not without criticism (Monnakgotla 1996; Wentges 1998; Pugh 2004; Karlsrud 2015; Tardy 2011). Further muddling the distinction between traditional peacekeeping and contemporary robust peacekeeping missions is the UN's hesitancy to categorise missions under Chapter VII, marking UN states' preference to 'fit' forceful missions within the category of peacekeeping rather than peace enforcement (Berdal and Ucko 2015), even when the mission mandate permits tactical force to 'take all necessary measures to neutralize and disarm' peace spoilers, such as the MINUSMA mission in Mali (Karlsrud 2015: 40). The boundaries of peacekeeping are quite blurry both in practice and in academic classification.

In addition, the practice of peace and security interventions by regional organisations, such as the African Union or the North Atlantic Treaty Organization (NATO), sometimes further blurs the distinctions of what 'peacekeeping' entails, particularly when peacekeeping missions are

termed 'stabilisation' missions and the limits on force are not clearly institutionally defined (Karlsrud 2015: 42). Joan Tronto, an ethicist, describes
peacekeeping as 'a term of art in international discourse' (2008: 180).
Tronto uses peacekeeping to describe 'all forms of military humanitarian
intervention in situations of conflict' (2008: 180). Her categorisation is
not intellectual illiteracy; rather, Tronto argues that these 'peace' distinctions all function as a justificatory use of military force in the name of
peace, an argument that feminist scholars have also identified as a glaring
paradox of peacekeeping (Razack 2004; Whitworth 2004; Krosnell and
Svedberg 2011; Wegner 2021a).

Traditional Peacekeeping's 'Trinity' and/as the Peacekeeper Myth

There is considerable academic attention paid to the distinctions of
forms of peace operations, but what I am interested in is how peacekeeping is imagined and defined in the peacekeeping myth. The mythologisation of peacekeeping does not account for the varying nuances in
peace operations across time and space; as myth, it simplifies these com-
plexities into a dominant and unidimensional trope rooted in the three
elements of 'traditional peacekeeping'. The trinity plays 'an important
ontological and semantic role: [it] refers to the essence of peacekeeping and distinguish[es] it from other methods of crisis management or
resolution' (Tsagourias 2007: 466). Therefore, the trinity functions as
the foundation of the peacekeeper myth because these rationales are the
reason that peacekeeping is positioned as (morally, ethically, militarily)
distinct from other forms of militarised interventions.[8] Peacekeeping has
been said to 'occupy the twilight between war and peace in which the
law has not yet been settled' (Weiner and Aolain 1996: 306), semanti-
cally establishing that peacekeeping is both distinct from war *and* understood to be the tool to prevent the resurgence of war.

Below I explore the three elements of 'traditional peacekeeping' to
tease out how these three components have reproduced certain predi-
cations of peacekeeping. In the section to follow, I illustrate how the
representations of peacekeeping as defined in the 'trinity' articulation
constitute the moral foundation of the peacekeeping myth. Relying
on discursive analysis as a method, I draw upon Roxanne Doty's use
of the concepts of predication, presupposition and subject-positioning as textual mechanisms used in the formation of the peacekeeping
myth.[9] Predication is the linking of descriptive qualities to a particular
subject, focusing on the adverbs and adjectives that affirm the subject
(1993: 231). Subject-positioning is attentive to the ways that a subject
is positioned in written or visual texts, for example the ways that 'the

peacekeeper' is positioned within doctrine and documents. Presupposition, finally, is the background knowledge in place when analysing a text, 'what kind of world the representation is constructing and what is considered true in the constructed world' (Åhäll 2015: 42). Drawing upon scholarly texts on peacekeeping and UN doctrines about peacekeeping, then, the peacekeeper myth is mapped through attention to the descriptions of and about 'peacekeeping' and 'peacekeepers' and involves presupposed knowledge about the worldly environment in which peacekeepers operate.

Non-use of force

If peacekeeping is seen as a 'sui generis category distinct from war-fighting' (Levine 2014: 5), it is often positioned so because of the rules of engagement that require peacekeepers to use restraint in deploying lethal force. As mentioned, early or 'traditional' peacekeeping missions (prior to the 1990s) limited peacekeepers' use of lethal force to self-defence, lending credence to the notion that peacekeepers conducted their responsibilities in a non-violent manner, or the representation of peacekeeping as less militarised in relation to combat or 'real war'. Yet the notion of 'self-defence' has shifted in UN doctrine, from individual self-defence of military personnel to defence of the mandate and the protection of civilian third parties (Tsagourias 2007: 473)[10, 11] calling into question whether contemporary missions fall into a new 'grey area' between the 'traditional' ceasefire monitoring and counterinsurgency operations. The DPKO/DFS Concept Note outlines concern about robust peacekeeping compromising the perception of impartiality (DPKO 2009; see also Tardy 2011), illustrating that the trinity's requirements are mutually reinforcing.

While restriction of force positions peacekeeping as distinct from peace enforcement or even war-fighting, it is based upon the relevant *scale* of military violence, *rather than an absence of it*. The delimitation of force to self-defence reinforces the imperative for peacekeepers to act impartially (Tsagourias 2007: 474), bolstering notions of a paternalistic umpire managing unruly participants in a sports match. This summons an image of who peacekeepers *are*; it is an instance of subject-positioning (Doty 1993: 306) whereby 'the peacekeeper' emerges as a construct both similar to, yet distinct from, the combat soldier. The restrained use of force positions peacekeeping as less militaristic or less violent than other forms of military interventions who use lethal force in offensive or strategic ways. Peacekeeping, as defined in the 'traditional' sense, only uses force in a responsive or reactive way, imbuing the activity with a sense of innocence, casting peacekeepers as restrained parental figures managing squabbling dependants. It also, as will be discussed below, feeds into the value of non-violence inherent to the myth.

The use of force is of central importance to the peacekeeper myth because justifying the use of force – the how, why and when (Doyle 2001; Annan 2005: para. 122) – is an enduring challenge for individual states and UN membership alike. Scholarship has noted that the UN and its member states have been reluctant to resort to force in peace operations and while this hesitancy is not shared equally by member states (Kagan 2002), the limitations on force have been equated to both an inefficiency of UN peacekeeping[12] *and* as the component that imbues peacekeeping with the moral legitimacy to intervene militarily and violate state sovereignty (Levine 2014).

Therefore, the presupposition that peacekeeping is less violent or more restrained than other forms of intervention (from peace enforcement to counterinsurgency to formal declared wars) is central to the legitimisation and distinction of the practice. Peacekeepers are cast akin to benevolent officials, upholding rules, laws or regulations.[13] Peacekeeping has been described as having a 'constabulary ethos' (Janowitz 1971) that positions its practitioners in the 'muddy transition' between war and peace (Levine 2014: 59). The 'restraint on force' tenet, therefore, provides powerful legitimacy to the peacekeeper myth because the relative scale of force is presumed to be ethically preferred to alternatives (such as peace enforcement) and, in comparison, can be used to legitimise martial force in a variety of peace operations.

Consent

The second tenet of 'traditional peacekeeping' is consent of warring parties to the presence and control of operations by a peacekeeping detachment. Again, the principle of consent distinguishes peacekeeping from other foreign military interventions. The principle of consent situates peacekeeping in a superior moral positioning, as the 'conditions of birth' of the external intervention – consent and the request of local parties – are perceived as distinct from the *mission civilatrice* (Paris 2010: 248) of historical European colonial and imperial invasions.

Legally, the host state must consent to the placement of a peacekeeping operation, otherwise violating Article 2 (7) of the UN Charter, but this is also an assumed component of peacekeeping operations by regional organisations. In inter-state conflicts, the respective governments provide consent, but in intra-state conflicts, often diverse and disputed groups are in conflict, resulting in difficulties identifying who the interested parties are, what their systems of communication look like, and how to verify the validity of their consent (Tsagourias 2007: 474).

In many peace processes, decision makers are often powerful men representing various factions and may not adequately represent the will of the general population or other affected groups, a criticism of UNOSOM I in Somalia speculated to have led to the failures of this mission (Tsagourias 2014). The UN Department of Peacekeeping Operations acknowledges that 'universality of consent' is not possible, particularly in volatile intra-state conflicts (UN DPKO 2008: 33). The presumption that consent bodes legitimacy for peacekeeping missions overlooks the ways in which consent is often not freely given by those without the power or authority to do so. However, the tenet of 'consent' is presumed to add legitimacy to peacekeeping as a form of international intervention because it distinguishes peacekeeping from other forms of international interventions – such as formally declared wars – where consent is not sought in any form.

Consent as a legal requirement for peacekeeping operations therefore imbues the missions with legitimacy because the presence of military operations does not violate established norm principles of sovereignty and non-intervention in international relations. Peacekeeping, therefore, is cast as an altruistic, volunteered use of UN member state resources to help other states and factions sort out disagreements in a supervised manner.

Impartiality

The third element of the peacekeeping trinity is impartiality or neutrality. While these terms are used interchangeably, neutrality refers to the character of the operation while impartiality is used to describe the conduct of the operation (Tsagourias 2007). I am using 'impartiality' as the third component of the trinity as, in contemporary missions, neutrality has been referred to as a legal fiction (Richardson 1995) and 'the claim to neutrality has been totally misrepresented to the extent that it mean[s] political and moral blindness or inaction' (Tsagourias 2007: 480). Nonetheless, there has been conflation of neutrality and impartiality in the mythologisation of peacekeeping. I want to flag how associated values of neutrality get mapped onto the notion of impartiality in the careless exchange of these terms to describe peacekeeping. Despite UN Secretary General Kofi Annan's claim that 'impartiality does not – and must not – mean neutrality in the face of evil' (Annan 1998), the 'doctrinal separation between neutrality and impartiality [has] not consolidate[d] in the discourse, nor in the practice of peace operations' (Malito 2017: 283, see also Donald 2002; Astor 2007).

The presumption is that if peacekeepers are impartial, they are so because they have nothing to gain personally from participating in the conflict. They are positioned as altruistic subjects motivated by a desire to help and to preserve the peace mandate. The analogy of peacekeepers as referees commonly is linked to the notion of impartiality. The United Nations explains that, 'Just as a good referee is impartial but will penalize infractions . . . a peacekeeping operation [addresses violations of the peace process] that a United Nations peacekeeping operation upholds'[14] (United Nations Peacekeeping, n.d.c). While impartiality is indeed referred to as the outcome of conduct in operations, the slippery linkages to neutrality occur in discussions of early or 'traditional' missions that monitored ceasefires.

Through the peacekeeping myth, states that fund and deploy peacekeeping troops are also cast as 'neutral', particularly as early peacekeeping missions' consent clauses included the consent of the composition of peacekeeping operations (not including military forces from the warring states, but also not including forces from the Great Powers on the Security Council). Therefore, peacekeeping mythologised casts peacekeeping actors in the subject positions of 'neutral helpers', removed from the political circumstances that have led to the requirement for externally imposed military force. Yet this vague and problematic representation of 'neutrality' does not actually align with UN operational requirements for impartiality. In doctrine, impartiality refers to the need for peacekeepers to coerce all parties in an even-handed way and to respond to the same infraction by various parties with consistency.[15] The predication 'impartial' therefore casts peacekeeping as a measured, rational and neutral activity.

It is worth noting that the doctrinal imperative for individual peacekeepers to perform to this standard fails to account for individual-level politics that play out in peacekeeping theatre, where individual peacekeepers may be frustrated, isolated and facing others who are recalcitrant and unable to match the level of force that peacekeepers wield, leading to great potential for 'temptation to violence' (Levine 2014: 65). Impartiality does not preclude the use of violence, rather it requires peacekeepers to be uniform in their application of force. It is not difficult to imagine how challenging this would be for peacekeepers under stress, duress or fatigue. The positioning of peacekeepers as subjects (within this discourse) capable of rational, apolitical and universally impartial capacity is how the peacekeeper myth manages to conflate impartiality with political neutrality. It assumes that both peacekeeping and peacekeepers are apolitical and rational constructs, absent of bias and preference.

Yet, impartiality is central to how the peacekeeper myth legitimises the (restricted) use of force. Howard and Dayal note that impartiality is 'the bedrock of peacekeepers' legitimacy' (2018: 75), again contrasting peacekeeping's impartiality clause with the absence of impartiality in peace enforcement missions[16] that may require uneven application of lethal force towards opposing parties to determine or secure a particular political outcome.

The impartiality–neutrality conflation is furthered by presupposed knowledge about liberal peace interventions built upon assumptions that 'external forces can intervene into the peace processes, maintaining a safe distance from parties' conflict' (Malito 2017: 281). Therefore, while the actuality for impartiality and neutrality have not escaped critical attention, these tenets have been mythologised in the peacekeeper myth as an element of the practice that distinguishes peacekeeping as an ethically superior use of military force in global affairs.

In sum, the trinity components are used not to describe peacekeeping's specific definitive activities, but to set peacekeeping apart from, or distinct from, other forms of militarised interventions. Peacekeeping is defined largely by what it is not (for example, peace enforcement or imperialist war). Peacekeeping has been described as having 'an identity as a security-related military function that is honourably separable from war' (Levine 2014: 3), and peacekeepers as agents have been specified as 'fundamentally not having enemies' (13). It is in this comparative construction of peacekeeping that the mythologisation of the concept has occurred, justifying the activities based on how they, relatively, are an ethically preferred option.

Myth Making, Militarisation and Martial Peace: Why Do Myths Matter?

Peacekeeping in academic and institutional discourse has been mythologised. The peacekeeper myth, or the assumption that peacekeeping is an ethically 'good' use of militarised force, has occurred through a widespread emphasis on the 'trinity' characterisations of peacekeeping in UN doctrine. The use of the trinity to define and typologise peacekeeping has led to a dominant understanding of peacekeeping according to these three principles. Yet, the emphasis on the trinity in peacekeeping has resulted in peacekeeping's positioning as a *distinct form of* international intervention. Peacekeeping is just one of many forms of liberal peace interventions used in international relations, yet its mythologisation has occurred precisely from efforts to distinguish it from others; to position it as superior to these forms because of implied values associated with the practice.[17]

Yet, as this book intends to demonstrate, peacekeeping is a political practice. The peacekeeping myth functions to obscure the politics of the practice by romanticising peacekeeping as ethically distinct from other forms of interventions using martial force. The widespread beliefs about peacekeeping's ethical use of force, reproduced through discourses about peacekeeping, normalised liberal peace apparatuses in global politics and legitimised the use of military force, technologies and techniques in the creation of limited political visions about the world. These technologies and techniques involve the lethal use of force, coercion, threat and martial presence to enforce 'peace' – martial peace – and in turn reinforce certain geopolitical and social relations.

As the peacekeeping myth does not manifest uniformly across cultural contexts, Chapters 3, 4 and 5 proceed to explore how these normative assumptions about the apolitical or 'ethical' nature of peacekeeping have influenced how martial violence by the Canadian state has been justified domestically and internationally.

Notes

1. Myths are co-constitutive of ideology; they are ideological paradigms that 'signify intertextuality of myths along a mythographical sign-chain' (Cooke 2016: 75).

2. Cynthia Weber (2014: 6) distinguishes conscious ideologies (like IR traditions of realism and idealism) from unconscious ideologies ('ideologies we don't have names for'). Militarism may be less overtly conscious than, say, political realism, yet it is intimately bound up within assumptions of political realism, making it both inescapable yet invisible (Jackson 2013: 214). Ideology is reproduced through stories that 'seem to make so much sense' (Weber 2014: 6), yet we rarely consider how these stories – myths – function politically. This is because myths are often wielded to transform one view of the world to seem to be true or natural.

3. For more, see BBC Bitesize. 'Reasons for westward expansion'. Available at https://www.bbc.co.uk/bitesize/guides/znhkpg8/revision/2.

4. Examples (not exhaustive) include Diehl et al. (1998); Demurenko and Nikitin (1997); Bellamy et al. (2010).

5. Early generation UN peacekeeping (what Bellamy et al. 2010 dub 'traditional peacekeeping') was used in inter-state conflicts when a ceasefire needed to be monitored. Later missions, including Cyprus (UNFICYP) and Somalia (UNOSOM I), were confounded with how to employ restraint on violence when there was an absence of ceasefire or wide-scale harm to civilians. The presumption was that the changing nature of conflict required peacekeeping strategy and mandates to adapt.

6. In contrast to the New War rationale for shifting peacekeeping practice, Alex Bellamy rejects the notion that the 1990s saw an increased number and complexity of peace operations as a result of changes in conflict areas themselves (2014). He instead notes that missions of this era were directed by the interests of the intervenors, rather than the targets of peace intervention, resulting in mismatched expectations of what was required for peace. Critical theorists such as Christopher Clapham (1998), Mark Duffield (2001) and Roland Paris (2002) have similarly argued that peace missions of the 1990s and 2000s attempted to transplant liberal democratic values of core nations to the host states in which 'peace' was enforced. This book will build more upon this critical literature in an investigation of martial peace and the peacekeeper myth, but here it is worth noting that while there is disagreement about the *intentions* of peace operation mandates, it is historically well accepted that 'traditional peacekeeping' missions of the 1950s operated very differently from modern missions that utilise much more robust and overt force, such as MINUSMA in Mali.

7. This chapter will not delve into the historical or nuanced overview in these shifts as this has been covered very comprehensively elsewhere (see Rikhye 1984; Goulding 1993; Segal 1995; Bellamy et al. 2010). In addition, there is not space for a full discussion the issues and controversies of peace operations, their mandates, or the abilities of contributing countries to effectively fulfil these mandates (see Sitkowski 2007; Diehl and Balas 2014; Berdal and Ucko 2015). Instead, I seek to highlight the lack of clarity, both within UN doctrine and academic study of peacekeeping in general, on what constitutes 'peacekeeping' as a distinct activity from other militarised interventions, or as Daniel H. Levine articulates, a *sui generis* activity, distinct from war, policing or intervening governance (2013: 5).

8. Andrzej Sitkowski has argued that the mythologisation of UN peacekeeping has caused the UN to cling to 'traditional' peacekeeping with unnecessary stubbornness and failed results (2007), arguing that the UN and members should either embrace contemporary, more militarised solutions to peace management or not intervene at all. This book departs from Sitkowski's recommendation and instead takes a firm anti-militarist stance.

9. I was inspired by this methodological practice, used by Linda Åhäll in her book *Sexing War/Policing Gender* (2015: 41–2), and am grateful to her clear documentation of this methodology to illustrate what she terms the myth of motherhood. I utilise the same methodological strategy to determine the semiotic approach to representing the peacekeeper myth ('how' the peacekeeper myth has been formed) as well as the discursive approach that considers the effects and consequences of this representation in latter chapters (see also Hall 1997: 6).

10. By way of example, Tsagourias (2007) notes that the language of 'self-defence' was used in ONUC's (1960–4) authorisation, even though the language was extended to include defence of territorial integrity of the Congo, rather than defence of military individuals.

11. Expanded mission mandates that include the tactical use of force are labelled 'robust peacekeeping' as defined in contemporary UN doctrine ('UN PK Operations Principles and Guidelines', Concept Note on Robust Peacekeeping', 2009),

not to be confused with peace enforcement, but instead defined as 'the use of force by a United Nations peacekeeping operation at the tactical level, with the authorisation of the Security Council, to defend its mandate against spoilers whose activities pose a threat to civilians or risk undermining the peace process' (UN DPKO 2008).

12. There has been attention paid to the legitimacy of extending UN mandates' use of force requirements beyond the traditional 'individual' self-defence (Berdal and Ucko 2015) as well as scholarly claims that peacekeeping is only efficient if it possesses and utilises capabilities akin to seasoned, developed armies (James 1990; Thierry 2007; Sitkowski 2007; Autesserre 2019).

13. While this positions peacekeepers as restrained in their use of violence, what is obscured in this mythologised representation are the ways that peacekeepers themselves may deliberately or indirectly cause harm to those under their tutelage.

14. For more, see UN Peacekeeping Principles, available at https://peacekeeping. un.org/en/principles-of-peacekeeping.

15. See Brahami Report, paras 48–50; see also Report of the Special Committee on Peacekeeping Operations (1977) that states 'such forces must . . . act with complete objectivity' (cited in Tsagourias 2007, fn. 82)

16. It has been argued that impartiality in peace enforcement or stabilisation missions is compromised when soldiers must fight directly to protect civilians, and this has cascading effects for non-governmental organisation (NGO) and civilian workers who may rely on the UN for transportation, thereby limiting the peacekeeping operation's perceived 'impartiality' (Howard and Dayal 2014: 75).

17. International relations has seen a proliferation of liberal peace approaches, which are positioned as 'value-neutral techniques where impartial international actors, immune from power relations or political preferences, mediate between rival parties' (Malito 2017: 281).

CHAPTER 3

Cultural Nostalgia and the Political Construction of the Canadian Peacekeeping Myth

As outlined, the peacekeeping myth involves the belief that peacekeeping is an ethically and practically distinct use of military force, set apart by its *intention* to create peace, rather than its means (militarised coercive force). This distinction positions peacekeeping as apolitical and functions to legitimise military interventions made in the name of keeping or making peace. Understanding peacekeeping as *myth* is a means to understand structural manifestations of military power; the peacekeeping myth reifies militarism through its ideological legitimation of violence. Part of the peacekeeper myth's appeal is because it shares ontological assumptions of mainstream international relations, including belief about the inevitability of violent conflict and the need for militaries to cease conflict through violence. Exploring peacekeeping as mythology helps to illustrate how violence is legitimised through discourses about the necessity of military force to create political change and about the value of militaries as essential institutions for creating peace and security.

Like all myths, the peacekeeping myth does not *look the same* across time and space because it contains culturally specific and fluid adaptations. In other words, the culturally specific values linked to the peacekeeping myth, and the manifestations of militarism that accompany this, vary across different spatial and temporal contexts. Cultural values shape military institutions and in turn shape how processes of militarisation, militarist ideologies and broader systems of martial politics unfold. We cannot comparatively measure militarisation's effects because of the ways cultural values shape military institutions and how this variably manifests across time and space (Lutz 2002: 275). Therefore, to illustrate how a particular manifestation of the peacekeeping myth has been used to legitimise militarism, military violence, and warfare in culturally specific ways, I now turn to an exploration of the peacekeeping myth in Canadian politics.

Myths develop in nuanced ways across cultural contexts and the Canadian peacekeeper myth is no exception. Canada's peacekeeping myth builds upon mythologised assumptions about UN peacekeeping, but manifests as the widely believed narrative that Canada's military is uniquely suited for international peacekeeping, exemplified by the state's role in the formation of early UN peacekeeping, its prominent Cold War contributions, and the presumed Canadian political ethos that aligns with a peacekeeping praxis. An examination of Canada's version of the peacekeeping myth illustrates the development, longevity and immutability of this myth in national context. The Canadian peacekeeping myth is perpetuated because it signals positive symbolism about Canada's place in the world.

Despite efforts by individual scholars and evidence of political events that could have or should have destabilised the Canadian peacekeeping myth, it has stubbornly endured. As I will outline, this is because myths are not static; rather, they evolve within political discourse and popular understandings. Importantly, myths' durability is enhanced when they affirmatively reflect something about who 'we' believe we are and who 'we' want to be. In the Canadian context, the peacekeeper myth is understood to reflect something about the unique moral and altruistic nature of Canadians, allowing the nation to ignore the ways that state-directed violence has been used against others at home and abroad.

The *Canadian* peacekeeping myth draws from the broader association of UN peacekeeping as an ethically superior use of military force and manifests into a culturally specific set of beliefs about Canada's roles in global peacekeeping. Key elements of the Canadian version of the myth position Canada's military as historically and practically an idealised peacekeeping nation, evidenced by its long-standing identity as a helpful-fixer middle power. Within the Canadian version of the peacekeeping myth, there is, of course, the assumption that peacekeeping is markedly different from other types of militarised force (for example, peacemaking or multilateral counterterrorist activities). In the Canadian myth however, the distinction of peacekeeping from other forms of militarised deployment is normatively significant because it is understood to reflect a 'distinctly Canadian political ethos and ethics' (Jefferess 2009: 712).

The Canadian version of the peacekeeper myth, therefore, promotes peacekeeping as the cornerstone of Canada's global identity and representative of the types of values that Canada, and Canadians, endorse and embody. Canada has been described as 'the world's foremost peacekeepers'

(Potter 2009: 4). According to the myth, peacekeeping is 'in our genetic code as a nation' (Off 2000: 2) due to the imagined compatibility of Canada's (often unstated) national political values with the romanticised elements of international peacekeeping (which, as we explored in Chapter 2, are understood to be impartiality, non-use of force, and consent). The alignment of Canada's imagined national identity with the mythologised requirements of international peacekeeping is how scholars and politicians alike have imagined Canada as 'the world's foremost peacekeeping nation' (Jockel 1994).

This chapter focuses on the contextual elements of the Canadian peacekeeping myth and how this myth has risen to prominence in the nation's political imaginary. I suggest that its permutations include positioning Canada's international identity – and ethico-political virtues signalled in the peacekeeping myth – as characterised by moral altruism, innocence, paternal helpfulness and non-violence. I map the evolution and existence of the Canadian peacekeeping myth, including the symbols associated with this branded identity. This chapter explores the evolution of the Canadian myth, including tracing its emergence as a core facet of imagined identity, and shows why this myth has been embraced: it gives Canada a special 'role' in the world, justifies Canada's military deployments as altruistic and helpful, smooths over gendered, racialised and colonial hierarchies within the Canadian polity, and positions the use of military force at home and abroad as helpful, innocent and benevolent: in the service of peace and order.

Normative Foundations of/in the Canadian Version of the Peacekeeping Myth

As explored in Chapter 2, the broad peacekeeping myth functions to obscure the politics of military interventions by romanticising UN peacekeeping and mythologising it according to the 'holy trinity' principles of consent, neutrality and restriction on force. The characteristics of traditional peacekeeping – consent (altruism), neutrality (paternal helpfulness and innocence) and restriction on force (non-violence) – are reproduced also in the discursive circulation of Canada's version of the peacekeeping myth and confirm peacekeeping as a desirable activity for Canada's military.

In the Canadian version of the peacekeeping myth, which assumes Canada is an ideal, perfectly suited nation/al military for international peacekeeping, the presumed values of international peacekeeping become associated with desired ethico-political values Canadians and the Canadian state wish to emanate. The association of altruism, non-violence, and helpfulness with peacekeeping is how militarism, militarisation and martial politics become legitimised: peacekeeping is understood as distinct from other forms of militarised force because of the assumption that peacekeeping is driven by these normative values. Importantly, violence by the Canadian state has been imagined as innocent – without intention to cause harm or violence, and with the intention to help in a paternal and helpful way. Yet, as this book seeks to illustrate, the Canadian peacekeeping myth that assumes peacekeeping by the Canadian military exemplifies altruism, non-violence, paternal helpfulness and innocence can explain how non-peacekeeping interventions, like the war in Afghanistan and numerous militarised violences towards Indigenous communities in Canada, have also been legitimised: the peacekeeping myth's reproduction and representation according to these four values conflates these ideals with *all* Canadian military activities.

Discursively, Canadian martial activities – including non-peacekeeping activities – have been represented as altruistic, non-violent, paternally helpful and innocent. This representation has been manifested through the Canadian version of the peacekeeping myth. The consequences have been that the normative assumptions in the myth have become conflated with the Canadian military itself. As I've sought to demonstrate through my examination of myths as symbolic, the problem with this conflation is that militarism and martial politics of the Canadian state become obscured.

Importantly, as I'll conclude later in this chapter, it matters little when scholars or political elites have exposed – or 'myth-busted' – occurrences where Canadian military activities have been driven by economic interest, excessive violence, unhelpfulness or malignance. The immutability of the Canadian peacekeeper myth endures *despite* its one-dimensionality or outright falsity; people like it. It is a politically effective brand and there is political utility in representing Canada in this manner (Wegner 2021a). Canadians like to believe that the peacekeeping myth reflects upon the nation in a positive way. Canadians – citizens and political leaders alike – love to believe that they are innocent, helpful, non-violent and altruistic; the peacekeeping myth is a well-loved and widely believed narrative that 'confirms' these values are somehow distinctly Canadian. These four values are implied and signalled through discourse underpinning the peacekeeping myth. The peacekeeping myth in the Canadian context, therefore, reproduces these romanticised ideals as inherent characteristics of peacekeeping and qualities that Canadians wish to associate with their national identity: altruism, paternal helpfulness, innocence and non-violence. These qualities are discussed in turn below.

Altruism can be understood as 'behaviour that benefits others at a personal cost to the behaving individual' (Kerr et al. 2004). This aligns with IR's preoccupation with actors (both states and individuals) as self-serving and dominant theoretical frameworks that see global power and interest in a zero-sum manner. Actions understood to be altruistic, therefore, assume that the *recipients* of altruism gain something, potentially at the expense of states acting altruistically. In Canada's peacekeeping myth, there is an assumption that by willing or eager participation in peace interventions, Canada has altruistic intentions that automatically translate into results aligned with the interests of, and benefit to, the target community(s). The association of altruism with Canadian peacekeeping imbues the military (and their various activities) with legitimacy (Barnett 2012: 486), particularly as these activities are represented as having the consent of those whose lives are being intervened. Rather than representing 'peacekeeping' as beneficial to the Canadian state, political economy or international power relations, the peacekeeping myth has represented the deployment of martial force as beneficial to the populations against whom force is deployed, and morally significant because it is assumed to be at a cost to the Canadian nation.

Paternalism is not simply defined by interference, but as *coercive* interference (Dworkin 1972; Barnett 2016: 26). Paternalism is a structure by which power relations flow: sometimes by direct and coercive means and sometimes through 'covert, indirect, and gentler mechanisms' (Barnett 2012: 500). The peacekeeping myth's embrace of paternalism as a virtue justifies military interference in the name of another's interests (Applebaum 2007; Barnett 2012: 493), encapsulated by the principle of consent that presumes the desired presence of martial forces. Peacekeeping, even in 'traditional' format, therefore, is paternalist because its 'gentler mechanisms' are utilised for the purpose of securing political preferences. Paternalism as a virtue of the peacekeeping myth reinforces power relations: it casts a distinction between those that can legitimately use violence (peacekeepers) and those whose violence is cast as illegitimate. In this representation, paternalism is desirable because martial violence by Canadian forces is legitimised through the association of peacekeeping with rational, restrained use of force by a paternal (or perhaps parental) institution against irrational aggressors. The myth's 'helpful paternalism' virtue is contiguous with other IR theories that justify state violence as a 'political-legal force . . . [contrasted with] "violence" that is used by citizens, denizens, aliens and other people' (Frazer and Hutchings 2019: 9).

Paternal helpfulness is also expressly gendered, as Canadian peacekeepers have been represented as 'white knights' challenging 'dark threats' (Razack 2004), and, as Chapter 4 will explore specifically, associated with white masculinity. In Canadian representations of peacekeeping, conflicts are often positioned as humanitarian crises, including the representation of the 'victim-rescuer model' (Pugh 2004: 48) that assumes that peacekeeping's primary objective is to help individuals and communities who are unable to solve issues themselves and require a benevolent paternal figure acting as 'referee' or 'champion' to help victimised communities. The myth casts a peacekeeping force as a parental figure helping child-like populations sort out their squabbles. In many representations, the myth has been mobilised as legitimising martial violence to protect feminised victims subject to effects of the illegitimate violence waged by aggressive insurgents. Both 'referee' and 'protector' tropes in the peacekeeping myth represent the actions of Canadian peacekeepers as altruistic, as if these acts primarily serve the populations who need 'help'.

In addition to infantilising and trivialising the politics that lead to peacekeeping deployments, this discourse is also heavily steeped in racialised assumptions. Sandra Whitworth explained that discourse about peacekeeping tells us 'A great deal about who conducts peacekeeping missions ("us") and who needs peacekeeping missions ("them")' (2004: 25), emphasising that this discourse is largely about the constitution of racialised identities of Canada's military and state, as well as those countries presumed 'in need' of peacekeeping's promises (Whitworth 2004: 44). In short, the values signalled in the Canadian peacekeeper myth centre whiteness as a subject position and casts upon those who are 'peacekept' Orientalist (Said 1978) reflections of us/them.

While paternalism in the peacekeeping myth is bonded to the notion of helpfulness, Jennifer Terry reminds us that 'the urge to "help" has rationalized many violent military adventures and is driven by a visual economy of the suffering of Others . . . their bodies become the grounds for intervention and further "peacekeeping" militarist practices' (2009: 206). The peacekeeping myth therefore interpellates relationships of victim and rescuer in ways that obscure the power politics in this relationship and instead cast military intervention as necessary, inherently good, and helpful. As 'traditional' UN peacekeeping requires consent, the peacekeeping myth has romanticised peacekeeping as a practice without imperial desire. The peacekeeper is mythologised as the altruistic helper, rather than, for example, a colonial overlord or a professional soldier doing paid work that facilitates specific political interests.

On this note, paternalism might not immediately be considered a virtue: it has been associated with past colonial projects viewed as 'in the interests of, for the good of, and as promoting the welfare of the colonized' (Narayan 1995: 133–4) or aligned with a 'deeply held belief in the need to and the right to dominate others for their own good' (Razack 2004: 10).

Despite academic critique of contemporary peacekeeping discourse and practice – labels which include 'mission civilatrice' (Paris 2002; see also Ayoob 2004; Chandler 2005) or 'imperialism's new disguise' (Schellhaas and Seegers 2009)[1] – Canada's peacekeeping myth's paternalist virtue is represented unidimensionally as helpful or useful. The Canadian version of the myth assumes that peacekeeping is an inherent good because of, rather than in spite of, paternal helpfulness. As will be discussed in greater detail in Chapters 4 and 5, this outlook is unsurprising considering how Canadian militarised force used against civilians has also been justified as helpful, non-violent and necessarily paternal. This positive understanding of paternalism as helpful is coded in Western epistemological perspectives that justify and naturalise gendered and racialised accounts of the world and sanitise imperial history and the dispossession and exploitation of Othered peoples in international relations (see Krishna 2001; Barkawi 2016; Barkawi and Laffey 2006).

The two other co-constitutive values associated with the Canadian myth are **innocence and non-violence.** In the Canadian peacekeeping myth, it is assumed that peacekeepers possess an inherent form of **innocence**, rooted in their altruistic desires to 'help'. The holy trinity principles in the peacekeeping myth (consent, restriction on force, and neutrality) reinforce the mythologisation of peacekeeping as innocent and non-violent. Traditional peacekeeping's restrictions on force (limited to self-defence) have been mythologised to position peacekeepers themselves as 'innocent'. This is evidenced in UN doctrine that described peacekeepers as 'soldiers without enemies' (Fabian 1971) and is articulated in scholarship that promotes the morality of peacekeeping (Levine 2014). Non-violence in the peacekeeping myth does not mean a complete absence of violence, although as I will show in the section to follow, the cultural mobilisations of the myth have presented Canadian and UN peacekeepers as stopping violence without any martial force, representations that show peacekeepers verbally evoking United Nations authority to deter aggressors but not actually using physical force themselves.

While 'violence' itself is a slippery term and a philosophically contested concept (Galtung 1969; Arendt 1970; Confortini 2006; Haan 2008), in the peacekeeping myth non-violence signals restrained or extremely limited physical violence by martial forces. '**Non-violence**' as a characteristic reproduced in the peacekeeping myth refers to limited – or absence of – martial violence. To borrow Katharine Millar's (2021) distinction, *martial violence* is differentiated from more expansive understandings of *political violence*, whereby martiality is constitutive of practices of war, combat and the deployment of militarised lethal capacities. Non-violence as signified in the peacekeeping myth suggests that physical violence is only used as a last measure, actions that leaders and soldiers begrudgingly and compassionately employ in self-defence or defence of innocent civilians. The peacekeeping myth justifies violence in the name of altruism and paternalistic benefit for those who are 'peacekept', justifying state-led martial violence as for 'the necessary maintenance of social order' (Frazer and Hutchings 2019: 98) and therefore not offensive or aggressively violent.

Yet within the peacekeeping mythology, it is not only civilians who are cast as innocent victims subject to violence. The peacekeeping myth has also been used to distort and stretch innocence to reflect this virtue upon peacekeepers themselves. The myth represents peacekeepers as witnesses to evil (Razack 2004) who are forced to intervene to uphold their moral duties. Innocence can be mobilised in many ways, yet I find Miriam Ticktin's definition most useful: innocence is 'a state of moral and epistemic purity' (2017: 578). Innocence as an implied virtue of peacekeeping positions states as without political intention and without political desires in their promotion or practice of peace missions. The 'holy trinity' requirements of neutrality/impartiality, when mythologised, also casts peacekeepers themselves as innocent and apolitical actors. As Ticktin explains,

> Those inspired by humanitarian sentiments may try to bypass politics, claiming to act only as witnesses to injustice or in response to the immediacy of suffering, but the political innocence they proclaim ignores the privilege that allows them to act – it is a refusal to acknowledge the structural inequalities that allow them to be humanitarians, witnesses, or saviours. (Ticktin 2017: 583)

Innocence can also be understood as an epistemological stance, a central characterisation of white subject-positioning that, as Meera Sabaratnam (2020: 13) explains, 'seek[s] to emphasise the *inadvertent, unintentional* and *exceptional* character' of racism, which I argue can be extended to the justification of racist, colonial, gendered or martial violence. Innocence, reflected in a white subject positioning, professes good faith and moral respectability for its referent (Wekker 2016). In the case of the peacekeeping myth, innocence becomes the position of peacekeeping soldiers or police officers, as well as the nations they represent. The belief that innocence is an ethico-political value inherent in, and exemplary of, Canada's peacekeeping myth is central for continued justification of martial force, and colonial/imperial violences informed by white supremacy inside and outside the polity.

Epistemologies of innocence, according to Sabaratnam, 'separate racially privileged peoples from the historical and contemporary production of the privilege or consequences of their actions' (2020: 14).

Innocence, therefore, not only justifies violence as a key virtue signalled in the peacekeeping myth but also explains why the myth has been beloved by the political actors that reproduce it. In short, the association of innocence with Canada's peacekeeping myth obscures the political nature of peacekeeping. It allows Canadians to deny their complicity, privilege and benefits in/from the status quo international order from which they benefit. Sherene Razack (2007) has emphasised this in her assessment of media coverage about Canadian peacekeepers in Rwanda that largely focused on the traumatisation of Canadian soldiers who were forced to 'witness the evil', diverting our focus to the pain of soldiers rather than that of Rwandans. These representations have positioned Canadian soldiers as innocent in the face of unspeakable violence they witness while deployed and position Canada as a nation who does not benefit from the international order that peacekeeping seeks to defend.

The altruism and innocence presumed in the peacekeeping myth reinforces Spivak's (1994) assertion that humanitarian interventions are understood to be white men who save brown women from brown men (see also Cooke 1996). In these constructions reproduced through the peacekeeping myth, 'we' saviours feel powerful in our ability to 'save' others, and the presumed altruistic, apolitical motivations of these missions enable us to simultaneously claim innocence – to purify or absolve peacekeeping as containing colonialist aspiration. These reflected virtues permit those that reproduce the peacekeeping myth(s) to absolve themselves from benefiting politically or economically from peace interventions. The perceived altruism of the myth, and its paternal tactics, are represented as compassion for feminised or racialised others. Ticktin explains that innocence is an inherently political concept that

> has become central to the politics of help, pity, and rescue . . . encourag[ing] a form of expansion, colonizing new landscapes to produce innocent victims, reproducing a certain sentimental political project of 'protection' in the process – one might call it a predatory compassion. (Ticktin 2017: 586)

Yet, as myths smooth, distract and repackage nuance into tidy narratives and aesthetic visions, the peacekeeping myth does not present Canadian military activities as predatory, but, instead, as helpful, non-violent endeavours for which the nation should be commended. This self-congratulatory theme is explored further in the ways that the Canadian peacekeeping myth has developed, largely through storytelling, narratives and theorisations that present peacekeeping in a positive light.

Canada's Peacekeeping Myth

I am not the first scholar to refer to peacekeeping-as-myth in the Canadian context. My novel contributions, however, are to flesh out what has been called the 'peacekeeping myth' as a rhetorical shorthand for inaccurate military historiography and to investigate this discourse as integral to the construction of peacekeeping as a *symbolic myth*, which has significant political power and consequences. Canada's peacekeeping myth illustrates a unique militarist ideology and a 'normative imaginary of violence' (Millar and Tidy 2017) that is celebrated in Canadian political culture.

Most scholarly discussions of the Canadian peacekeeping myth have centred upon the fallaciousness of the myth. These critics seek to 'reveal' that Canada has a robust war history that is overlooked in the promotion of the peacekeeper myth (Granatstein 2002a; Wagner 2006; McKay and Swift 2012; Summerfield 2018), or to show that there has been a relative decline of Canadian contributions to peacekeeping since the Cold War, making the myth little more than inaccurate or over-stated nostalgia (Staples 2006; Dorn 2007, 2009; Carroll 2016).

Other scholarship about Canada's peacekeeping myth has considered the violent, racist or misogynist practices that peacekeepers have committed, noting an absence of these transgressions in the myth's sanitised visions of peacekeeping (Razack 2004; Whitworth 2004). These critics seek to reveal that the inherent feel-good sentiments of the peacekeeping myth should be questioned, considering nefarious elements of Canada's peacekeeping history and contemporary practices (Härting and Kamboureli 2009).

Finally, interdisciplinary scholarship has looked at the ways in which this myth has been reproduced culturally and sustained through various social and political practices (Gough 2002; Dorn 2005; Richler 2012; McCullough 2016; Mutimer 2016), where the selectiveness of historical storytelling about Canada's roles in peace and war is highlighted. Across the various literatures, what is relatively consistent is an understanding that the Canadian peacekeeping myth is the product of long-standing nostalgic desire for Canada's identity to be associated with peacekeeping (Jefferess 2009), despite the myth's one-dimensional construction, outright embellishments and historical inaccuracies.

Scholarship on the Canadian myth, with few exceptions (Härting and Kamboureli 2009; Jefferess 2009), has contained a dominant focus on what the myth 'is' and therefore lacked a sustained theoretical investigation about what the myth *does*. Considerations of the peacekeeper myth have largely centred on the ways that the myth functions to summon a cohesive 'national identity' or consistent historical narrative about Canadian foreign policy; scholarship has both criticised and celebrated the peacekeeper myth for bolstering a sense of Canadian patriotic nationalism. The peacekeeper myth has dominantly been reproduced by/in academic literature and has also been mobilised in political elite rhetoric, as will be outlined in greater detail in sections to follow. The discursive articulation of 'us' (the citizenry) and 'them' (all others outside of an envisioned boundary) occurs in foreign policy narratives crafted by academics and political leaders alike (Walker 1993). Through foreign policy narrations, the vision of whom 'we' are or what 'we' are like is attached to conceptions of national identity. While national branding does not describe an individual's personal self, many foreign policy narrations, including the Canadian peacekeeping myth, are effective in their ability to evoke personal identification with their messages. Promoting the 'identity' of the nation (as defined by affirmative characteristics) reflects individual desire to have those imagined, self-professed nationalistic qualities reflect their personal self. This may explain how and why peacekeeping as a prioritised foreign policy activity has historically held great traction in Canadian public opinion (Martin and Fortmann 1995; Anker 2005; McCullough 2016; Mutimer 2016).

Benedict Anderson considered how nationalism has been hypostasised as a mechanism for personal identity demarcation. He defined the nation as an *imagined* community, rather than a *sui generis* category in itself (1991: 49). As the community distinguishes itself 'in the style in which they are imagined' (49), the individual associates his or her personal identity as bound up in this same image. Anderson explained that despite actual inequality or exploitation that may prevail in each community, the nation is always conceived as 'a deep, horizontal comradeship' (50), the imagined bond for which citizens are willing to die and to kill for. The national imagined community reinforces racialised, sexualised, classed and gendered hierarchies that sustain the ways that political communities justify and desire to die and kill for. The peacekeeping myth obscures these hierarchies by representing peace and order as the normative unifying objective definitive of Canada's imagined political community. Canada's relatively short history of overseas military endeavours, from supporting the British in the South African 'Boer Wars' and the First World War to its independent sovereign choice to deploy in the Second World War, the Korean wars, the Gulf wars, and the Afghanistan war, have all been 'performed under the pretence of the interests of peace and order' (Jefferess 2009: 716).

Historical narratives have promoted the ideal of the peaceable nation and position Canada's emergence as a settler colonial nation as without war or excessive conflict violence, a false account criticised in emerging contemporary scholarship (Jefferess 2009; Choquette 2019). Canadian historiography has often reinforced state-making endeavours as non-imperialist. Canadian historiography is complicit within nationalistic and political meaning-making about Canada's political community. The peace-oriented nationalist identity was developed as a sort of 'civic ideology that [is] continually recreated and reinforced' (Francis 1997: 10, cited in See 2018) in response to a lack of common religion, language and ethnicity in Canada.

The notion of peacefulness as a central component of Canadian state-building history was often expressed in contrast to the presentation of Western Europe's undemocratic nature and excessive bloodshed in the nineteenth century. Canada's formal establishment as a state in 1867 was described as a 'peaceful antidote to the violent spectacle of . . . the failed American experiment of republicanism' (See 2018: 515). Canadian nationalism in these accounts therefore developed as an attempt to distinguish the country from the United States (Cook 1986; Champion 2010; See 2018). Constructions of Canadian history contrast Canadian martial forces (the North-West Mounted Police) with a 'violent, sometimes tyrannical, and increasingly imperialistic United States' (See 2018: 513) and the American mythology of the Wild West settlement of the 'frontier' involving explicit violence. Canada's settlement history has been presented as one of civility and the creation of order through diplomatic relations with Indigenous groups, a presentation that employs egregious oversight of the ways in which violence, excessive force, and colonial land acquisition occurred in explicitly imperialist means (Choquette 2019), or how latter genocidal practices, including the establishment of residential schools, relied upon martial policing forces for enforcement. The representation of Canadian martial force historically has leaned upon notions of 'peaceful' military tropes to legitimise violence and warfare against Indigenous communities.

As will be discussed in Chapter 5, Canada's domestic deployment of militarised force against citizens, from the Red River Rebellion in 1869 to the ongoing Wet'suwet'en land protests, has employed narratives about the use of benevolent militarised force in the name of peace and order. The use of force against Indigenous populations has been positioned as a form of benevolent paternalism, rather than explicit neo-colonialism. This is perhaps unsurprising. Eric Hobsbawm (Hobsbawm and Ranger 1992) theorised that nationalist discourse promotes *select* values, norms and accounts of history, and Canada's nationalist narratives about peacekeeping and the peaceable nation have therefore focused on select events of the past and thematic discourses that make peacekeeping as a national tradition appear historically congruent. The idea of the 'peaceable nation', captured in Canada's version of the peacekeeping myth, has distracted Canadians from history and contemporary politics defined by overt colonial violence.

Peacekeeping as a cornerstone of national identity has been promoted through seductive storytelling about who Canadians are, and what Canada does in the world. The Standing Committee on National Defence and Veterans Affairs explained: 'Canadians have always seen peacekeeping as an important element of their identity and of their country's position on the international stage, even when peacekeeping meant little for much of the international community' (Parliament of Canada 1993: 7) Peacekeeping has been articulated as 'firmly embedded in the national psyche' (Martin and Fortmann 1995: 384; see also Mueller 1992), a 'touchstone of our identity' (Cohen 2008: 124). Support for peacekeeping has been claimed to be 'virtually unanimous' among Canadians (Citizens' Inquiry into Peace and Security 1992: 23), and Canada has been called a 'peacekeeping country *par excellence*' (Jockel 1994: 1). Peacekeeping, as a celebrated national mythos, is understood to reproduce particular 'Canadian values' that are inherent in Canadian culture: 'a commitment to tolerance, to democracy, equity and human rights, the peaceful resolution of differences' (as cited in Howell 2005: 8), reiterated by political elites as 'an unswerving commitment to peace' (cited in Cox and Sjolander 1998). Sandra Whitworth explains that the peacekeeper myth 'locates Canada as a selfless middle power, acting with a kind of moral purity not normally exhibited by contemporary states' (2004: 14).

In the 1990 Citizens' Forum on Canada's Future, a synthesis of feedback provided by 400,000 Canadians through letters, poems, discussion groups and a toll-free 'idea line', the report noted that 'Our view of ourselves, and the world's view of us, as a free, peaceable, non-violent people is of great importance . . . [participants] express substantial support for non-violence and for Canada's historical role as an international peacekeeper' (Canada, Privy Council Office 1991: 44) There is a strong association with Canada's international reputation as a peacekeeper that is tied to the ideas of altruism, paternal helpfulness and non-violence, elements of the Canadian peacekeeper myth to be explored later in this chapter. These narratives are illustrative of how the broader peacekeeping myth (the belief that peacekeeping is distinct and normatively superior from other forms of militarised force) intertwines with Canada's peacekeeping myth (Canada's military is inherently well suited for peacekeeping due to normative national values) that promotes a vision of who Canada and Canadians are in the world: altruistic, peaceful and helpful actors seeking to secure peace-oriented, non-imperialistic or non-violent goals. The evolution of this mythological relationship is discussed in greater detail in the sections to follow.

In addition to the signification that peacekeeping reflects about Canadians' personal and political ethos, it is the affirmative association of the myth with militarised institutions that is also of importance. The presumed values of the Canadian peacekeeping myth (helpfulness, altruism, non-violence and innocence) have become associated not only with individual and collective identities, but also with the Canadian *military*. This will be explored in greater detail in Chapter 4 as internal dissent against the promotion of the peacekeeping myth has largely come from within the defence community which has not wanted to see the military and its history painted as restrained, altruistic or non-violent. Despite criticism of the peacekeeping identity by defence elites and academics, the peacekeeper myth has been both strategically and inadvertently promoted by various sources and has resulted in a widespread public affinity for foreign policies associated with peace(keeping).

Where Did the Peacekeeping Myth Come From?

The Canadian peacekeeper myth, or the widespread belief that Canada's military is a specialist in international peacekeeping based upon imagined national normative values, is both related to and bound up within the broader peacekeeping myth discussed in Chapter 2. Specifically, the broader peacekeeping myth that peacekeeping is a practically and morally distinct use of military force that is a tool for creating peace in the world has been extrapolated in the Canadian cultural environment to not simply be a unidimensional representation about what peacekeeping *is*, but also a representation about the Canadian state: presumed and promoted as an anti-imperialist, benign and helpful nation.

The Canadian peacekeeping myth evolved and grew from nostalgic foreign policy discourse, theorisation by academic scholars, and cultural celebrations and educational initiatives. While I outline these three sites separately, the discourse and practices in each area overlap and reinforce one another. It is because of the intersections of these discursive promotions of Canada-as-Peacekeeper that the myth has firmly embedded in the national imaginary and continues to hold nationalistic resonance, despite efforts by scholars and political elites alike to dismantle it.

Foreign policy storytelling: Canada's peacekeeper myth as historical nostalgia

The origin story of Canada's naturalised peacekeeping identity is told alongside narratives about the 'invention' or birth of UN peacekeeping practice. Canadian peacekeeping myth as historical nostalgia is promoted by both academic experts in foreign policy as well as other elite narratives by journalists, politicians and celebrities. While the League of Nations had ambitions to create methods and procedures to manage conflict, peacekeeping's formal establishment under the United Nations occurred in the deployment of an emergency force, UNEF-1, following the 1956 Suez War (Rikhye 1984). Narratives by foreign policy elites have frequently emphasised Canada's role in the formation of UNEF-1 as evidence of Canada's unique and special role as a global peacekeeping expert. While UN peacekeeping has evolved from UNEF-1, including the 1965 establishment of the UN Special Committee on Peacekeeping Operations and the 1992 establishment of the Department of Peacekeeping Operations (Bellamy et al. 2010), it is Canadian political and military involvement in the 'founding' of the 1956 mission that roots the myth in historiography.

As all good myths are built on seductive storytelling, it is unsurprising, then, that Canada's peacekeeper myth contains a central hero; societies love to imagine their collective identity as represented in remarkable figures (Cohen 2008: 1). The founding hero of the peacekeeping myth is Lester B. Pearson, Canada's foreign minister in 1956, who has been called the 'father of peacekeeping' (Dorn 2006). Celebration of Pearson's political history has primarily focused upon his acclaimed role in forming the first United Nations Peacekeeping force to manage tensions in the 1956 Suez Crisis. Pearson would go on to become Prime Minister and Canadian political elites would go on to promote the nation's role in the formation of peacekeeping internationally and Canada's perceived niche for peacekeeping leadership.

As the story is told, when Egypt strived to nationalise the Suez Canal in 1956, Israel, Britain and France invaded Egypt to regain Western control of the waterway. With fears about the growing tensions in Egypt, Lester Pearson drew upon his clout and networks as former president of the United Nations General Assembly and proposed the formation of a UN emergency 'peace and police' force (Carroll 2016: 247). Pearson's informal, back-room organisation strived to facilitate the peaceful withdrawal of France, Great Britain and Israel and to monitor a ceasefire agreement in Egypt. For his efforts, Pearson was rewarded with the 1957 Nobel Peace Prize. Pearson's 1957 award is often touted as evidence he was the 'father' of UN peacekeeping and that Canada's political ethos was recognised internationally as being the most suitable approach to global peace and order. As the Canadian peacekeeper myth's starring hero, Pearson's motivations and actions have been interpreted by foreign policy elites as representative of the kinds of values and ethics that Canadians endorse and uphold. Philosopher John Ralston Saul commented that Pearson 'instinctively' understood that the world was not being served or expressed by the system of leftover colonial habits which was still in place. What had to change was how we organized our society, how we projected justice among ourselves, how we explained and presented ourselves to ourselves, how we dealt with the rest of the world. (Cohen 2008)

Colonialism, in this passage, refers to the post-Second World War formal state-structured colonies and did not embrace broader conceptualisations of colonialism that recognise the ongoing systemic exploitation of marginalised groups, including Indigenous populations, characteristic across much of contemporary global politics. In this quote, Canada's vision of peacekeeping is envisioned as some sort of post-colonial vision for justice and Pearson was positioned as the champion of this vision. The irony of Canada's Nobel-winning peace-hero, who according to Ralston Saul, wished to move beyond the colonial habits of the nineteenth century, was that Pearson was an active supporter of the creation of the state of Israel in 1947, despite the lack of support of Palestinian Arabs who made up two thirds of the population. In addition, Pearson's political leadership failed to meaningfully alter domestic colonial practices, including federal-Indian policies in Canada that, at the time of his Nobel award, actively recruited Indigenous children into residential schools where they were subject to high levels of neglect, cruelty and abuse in the name of assimilation (Truth and Reconciliation Commission 2015) and quelled resistance by Indigenous communities through a variety of legal and martial measures. Colonialism, in the Pearsonian vision, was a narrow construct about justice in the world, but appeared only to reckon this at the external state level.

Canada's peacekeeping mythology and its origin story that espouses Canada's altruistic global vision, is clearly one of partial account. Pearson, as the central hero, anchors the peacekeeping mythology in Canada's foreign policy, evidenced in material form by the naming of the Canadian Department of Foreign Affairs, Trade, and Development building 'The Lester B. Pearson Building', erected in 1973. In the lobby of this building is a large display of Pearson's Nobel Peace Prize from 1957, as well as the 1988 Nobel Prize awarded to UN peacekeeping, which many Canadian politicians claimed as a secondary recognition of Canada's contributions (McCullough 2016; Mutimer 2016: 215).

The Nobel Prizes have been a source of national pride that solidified the mythologised narrative that peacekeeping was a Canadian invention. Canada's involvement in the Suez Crisis management was the first of many decades of peacekeeping contributions internationally. Canada's subsequent participation in UN Cold War missions, including the contribution of 10 per cent of all personnel serving in Cold War peacekeeping missions (Dorn and Libben 2018), reinforced the peacekeeping myth through historical nostalgic narratives that celebrated Canada's willingness to undertake this paternal, helpful and altruistic practice. The willingness of the Canadian public to support peacekeeping, even when it was not in the national interest, is used as 'evidence' of the alignment of Canadian values with UN peacekeeping, with elites citing the intense pressure Canada's government faced to participate in the 1960 UN mission to the Congo, despite active opposition from military officials (Martin and Fortmann 1995).

The story of peacekeeping as a Canadian invention was one that gained significant traction following Pearson's Nobel award. Following this, narratives about Canada's willingness and central starring role in UN peacekeeping continued. Political leaders and scholars alike point to Canada's participation in every UN-led peacekeeping initiative during the Cold War, emphasising that Canada contributed the most peacekeepers to UN missions during this period (for extensive mapping of political elite promotion of peacekeeping, see McCullough 2016). When the 1988 Nobel Peace Prize was awarded to 'UN peacekeepers', this too was viewed as a Canadian victory (McCullough 2016: 45).

In the 1990s, values of altruism, paternalism and non-violence associated with peacekeeping were also discursively linked to other Canadian foreign policy priorities, such as the assertive promotion of human security through campaigns against landmines (the Ottawa Process) and the Responsibility to Protect. These human security initiatives were a means for Canada to 'set itself apart' and emphasise that Canadian foreign policy was value based, a 'moral foreign policy that . . . helped shape Canadian identity' (Kitchen 2002: 53–4). Human security as foreign policy priority aligned with the sentiments of the Canadian peacekeeper myth, namely that Canada's foreign policy is not anchored in material interests, but rather in values like altruism and idealism (Middlemiss and Sokolsky 1983; Martin and Fortmann 1995). The durability of the myth that Canada's foreign policies and exceptional nature to conduct international peacekeeping stems from national values like freedom, peace, and the rule of law has extended into contemporary political discourse, despite contestations that this linkage is untrue or problematic (see Howell 2005). Yet, it is not solely the proclamations of political elites or the reiteration of the Lester Pearson story that have reified the peacekeeper myth in national imaginary; it is also the ways in which international relations theory has promoted other ontological presumptions about the world – specifically, the extensive focus on Great Power politics.

Scholarly theorising: Canada's peacekeeping myth as evidence of IR power politics

The origin story of Canada as 'founding nation' of international peacekeeping occurred within academic theorisation as well as popular and political discourse. Yet, the 'birth' of international peacekeeping occurred within the same temporal period as the 'birth' (or rather, institutional growth) of international relations (IR) as an American and European academic discipline at the turn of the twentieth century. Primarily concerned with the horrific outcomes of decades of inter-state war and a desire to prevent future instances, IR sought to develop grand theories to help explain and predict state tendencies and behaviours towards conflict. IR's early focus on balance-of-power approaches meant that Canadian foreign policies (including Cold War peacekeeping) were understood predominantly through realist frameworks that theorised Canada's status as a middle power. The Canadian peacekeeper myth, in short, was reproduced through extensive academic theorisation that middle powers did peacekeeping and that Canada was an exemplary middle power. Implicit in these theorisations is an acceptance that structural conditions of global politics limit or empower states' ability to influence international affairs based upon military capacity and that peacekeeping is an obvious military role for middle powers, described as a 'classic middle-power activity' (Hayes 1997).

Middle power-hood is a concept employed by grand theory IR scholars who analyse global relations as dependent upon a 'balance of power' between states operating in an anarchical realm. Lionel Gelber (1945) wrote that the middle power idea 'adopt[s] the conclusions of realism and extend[s] them. Since major powers are differentiated by their greater functions than the rest, the Middle Powers ask that they be distinguished from the lesser ones by the same criteria' (280–1). The rise of neo-realist analysis in IR during the 1970s influenced discussions about a hierarchy of middle power-hood. Scholars theorised secondary 'influencing' powers as distinct from middle 'affecting' powers (Keohane 1969), or distinguished middle power states such as Canada, Mexico, Brazil and Australia from 'second tier' powers such as Britain, France, Germany and Japan.[2]

Canada, like other small middle power nations such as Australia, Sweden, Denmark, Ireland, New Zealand and South Korea, has been envisioned by historians and political scholars as a non-dominant state with a moderate ability to influence the behaviour of other states. Canada's middle power 'identity' is understood to be an evolution of a rhetorical self-promotion by diplomat Hume Wong in 1942 (and subsequent political elites) into a widely used but poorly defined academic concept in the study of Canadian foreign policy (Chapnick 2000). Canada's middle power-hood characteristics have been linked to using multilateral solutions (Cooper et al. 1994); performing a 'helpful-fixer' role (Dewitt and Kirton 1983); endorsing mediation (Gordon 1966); normatively projecting ideals (Stairs 1994); using strategies of diplomacy and conflict resolution (Keating 1993: 204–23); or prioritising foreign policy related to the international political economy (Pratt 1990). The holy trinity of the peacekeeper myth – neutrality, non-violence and consent – therefore map easily onto these other scholarly articulations about what Canada as a middle power does and should do.

More broadly, in realist theory the link between middle powers and peacekeeping has been explained as a means for middle powers to gain influence without the material capacities of Great Powers (De Carvalho and Neumann 2015). Scholarship assumes middle powers' engagement in peacekeeping to be a reflection of their relative lack of (military) capacity to easily generate change in the international system. This draws upon realist assumptions that all states are motivated by self-interest and limited by their military and economic capacities to wield power (Gordon 1966; Holmes 1982; Melakopides 1998; Keating 2002). In the Canadian context, these assumptions have been echoed by political elites whereby peacekeeping has been promoted as an area of competitive advantage (quoted in Whitworth 2004), a way to exert influence without bolstering Canada's limited military capacity.

Academics and political officials assumed that since Canada lacked the equivalent technological resources or breadth of military powers such as the United States, the military was better suited for peacekeeping, because this military role did not require as much capital expenditure (Whitworth 2003). From a 'functionalist' perspective, peacekeeping was viewed as a niche role in which Canada could gain reputation and power (McCoullough 2016) without having to significantly invest in defence expenditures (see also Keating 1993; Nossal 1997; Murray and McCoy 2010). Canada's ability to influence international affairs through peacekeeping was considered disproportionate to its military or economic power (Cooper 1997: 20). Peacekeeping was believed to 'have strengthened [Canada's] position in the UN across a wide range of issues on the world agenda' (Jockel 1994: 15). Peacekeeping was understood to allow the nation to 'punch above its weight in international politics' (Montgomery 2017: 116). Peacekeeping has been presented in both scholarship and by political leaders as a pragmatic use of the military that permitted Canada to influence global affairs without a significant reinvestment in defence expenditure. Some scholars have even suggested that, following the Second World War, peacekeeping provided a purpose for many middle power nations, such as Canada, Ireland, Denmark and the Scandinavian nations, making 'some militaries possible *as* militaries' (Whitworth 2004: 34).[3]

Scholarship has also framed middle powers as well suited to engage in peacekeeping to bolster moral commitments to a particular world order (Neumann and de Carvalho 2014). In this framing, peacekeeping is a form of 'social power' or 'norm entrepreneurship' (Ingebritsen 2002) for middle powers. The 'soft power' framing positions peacekeeping as a *moral vocation* that naturally extends from the values of nations that undertake this role, a key presumption of Canada's version of peacekeeping myth. This is contentious as scholarship has shown participation in UN peacekeeping missions for majority-world nations has strategic advantages, such as the acquisition of up-to-date technology paid for by the UN (Whitworth 2004; Ulery, 2005; Pelaez 2007), and suggests that peacekeeping provides a form of international service recognition able to influence countries' nominations for UN Security Council seats (Krishnasamy 2001; Karlsrud 2019). The assumption that middle powers are naturally, morally, suited for peacekeeping also ignores the stark difference in which countries contribute labour (primarily developing world nations) as opposed to financial contributions (the heralded 'peacekeeping middle powers' like Canada or Norway) to UN peacekeeping (Henry 2012). Nonetheless, the association of peacekeeping with moral values of middle power countries is a common framing (Lyon and Tomlin 1979) and is particularly salient within the Canadian context. The Canadian version of the peacekeeper myth that assumes peacekeeping is a morally superior use of military violence and that Canada is a morally (reputable) nation suited for this task is clearly linked to academic theorisation about these broad ideas.

The peacekeeping–middle power link in scholarship is not without critique. Some scholarship has challenged the middle power peacekeeping conflation, noting this romanticises Canada as 'an altruistic middle power . . . "saints and crusaders" in the cause of the just and the weak' (Sjolander 2010: 322). Others have cautioned the 'moral arrogance [that] has crept into the concept of middle powers' (John W. Holmes, cited in Sjolander 2010: 324). Further critique challenges the lack of explicit articulation of what 'values' Canada is perceived to promote (Howell 2005) and suggests that the promotion of Canada as a penultimate peacekeeper has instead prioritised *order* as a value, rather than Government of Canada promotion of tolerance, diversity and rule of law (Government of Canada 2005). The 'moral' suitability of Canada as a peacekeeping middle power has been criticised often by those offering 'functionalist' explanations for Canada's middle power peacekeeping niche. These scholars argue that virtuosity is a self-declared identity feature of a middle power, not an actual characteristic (Holmes 1982; see also Stairs 2003; Granatstein 2007b): 'middle powers are middle powers because they are weaker, not because they are more virtuous' (Holmes, cited in Sjolander 2010: 324). Opposition to the peacekeeping myth will be outlined in greater detail below, but despite academic resistance to the middle power–peacekeeper conflation, this is still an embedded and theorised element of contemporary IR theories (see Jordaan 2003; Ko 2012; Roehrig 2013; Easley and Park 2018; Ayhan 2019; Karlsrud 2019).

Canada's peacekeeping myth in cultural symbols and symbolism

A third mechanism where the Canadian peacekeeping myth has been reproduced is through cultural practices and symbolism; cultural reproduction of this myth has many mediated forms. Peacekeeping as symbolic of a kind of uniquely Canadian practice has been enshrined in institutional memorialisation, in popular culture, in art, music, and educational curricula. Material symbols (statues, art, museum displays, paraphernalia) are mechanisms for reinforcing Canada's international image as a peacekeeping nation, signifying the importance and political relevance of the myth. Paul Gough (2002: 214–15) notes that these sites of memory are 'rarely arbitrary assignations: instead, they are consciously situated to connect or compete with existing nodes of collective remembering . . . [they] exist not only as aesthetic devices but as apparatus of social memory'.

An iconic cultural representation of peacekeeping is exemplified by *The Reconciliation* statue, colloquially called 'the Peacekeeping monument', featured in downtown Ottawa. Situated at the intersection between Parliament House, the United States Embassy and the Prime Ministerial residence, the memorial sits within a pie-shaped traffic island. The monument was part of a commission contest, 'Creating a National Symbol: The Peacekeeping Monument Competition', and was meant to be 'immediately meaningful to the Canadian public and to people visiting Canada's Capital from abroad' (cited in McCullough 2016: 181). *The Reconciliation* was unveiled in 1992, telling 'a story that every Canadian can be proud of' (Department of Canadian Heritage 2014). The monument contains three bronze figures of bereted peacekeepers, presumably in the image of deployed soldiers in Canada's long-standing role in the UNFICYP Cyprus. One figure is a kneeling female signaller, wearing a backpack, a second male figure stands behind her holding binoculars and a third figure keeps watch in the opposition direction, a slender gun slung over his shoulder. All three figures wear berets and appear without excessive militarised aesthetic or menacing expression.

The monument has two inscriptions, 'Reconciliation' and 'At the Service of Peace/Au Service de la Paix'. The design motif is explained on a plaque, whose English translation reads,

> Members of Canada's Armed Forces, represented by three figures, stand at the meeting place of two walls of destruction. Vigilant, impartial, they oversee the reconciliation of those in conflict. Behind them lies the debris of war. Ahead lies the promise of peace; a grove, symbol of life.

The architect and designers of *The Reconciliation* were said to have created the image to represent 'the reality of our soldiers' place between the two forces of conflict', calling the figures 'guardians of peace' (McCullough 2016: 182). Engraved in a secondary location on the monument are English and French translations of Lester Pearson's 1956 UN speech:

> We need action not only to end the fighting but to make the peace . . . my own government would be glad to recommend Canadian participation in such a United Nations force, a truly international peace and police force.

Notably, this quote is from different components of Pearson's address, edited together to reinforce a particular image of peacekeeping and the centrality of Canada in its international formations (McCullough 2016: 182), These narratives cast Canadian peacekeepers in the image of a referee, whereby Canadian peacekeeper actions are understood as 'non-violent observation whose presence prevented conflict' (English 2003: 1). The inscription plaque refers to peacekeepers, 'standing on two sharp, knifelike edges of stone, cutting through the rubble and debris of war and converging at a high point, which symbolises the resolution of conflict' (Veterans Affairs Canada 2014).

The monument's figures represent the assumed impartiality, restrained violence and altruism in the peacekeeping myth. It is this image – Canadian peacekeepers as rational, cautious referees – that is institutionally memorialised, and which reinforces both broader and culturally specific versions of the peacekeeping myth. At the monument's unveiling, Prime Minister Brian Mulroney expressed the notion that peacekeeping was a 'Canadian idea, pursued in the midst of conflict, and now recognized globally as pivotal to world peace' (cited in McCullough 2016: 186). Politicians since Mulroney recreate nationalistic narratives annually at *The Reconciliation*, to commemorate National Peacekeeper's Day on 9 August. Yet *The Reconciliation* does not just signal peacekeeping as a part of Canada's past. The monument's side wall is inscribed with forty-eight locations where Canadians have served in peacekeeping roles. Sufficient additional space was left for thirty future inscriptions. The significance, Gough (2002: 221) explains, is that 'it presupposes a future peacekeeping role for Canadian troops into the next two decades. In this sense it *projects* a future role with some certainty, suggesting the Canadian values of impartiality and fairness will be constants worthy of continuous aggrandizement'.

The Reconciliation's image can be found in other artefacts. In 1995, the Canadian mint released a one-dollar coin – the 'loonie' – with an engraved image of the monument's three peacekeepers replacing the typical loon (bird) image on the reverse of the coin. This was one of only three times a specialised image was used on the coin, and the Royal Canadian Mint chose this image to celebrate the fiftieth anniversary of the founding of the United Nations (McCullough 2016: 187). The feature of peacekeeping imagery on the currency reinforces the nostalgic discourse about Canada's international identity and UN service; Colin McCullough suggests that the official launch of the peacekeeping loonie at Lester B. Pearson High School further reified the perceived connection between Pearson's role in the 1956 UNEF-1 mission, the formation of UN 'traditional' peacekeeping and the centrality of Canada to this practice (2016: 187). From 2001 to 2013, Canada's ten-dollar bill also featured peacekeeping imagery. The bill's reverse side featured a female Royal Canadian Air Force officer in a blue beret, below which appears the text 'In the Service of Peace', quoting *The Reconciliation* monument's iconic text.

In addition to *The Reconciliation*, other peacekeeping memorials and monuments have been erected across Canada. Calgary's Peacekeeper Park, Winnipeg's 'Peacekeeping Cairn', and an outdoor training facility in Malhide, Ontario also named 'Peacekeeper's Park' are intended to honour fallen peacekeepers and the missions served during the twentieth century. These monuments provide a public site to honour soldiers, and in turn, publicly romanticise this form of international military service. Calgary's Peacekeeper Park contains a bronze statue of a peacekeeper handing a doll to a little girl. This image is a representation of a Canadian soldier, Mark Isfeld, killed in Croatia in 1994; the doll represents the many hand-knitted dolls Isfeld gave away while deployed (McCullough 2016: 196). The dolls were knitted by Isfeld's mother and, after his death, other soldiers and healthcare providers in conflict or disaster zones continued the practice, supported by Carol Isfeld and other doll-knitting volunteers (Canadian War Museum 2021). The Canadian War Museum features a display of 'Izzy' dolls crafted by Isfeld's mother, with a note that reads 'IZZY DOLL Made for you with love in memory of Mark Isfeld killed in Kakma, Croatia 21 jun 94 removing landmines serving with 1CER Unprofor' (Canadian War Museum 2021). The imagery of Isfeld's 'peacekeeper' statue in Calgary is contiguous with *The Reconciliation*: it signals a type of altruism, paternalism, non-violence and innocence about who peacekeepers are and what peacekeepers do. Yet, Calgary's Peacekeeper Park also contains an element of contradiction. Despite the Department of Defence's insistence that Afghanistan was not a peacekeeping mission, the organisers of the Calgary monument intentionally put the names of those killed in Afghanistan on the wall (McKay and Swift 2012: 241). This is one of several symbolic attempts to link the war in Afghanistan to values and imagery of Canadian peacekeeping, which will be explored in greater detail in Chapter 4 as a mechanism that legitimises warfare and justifies militarism.

The Canadian version of the peacekeeper myth and narratives about Canada's presumed affinity for peacekeeping have also been reinforced in popular media and the arts. An example is Canadian country singerwriter Stompin' Tom Connor's song 'The Blue Berets', which evokes a sentiment of Canadian peacekeepers as helpful, altruistic and paternal. The lyrics state:

> We're always proud to say
> We'll stand between the mighty and the frail
> And where children cannot play because war is in their way
> We shall send in our blue berets without fail.
>
> We try to bring some hope to an ugly world . . .
>
> With another UN flag to be unfurled
> Till the factions are at bay and peace is on its way
> We'll display our Blue Berets around the world (Stompin' Tom Connors
>   2020)

In the 1994 music video for this song, there is an opening vignette where news footage from Sarajevo shows a blurry image of a blue-helmeted soldier crawling on the sidewalk amidst broken concrete to drag a wounded, blonde woman from the wreckage while gunfight sounds in the background. The soldier does not fire back, but instead drags the woman to safety. Connor's voiceover declares the song is dedicated to Canadian peacekeepers, and the remainder of the video that accompanies his song contains images of blue bereted soldiers and UN imagery (Stompin' Tom Connors 2020). This representation of Canadian peacekeepers exemplifies the presumed non-violence, helpfulness and altruism embedded in the Canadian version of the peacekeeping myth.

Other examples of popular media's reproduction of Canadian peace-keeping also include an explicit mention in a 2000s commercial for one of Canada's largest breweries, Molson. In the commercial, 'Joe Canada' rants onstage about the perceived characteristics and cultural uniqueness of Canadians, including explicit references to how Canada is culturally distinct from the United States. From his narrative, Joe declares: 'I have a prime minister, not a president. I speak English and French, not American. And I pronounce it about, not aboot. I can proudly sew my country's flag on my backpack. *I believe in peacekeeping, not policing.* Diversity, not assimilation, and that the beaver is a truly proud and noble animal.'[4] Peacekeeping is cast as a distinctly Canadian enterprise, juxtaposed with the presumed imperialistic 'policing' of American foreign policy, and linked to other practices understood to align with a distinct *Canadian* political ethos, including the Westminster governance system and the idea of Canada's multicultural mosaic (the practice of celebrating diversity) rather than the American 'melting pot' (understood as an intolerance of diversity and a requirement to assimilate into dominant culture).

Finally, peacekeeping featured prominently on both Canadian network television and in Canadian classrooms through historical foundations, such as the National Film Board and Historica Canada, which created short films that reproduced romantic depictions of Canada's peacekeeping history. One example is a Heritage Minute titled 'Dextraze in the Congo'. Heritage Minutes were funded by Historica Canada and shown on Canadian television at no cost to the networks as a means to fulfil a required quota of Canadian programming content each day (McCullough 2016: 6). There were three Heritage Minutes devoted to illustrating Canada's peacekeeping history, and 'Congo' represents Canada's peacekeeping myth in an exemplary way. The clip narrates that 'Canada proposed the United Nations peacekeeping force in 1956' (Historica Canada 2016a) and the theme of the clip is a confrontation between an angry African male figure threatening to execute priests and nuns if his demands are unmet. As the 'angry rebel' points his pistol at the missionaries and calls them 'cockroaches', a gun appears in frame and a figure – Canada's General Jacques Dextraze – flanked by two blue-helmeted peacekeepers, demands he drop his weapon. The video's voiceover affirms 'it was Canada who proposed the 1956 peacekeeping mission. General Jacques Dextraze would go on to become head of our armed forces'. This reifies the culturally widespread assumption that Canada's military was primarily comprised of peacekeepers, not lethal, martially capable soldiers, and evokes the peacekeeping myth's virtue of non-violence: Dextraze himself stands with hands behind his back while two unspecified UN peacekeepers hold the gun that forces the 'rebel' to surrender.

In a second Heritage Minute vignette titled 'Lester Pearson', there is an argument in a Cyprus street between two angry men – one identified as a 'Turk', the other as a 'Cypriot' – where the Cypriot accuses the Turkish man of killing his brother. The exchange involves threats to kill one another, with the Turkish character's rifle pointed at the Cypriot character's chest, until an open-roofed UN jeep pulls up and a blue-bereted peacekeeper grabs the gun and yells 'Stop it!'. The peacekeeper declares, 'I'm here as a member of the United Nations peace force, now, both of you go home: nobody is going to shoot anybody!' This assertion diffuses the conflict. The voiceover that concludes the Heritage Minute states: 'The UN peace force was designed by a Canadian, Lester Pearson, 1957 for his dream that soldiers could make peace instead of war. He received the Nobel prize' (Historica Canada 2016b). In this vignette, Canadian peacekeepers were able to cease violence by simply verbally evoking the authority of the United Nations. The peacekeeper carried no weapon and skilfully, within a matter of seconds, resolved the escalating conflict. As other scholars have noted, the Heritage Minute represents peacekeeping as adjacent to the moral authority of UN peacekeepers, a type of heroism that requires no exchange of gunfire, and 'an exciting vignette about peacekeeping in which no one is killed and Canada plays a starring role' (McCullough 2016: 8). Colin McCullough's (2016) extensive analysis of over a hundred English and French high school historical textbooks and National Film Board movies, fourteen of which contained peacekeeping as a dominant focus, demonstrates that through this mediation of Canada's peacekeeping history, Canadian high school education contained the peacekeeping myth as a central topic in curricula.

Throughout these cultural artefacts, what is clear is that the visual representations of Canada's peacekeeping roles and the aesthetics of peacekeepers was centred strongly towards imagery of early-generation peacekeeping missions. The blue berets and lack of overt militarised equipment or guns position Canada's international brand as akin to the helpful fixer role promoted by elites and academics, a role imagined to be idealised in the traditional peacekeeping missions of 1956–70. These elite narratives and cultural reproductions of the Canadian version of the peacekeeping myth blended the mythologised 'traditional peacekeeping' holy trinity values with the values presumed to make up Canada's political ethos: paternal helpfulness, altruism, non-violence and innocence.

Myth-Busting Nostalgia in/of the Canadian Peacekeeper Myth

Despite popular reproduction, the peacekeeping myth has also been subject to critique. The peacekeeping myth has not been universally endorsed or reproduced, particularly from within the Canadian military itself (Whitworth 2004; Mutimer 2016), a topic explored in greater detail in Chapter 4. Critics seeking to prove the falsehood or inaccuracy of the Canadian peacekeeping myth can be organised around two lines of argumentation: peacekeeping as a false, feminised vision of Canadian military history, and peacekeeping as falsely represented according to altruism and non-violence.

The first critique, promoted largely by military historians, is that the peacekeeping myth obscures historical 'facts' that the Canadian military has actively participated in warfare throughout history, emphasising the perceived important roles the military played in the war of 1812, the First World War, the Second World War and the Korean War. Critics explain the myth of 'Canada as Peacekeeper' as a story that ignores the Canadian Armed Forces' eagerness and skilled contributions in combat activities throughout the twentieth century. Those wishing to myth-bust peacekeeping offer alternative historical narratives that tell a story of how Canada proved its military capacity and forged its identity as an autonomous, sovereign state that 'stood its own' in global conflicts. Donald Schurman (1990), J. L Granatstein (1998, 2002a, 2004b), Norman Hillmer (Hillmer and Granatstein 1994), Eric Wagner (2006) and Michael K. Carroll (2016) have cast the Canadian peacekeeping myth as a historical record that does a disservice to the Forces due to the inaccurate and incomplete account of Canada's military history. These scholars point to Romeo Dallaire, 'arguably Canada's most famous peacekeeper', who himself claimed that 'Canada's soldiers are first and foremost specialists in combat' (cited in Carroll 2016: 169). These scholars have lamented public ignorance about Canada's 'real' military history. Rather than dispute or deny the existence a history of peacekeeping as a *past* priority of the Forces, most of these critics emphasise that the myth has been overstated and has resulted in an inaccurate representation of Canada's military history.

There is some nuance to this critique. Some historians criticised the 'traditional' peacekeeping trope as a dangerous distraction and an outdated vision of what peacekeeping evolved to in the late 1990s (Granatstein 2004a). There were concerns that peacekeeping, in Canadian nostalgia, aesthetically imagined according to the Suez or Cyprus 'traditional peacekeeping' missions, did not accurately capture the changing nature of UN missions. These critics pointed out the ways in which Cold War peacekeeping missions were more robust, dangerous and intensive than the mythos of 'traditional peacekeeping' allowed for, and thereby sought to show how Canada's role in peace enforcement was more 'war-like' than mythological conceptualisations accounted for (Summerfield 2018). The 'traditional' or Pearsonian model of peacekeeping embedded in the peacekeeping myth was criticised as a 'vague and often euphemistic concept' (Montgomery 2017: 117), an outdated representation of peacekeeping as a neutral force deployed to a buffer zone where two consenting parties had agreed to a ceasefire, referred to in demeaning manner as the 'umpire' image of Canada's military (Hillmer and Granastein 1994). Granatstein points to the awarding of the Nobel Peace Prize to Pearson and subsequent politician obsession with this accolade as the primary means by which the peacekeeper myth was promoted that inaccurately captured the gritty, tough and risky environments that peacekeepers during the Cold War encountered (2004b).

Military critics rebutted the idea that military activities could be altruistic or non-violent, with Colonel Bernd Horn explaining that the 'flattering image of a benevolent country that dispatches its reluctant warriors throughout the world to do good is somewhat simplistic and naïve' (Horn 2006: 12). Scholars have also documented careful analyses of political leaders who were reluctant to embrace Pearsonian peacekeeping or the helpful-fixer international role (Preece 2010; McCullough 2016), to highlight the mythologisation and one-dimensional nature of the peacekeeping myth, demonstrating that it was wishful thinking, rather than accurate representation.

For other scholars critical of the Canadian peacekeeping myth, there was also concern that the peacekeeping myth's seductive nostalgia permitted governments in the 1970s, 1980s and 1990s to divest resources, specifically funding and procurement, from the Forces. For many military supporters, the peacekeeping myth devalued the image of the Forces by presenting a feminised, passive institution not associated with traditional combat activity, and thereby influenced governments to cut defence budgets in a way that led to the 'rusting out' of the Canadian Forces, a theme explored further in Chapter 4. Akin to these critiques, other scholars have myth-busted peacekeeping through an examination of Canada's declining contributions to post-Cold War peacekeeping missions, noting the diminished troop and financial contributions since 1993 (Carroll 2016; Dorn and Libben 2018). Scholars who utilise this tactic concede that while Canada previously was a primary contributor to UN peacekeeping, its contributions following the early 1990s had dropped significantly. Therefore, the various critiques that the peacekeeping myth failed to accurately capture Canada's military past and to properly celebrate (and fund) Canada's defence history in combat activities, all rely upon challenging the peacekeeping myth's accuracy.

The secondary means in which Canada's peacekeeping myth was challenged was by critical scholars and military enthusiasts who sought to myth-bust the assumptions within the myth itself. Some myth-busting involved claims that peacekeeping was not altruistic, but rather within the strategic (realist) interests of the Canadian state (Chapnick 2000; Wagner 2006). Some challenged the idea that Canadian soldiers were somehow uniquely suited for the tasks required in peacekeeping, emphasising that the expectations and tasks of peacekeeping duty did not align with soldiers' training in warfighting (Granatstein 2007c: 24). This issue rose to prominence following the 1993 National Inquiry involving Canadian Armed Forces members' luring, torture and murder of a Somalian teenager, whereby critics flagged the disconnect between peacekeeping expectations and soldiers' combat training (Klep and Winslow 1999; Razack 2004; Whitworth 2004). While military enthusiasts were quick to try to dismantle the peacekeeping myth's altruistic symbolism and stress that Canada's soldiers were better suited to combat tasks (since that is what they were trained for), critical scholars who problematised the assumed altruism of Canadian peacekeeping did so with different, anti-militarist objectives.

Exploring the disconnect whereby soldiers are trained in combat and then 'told to keep a lid on warrior traits . . . [and therefore] can contribute to some of the explosions of hypermasculinity' (Whitworth 2004: 184), feminists have linked excessive and illicit use of violence by peacekeepers to the problem of having military personnel trained in combat deploy to maintain and contain peace missions that require different skill sets (Razack 2000; Sion 2006; Higate 2007). Sherene Razack (2004) details how nearly every peacekeeping mission involving Western peacekeepers has involved violence directed at local, civilian populations. This includes unsanctioned violence by Canadian peacekeepers involving abuse of youth detainees in Haiti, the cruel punishment of civilians by peacekeepers for petty thievery, the abuse of mental patients in Bosnia, and the unsanctioned murder of unarmed civilians in Somalia (Razack 2004: 53). For Razack, peacekeeping violence is not simply the result of institutional training that predisposes peacekeepers to violence, but also explicit colonial and racialised attitudes by peacekeepers inherent within peacekeeping as an international practice. These scholars have rightly noted that the *power* of the peacekeeping myth is bound up in what Interpal Grewal calls 'the interrelation between the sovereign right to kill and the humanitarian right to rescue' (Grewal 2003: 537, cited in Terry 2009).

Despite both 'camps' of scholarship who sought to falsify the peacekeeping mythology, it has stubbornly endured in Canadian popular imagination. The Report of the Commission of Inquiry into the Deployment of Canadian Forces to Somalia, titled *Dishonoured Legacy*, may have shocked Canadians, but the outrage was over the few 'bad apples' or the lack of professionalisation (Bercuson 2009) in the CAF, rather than a broader acceptance that 'Canadian values' of altruism, paternal helpfulness, non-violence and innocence were perhaps not central to Canadian foreign policy or that peacekeeping as a practice was perhaps not the romantic version Canadians thought it was. In an October 1992 Angus Reid poll (prior to the deployment of the CAF to Somalia), almost 80 per cent of Canadians had a favourable impression of the CAF, yet in 1996, 45 per cent of Canadians expressed concern about 'fundamental problems' in Canada's armed forces (Bratt 1998).

Yet, despite the temporary dip in support for the CAF, peacekeeping as a practice was still widely favoured in opinion polls. In 1993, the Senate Standing Committee on Foreign Affairs stated that peacekeeping was 'the sole military activity that Canadians fully support' (Dorn 2005). Angus Reid polls showed that Canadians identified their country as a world leader in international peacekeeping, expressed by 90% of respondents in 1992 and 94% of respondents in 1997 (Dorn 2005). In 2003, polls reported almost 90 per cent of Canadians believed Canada should provide troops for peacekeeping when asked by the UN (Dorn 2005). In 2008, Ipsos Reid survey found that 'peacekeeping', following 'the maple leaf', 'hockey', 'the beaver' and 'Canada Day', was in the top seven most important things that define the nation. In 2016, Nanos Research Survey found that 74 per cent of Canadians thought participation in UN peacekeeping missions was a 'good' or 'very good' idea (McPhedran 2016). In 2012, the Environics Institute's annual 'Focus Canada' survey showed that peacekeeping was the most common, *unprompted* response to the question, 'What is the most positive contribution that Canada, as a country, makes to the world today?' Forty per cent of respondents indicated peacekeeping was Canada's primary global contribution in 1993, and although the response rates fell to 36 per cent in 2004 and to 20 per cent in 2012, 'peacekeeping' was still the most common response to the question in 2018 (found in 24 per cent of responses) (Environics 2018: 31). Therefore, despite efforts to 'myth-bust' the Canadian peacekeeping myth, it has retained strong support among public audiences, including being used as a central campaign theme in the 2015 Justin Trudeau election campaign (Brown 2017).

In the chapters that follow, I explore two other empirical phenomena that *should* have challenged the peacekeeping myth, but, as indicated above, have not managed to disrupt it: Canada's 2001–14 war in Afghanistan, and Canada's long-standing use of militarised force against Indigenous populations. These phenomena will be explored in turn to show how the peacekeeper myth – and its implied 'Canadian values' – has functioned to legitimise warfare and violence in Canada and abroad, and what this can show us about the power of myths in sustaining militarism, militarisation and martial politics.

What Does the Canadian Version of the Peacekeeping Myth Do?

As outlined in Chapter 2, myths are not universal in content or structure. The peacekeeper myth, therefore, also takes on unique constellations of meaning across various cultural manifestations, where the fluidity of this myth makes its configurations take on nuanced forms across time and space. It is not uncommon for states and political elites to link nationalism to the activities of their armed forces (Brighton 2011).

The Canadian version of the peacekeeper myth, therefore, involves the widespread belief that Canada's military is a specialist in international peacekeeping based upon the country's inherent normative values. The myth's symbolic value is that is promotes altruism, paternal helpfulness, non-violence and innocence as normative values of the state and of Canada's militarised forces. The Canadian version of the myth is reproduced alongside narrative 'evidence' of Canada's peacekeeping status and history and is a discourse beloved by many Canadians who envision a foreign policy rooted in altruism and virtue (Sjolander 2010: 326). Despite efforts by scholars or some political leaders to disrupt the Canadian peacekeeping myth, it has stubbornly endured. Historians have remarked that 'it is certainly better for Canadians to think of themselves as umpires, as morality incarnate, than as mass murderers or warmongers' (Hillmer and Granatstein 1994: 350).

Like the broader UN peacekeeping mythos, Canada's national mythscape has failed to capture the technical nuances between Canada's peace enforcement missions and 'traditional' peacekeeping practices. Instead, Canada's myth is driven by emotional connection to the moral sentiments associated with 'peacekeeping' identity; in other words, the presumed altruistic and morally just nature of Canada and Canadians. While it has been theorised that the myth's reproduction in Canadian history has contributed to a coherent national identity for an otherwise diverse and vast population – with explicit non-American, anti-imperialist narratives – I suggest that this myth serves other ideological purposes, specifically related to militarism. The peacekeeper myth is a 'dream . . . [that] neatly enables Canada to tell a story of national goodness and to mark itself as distinct from the United States' (Razack 1996: 134). More specifically, though, the peacekeeper myth functions to legitimise Canadian martial violence by casting it as distinct from other (read: non-peaceful, American, terrorist, disorderly) uses of violence.

This simplified mythscape obscures domestic and international deployment of lethal state force and limits our ability to think critically about these practices. The paradox is that Canada's peacekeeping myth has been recognised as a 'persistent cultural fable that continues to thrive [even as] it is being questioned, [sometimes] in the same context' (Härting and Kambourelli 2009: 660). I suggest the myth, therefore, is not really about peacekeeping. Peacekeeping becomes the symbolic referent for the desired normative qualities that political elites and public audiences like to see as representative of the military, the state and the nation: altruism, paternal helpfulness, non-violence and innocence. These values explain how other, non-peacekeeping uses of martial force become legitimised. The legitimisation of warfare and violence occurs through the repackaging of the peacekeeping myth and through the unproblematised ontological acceptance of military violence as a 'force for good' (Duncanson 2009). These themes will be explored in the following chapter where I explain how the symbolism and values of the Canadian peacekeeper myth were used to justify and legitimise violence in the war in Afghanistan.

Notes

1. While some scholars take care to distinguish humanitarianism (relief workers, NGOs, medical staff) who assist civilians, distinct from peacekeepers who 'dampen down the potential for conflict' (Pugh 1996: 215), the peacekeeping myth blurs any sort of distinctions so that peacekeepers themselves are viewed as helpful humanitarians, a problem with the 'new humanitarianism' and the securitisation of aid that occurs in contemporary peace operations (Duffield 2001).

2. There is lack of scholarly agreement on what specifically constitutes middle power-hood (Cooper et al. 1994; Ungerer 2007; Behringer 2012; Patience 2014). Theory about middle powers was not only generated by realist theorists, but the English School and other constructivist branches also made use of the concept. Martin Wight described a middle power as 'a power with such military strength, resources, and strategic position that in peacetime the great powers bid for its support, and in wartime, while it has no hope of winning a war against a great power, it can hope to inflict costs on a great power out of proportion to what the great power can hope to gain by attacking it' (Wight 1995: 65). Robert Cox described a middle power as 'a role in search of an actor' (1981: 827). Cox insinuated the term does not contain an inherent meaning, but rather can be applied to states that behave in *normative* ways associated with this term (Chapnick 1999: 75).

3. Canada is not the only nation to associate peace activism or peace-oriented policies with state survival in a world of Great Powers; this has also been a discursive association and explanation for Norwegian foreign policy (Skånland 2010; Neumann 2011; Leira 2013; Karlsrud 2019) and South Korean middle

power-hood (Ko 2012; Roehrig 2013; John 2014; Easley and Park 2018; Ayhan 2019). Peace-oriented middle power identity in these three countries is distinct from scholarship assessing other middle powers who have engaged in peace-keeping as a middle power activity but do not actively centre peacekeeping as a *celebrated* or promoted element of foreign policy and identity – for example, Australia (Hocking 1997; Ravenhill 1998; Beeson 2011; Scott 2013; Carr 2014). Nonetheless, the mobilisation of 'functionalist' explanations for middle power peacekeeping – namely that it is a prudent strategy for small powers in a Great Power environment – extends across several national contexts and often hinges upon the assumption that middle powers have a perceived 'neutrality' as 'honest brokers' that makes them well suited for mediation and diplomacy (Jordaan 2003) and allows these middle powers to 'punch above their weight' in international power politics.

4. A full version of the Joe Canada ads is available on YouTube at https://www.youtube.com/watch?v=VZ-UTvLHb4U.

CHAPTER 4*

The Peacekeeping Myth and the War in Afghanistan

What Happens to the Myth When the Military Is Not Peacekeeping?

Afghanistan was the longest formal sustained war effort in Canadian history. How is it that, despite long-standing and ongoing public preference for 'peacekeeping' throughout the Afghanistan war, with 'tepid' public support for the various mission extensions in 2003, 2006, 2009 and 2011 (Boucher and Nossal 2015), Canada's war efforts were legitimised and promoted? With the peacekeeper myth embedded in popular and political memory, why was there was not greater resistance to the war in Afghanistan, or *outright dismissal of the peacekeeping myth*? This chapter explores this puzzle. In doing so, I endeavour to show how the peacekeeper myth in Canada was not disrupted by CAF participation in violent warfare, but rather symbolically manoeuvred to legitimise military violence. I argue that the power of the peacekeeping myth is not in its ability to accurately capture its referent subject, but its symbolic ability to fluidly obscure and sanitise militarised violence and the politics that drive it.

Focused on the Canadian Armed Forces and the war in Afghanistan, this chapter explores how the peacekeeper myth has made it possible to 'rebrand' war as global humanitarianism and combat-trained soldiers as helpful heroes. Although Canada's contribution to military operations in Afghanistan did not constitute a peacekeeping operation, elite discourse was able to manoeuvre the myth to represent Afghanistan according to the politics of idealised white masculinity (innocent and altruistic) and the representation of martial force as civilising (non-violent and paternally helpful). Investigating the process and manoeuvres involved in this

* Material in this chapter was originally published as part of: Wegner, Nicole, 2021a, 'Helpful Heroes and the Political Utility of Militarized Masculinities', *International Feminist Journal of Politics* 23 (1): 5–26; Wegner, Nicole, 2020, 'Militarization in Canada: Myth-Breaking and Image-Making through Recruitment Campaigns', *Critical Military Studies* 6 (1): 67–85. Available: https://www.tandfonline.com/

'rebranding' is essential to understanding how logics of war are sustained. While Afghanistan might have been events that dismantled the peacekeeping myth (myth-busted the myth), what a discourse analysis of this endeavour shows is the power of the myth to symbolically sanitise and obscure imperialist violence in the name of 'peace'.

With attention to gendered and racialised anxieties present in Canadian visions of peacekeeping, this chapter introduces four manoeuvres (Enloe 2004) used to explain and justify Canada's military contributions to Afghanistan. By manoeuvres, I mean targeted discursive shifts aimed at rejecting and rebranding, then reclaiming and reinforcing a version of the peacekeeper myth throughout elite discourse on the war in Afghanistan. The first manoeuvre involved evoking gendered ideals of militarised masculinities and racialised notions of 'white saviours' and dark threats (Razack 2004) to reject and reframe peacekeeping as inadequate for protecting the nation. The second series of discursive manoeuvres involved racialised narratives justifying military action in a non-peacekeeping mission as protecting 'vulnerable' Canadians from future 'dark' terrorist security threats. The first two manoeuvres were not very successful. Therefore, in the face of initial public resistance, a third manoeuvre occurred when CAF activities were reframed and discourse on Afghanistan reclaimed values of helpfulness, altruism, paternalist care for Afghan 'womenandchildren', and non-violent strategies in the construction of the 'helpful hero' idealisation of Canadian soldiers. Finally, a fourth manoeuvre sustained legitimisation for the war through Support the Troops discourse that focused on the sacrifice and death of Canadian soldiers, rather than specifics of the military operation or Afghan civilian deaths.

This chapter begins by outlining the ways that military operations in Afghanistan departed from 'traditional' peacekeeping operations, before exploring each of the four manoeuvres outlined above. The goal of the chapter is to demonstrate how gender and racialised assumptions surrounding the peacekeeping myth function were negotiated and how the Afghanistan mission was rebranded to represent CAF activities as altruistic, helpful, non-violent and innocent. This rebranding capitalised upon the peacekeeping myth even while the military was not peacekeeping. I will show that the mobilisation and manoeuvring of the peacekeeper myth is how violent warfare by the Canadian state (and its allies) was justified in Afghanistan, explaining how combat and counterinsurgency could have, but did not, destabilise the Canadian peacekeeping myth. I explore how the peacekeeping myth was manipulated in representations of the Afghanistan war to align with desires for Canada's military and national identities to be represented as helpful heroes. These representations are a contemporary manifestation of what Sherene Razack has called 'white knights' combating 'dark threats' (2004) and rely on gendered and racialised tropes that reproduce nostalgic support for the peacekeeping myth.

Afghanistan Was Not a Peacekeeping Mission

The US-led war in Afghanistan was understood to be a collective self-defence response to terrorist attacks on American soil. On September 11, 2001, co-ordinated terrorist attacks involving airline hijacking targeted major sites in the United States killing an estimated 3,000 civilians, including twenty-four Canadians. US President George W. Bush responded with an international military campaign, infamously termed the 'Global War on Terror(ism)', and invaded Afghanistan to oust the Taliban regime in a campaign titled 'Operation Enduring Freedom'. Following the initial objective to remove the Taliban government from power, the war in Afghanistan endured for twenty years under a NATO-led coalition of forty national military forces. Canada supported Operation Enduring Freedom and the NATO coalition's various missions between 2001 and 2014. This coalition was known as the International Security Assistance Force (ISAF), established in December 2001 by United Nations Security Council resolution 1386. The ISAF was formed to train, support and fight alongside the Afghan Armed Forces and to establish new government institutions.

While multilateral in nature, the war in Afghanistan was not a peacekeeping mission. It did not have the consent of all parties involved, it was not politically impartial or neutral, and the active employment of counterinsurgency (COIN) strategies meant that force was widely used in an offensive, not defensive manner. Civilian casualties were extraordinarily high, estimated by the Costs of War Project (2021) at 47,245 Afghan civilians.[1] As the Report on the Standing Committee on National Defence explained, 'Canada has taken sides in this issue . . . the mission is not, and never has been, anything akin to a peacekeeping mission' (Report on the Standing Committee on National Defence 2007: 7, 14, 115).

The timeline of Canada's involvement in Afghanistan spanned from 2001 to 2014. Afghanistan, for many foreign policy elites, was understood as an opportunity, representative of gendered desires for international prestige. Defence elites had long loathed the peacekeeping mythology and were keen to rebuild defence funding and procurement following the post-Cold War period referred to as the 'Decade of Darkness' (as cited in Berthiaume 2013). Funding cuts in the 1990s, and the 30 per cent decrease in CAF active members,[2] were criticised as the 'rusting out' of the Canadian Forces (see Bland 1998; Granatstein 2004a: 67). The 9/11 attacks caused defence elites to fret that Canada had neglected to maintain its military capacities due to a 'legacy of neglect' (Parliament of Canada 2005). Participation in Afghanistan, therefore, was presented as an opportunity to 'shift away from midddlepowermanship' (Murray and McCoy 2010: 177) and to embrace counterinsurgency as a key role for the CAF in the twenty-first century.

Afghanistan illustrated a tension within the peacekeeping myth: defence officials hated it, but public audiences and many political elites loved it. Despite efforts to re-masculinise the image of the CAF and to 'shed' the peacekeeping myth, what this political discourse eventually negotiated through 'ambiguous' messaging was a way to justify Canada's warfare contributions in a way that did not abandon the symbolism of the much-loved peacekeeping myth. Gender and racialised tropes were key to this messaging.

Rejecting the peacekeeping myth through gender

Branding the Canadian military involves representing military activities according to gendered tropes that represent a cohesive and appealing image. Peacekeeping has been central to the Forces' historical brand, and gender informs this militarised image and the long-standing tensions over whether CAF personnel should be manly warriors or feminised peacekeepers: both tropes that signal a form of idealised militarised masculinity. Jane Parpart and Kevin Partridge (2014: 551) propose that 'militarized masculinities are specific configurations of gendered characteristics and behaviours that are visible at the levels of individuals, families, communities, and states'. These idealisations are neither homogeneous nor static, but rather a negotiated set of gendered (and sexed and racialised) traits that are socioculturally and politically reproduced as desirable for militaries and their members to perform, even if many individuals themselves fail to fully embody them (MacKenzie and Foster 2017). These qualities are culturally privileged within Westernised culture as signifiers of 'manliness' and normatively (re)produced as desirable attributes for masculine identity within the military (Enloe 1993; Morgan 1994; Higate 2003; Whitworth 2004; Belkin 2012). Characteristics of strength, toughness, rationality and aggression have been historically associated with militarised masculinity[3] and a strong focus of scholarship has been warrior ideal types in military settings (Enloe 1993; Dawson 1994; Morgan 1994; Woodward 2000; Goldstein 2001; Barrett 2001; Higate 2003; Whitworth 2004).

Gender is not the only idealisation that goes into 'making soldiers'. An 'explosive mix of misogyny, racism, and homophobia, coupled with siege mentality' (Whitworth 2004: 99) is also embedded in hegemonic forms of militarised masculinity; an intersectional medley that feminists have found problematic for both intra-military relations and the political utilisation of soldiers as agents in peacekeeping missions.[4] Yet, intersectionality has only partially informed scholarship on militarised masculinities and gender has often been prioritised at the expense of other power vectors, including race (Sasson-Levy 2003; Henry 2017[5]). The execution of warrior violence has most easily been condoned when done by Western white bodies, evidenced by the ways that militarised masculinity idealisations are often contrasted with or foiled by Orientalist representations of 'bad' brown and black men both inside and outside formal military institutions.[6]

Feminists have also theorised that while the 'warrior masculinity' ideal has largely been idealised in Western militaries, there are alternative forms of militarised masculinities that have been cultivated among some peacekeeping units (Eichler 2012; Duncanson 2013, 2015; Parpart and Partridge 2014). Peacekeeper masculinity idealises the performance of impartiality, sensitivity, compassion and empathy (Higate and Henry 2004), the ability to network and use diplomatic strategies, and the ability to use self-restraint in executing physical force (Duncanson 2009). Claire Duncanson noted that British peacekeeper masculinity involves the portrayal of British soldiers as controlled, civilised and intelligent (2009: 73). In the Canadian context, these same gendered traits are idealised in the peacekeeping myth. Peacekeeper masculinity has also been theorised to be represented as distinct from masculinity of foreign 'Others', cast as aggressive, irrational and violent. Within the peacekeeping myth, this juxtaposition of ideal versus condemned masculine idealisations is distinctly racialised whereby white violence is positioned as legitimate and violence by men of colour has been positioned as barbaric.

Peacekeeping has been represented both metaphorically and aesthetically as white masculinity in many of the popular representations of Canadian soldiers discussed in Chapter 3.[7] Peacekeeping in myth, therefore, is not just the representation of these activities as the idealised realm of men from middle power nations, but the representation of these activities according to logics of whiteness (Sabaratnam 2020), cast as contemporary crusades to provide order and civility to uncivilised or disorderly 'dark threats' (Razack 2004). This is key to understanding how violence by peacekeeping or peacekeepers has been legitimised: it has been represented as orderly, civilising and necessary largely because it has been a practice of white, Western states targeting racialised populations around the world.

The peacekeeping myth does not only contain narratives about what peacekeeping 'is', but also about who peacekeepers 'are', including gendered and racialised assumptions about the idealised agents who conduct peacekeeping. Peacekeeper masculinity central to the Canadian peacekeeping myth (Wegner 2021a) privileges the attributes required for 'traditional UN peacekeeping' and the values of helpfulness, altruism, non-violence and innocence. These values are both gendered and racialised as their promotion and celebration has hinged upon white subjects performing and embodying them. Referring specifically to Canadian peacekeepers in Somalia, Razack notes how 'impressed with their own nobility and superiority, and not at all equipped to understand the West's implication in the civil war in Somalia, peacekeepers were surprised and outraged when they found ungrateful natives and a complicated conflict' (2004: 48). Peacekeeping masculinity, therefore, assumes a form of saviour complex whereby those that embody this idealisation should be celebrated and exalted for their paternal helpfulness, altruism and non-violent efforts.

Why do military masculinities matter for understanding the war in Afghanistan's effect on the Canadian peacekeeping myth? As I will show in the remainder of this section, political legitimisation of Afghanistan was fostered through 'official' and 'unofficial' representations of Canadian militarised masculinity. Militarised masculinity is not only about how the 'ideal soldier' is imagined within militaries but also how the desired archetype of soldiers, in turn, reflects the perceived gendered (and racialised) identity of the nation/state. Military masculinities 'can be as intimate and precise as the proportions of a particular soldier's body but can also include an entire nation's belief about whether war is an occasion for service members to demonstrate toughness' (Belkin 2012: 4). Therefore, I now turn to the ways that militarised masculinities were negotiated by political and military elites to justify Canada's not-peacekeeping mission in Afghanistan between 2001 and 2014.

In the early years of the war in Afghanistan, peacekeeping was represented as a feminised international role, and combat in Afghanistan was represented as an opportunity to re-masculinise Canada's middle power identity and 'prove' that the CAF was a 'serious' international combat force capable of the kind of martial violence that made other countries powerful, narratives that aligned with Great Power politics in international relations theory. The early years of the Afghanistan war saw political and defence elites attempt to 'brand' the CAF in a new foreign policy image, one that would help the Forces 'shed' their feminised peacekeeping image through combat and counterinsurgency. For defence elites, it was time for the peacekeeping myth to be extinguished.

The engendering of peacekeeping as a 'feminised' use of the military, and the pejorative connotations of this representation, was not new. As Sandra Whitworth documents in her study UN peacekeepers, many soldiers have described peacekeeping as 'boring' (2004: 86) and felt that 'real soldiering' included the opportunity to engage in fighting; soldiers expressed that 'non-blue-beret-fight[ing] . . . had more prestige' (2004: 100). As one Canadian soldier explained during the Somalia mission, 'We're training for war all our lives, and the guys all want to know what it is like. That's why they join the army, to soldier' (Winslow 1997: 198; cited in Whitworth 2004: 86). The desire to fight 'real wars' is indicative of the link between masculinity and military values, demonstrative of warrior 'militarised masculinity' that symbolises masculine power and prestige. Peacekeeping, according to some peacekeepers, limited warrior masculinity.

Gender is therefore important for understanding the early years of the Afghanistan mission when defence and political elites promoted counterinsurgency as a form of muscular nationalism to dismantle the perceived 'feminised' peacekeeping brand of the Forces. Defence elites were few but vocal. They included academics Jack Granatstein and David Bercuson, featured prominently in newspaper editorials and think tank essays, and military officials General Rick Hillier and Colonel Bernd Horn, all of whom took issue with the feminised image of blue-helmeted peacekeepers. Brigadier General Peter Devlin, commander of Operation Athena, declared, 'God, I hate it when they call us peacekeepers. We loathe the term, abhor it' (cited in Anker 2005: 28). Fear that Canada's reputation as a peacekeeper made other nations view Canada as 'weak' was expressed by General Rick Hillier, who claimed that at the start of the Afghanistan conflict, European countries were wary of Canadian involvement; 'the British in particular believed that Canada had "lost its ability to be a war-fighting nation". . . They had "no faith that Canada would pull its weight, especially if things got tough"' (cited in Comte 2009).

As Chapter 3 explained, part of Canada's peacekeeping mythology has centred around the notion of peacekeeping as an 'ideal' practice for middle power nations. In the early years of the Afghan conflict (2001–2005), elite representatives expressed concern that Canada's mythologised image of a global peacekeeper prohibited Canada from exhibiting power and influence among dominant state actors in international affairs. These concerns were often expressed in explicitly gendered and euphemistic language. Academic turned Liberal politician Michael Ignatieff explained: 'Canada can acquire influence internationally and sustain its reputation as a leader in peacekeeping only if it puts military muscle behind its good intentions . . . I work in a policy environment where Canada is considered a well-meaning herbivore vegetarian boy scout. We're not taken seriously' (quoted in Fraser 2002). It was assumed that militarisation was required for influence, even in peacekeeping, despite the myth's long-standing promotion of non-violence as a tenet. Afghanistan, and the new combat role it required, was therefore a solution to 'prove' the Forces' capacity as manly warriors.

The Commander of Canadian ground troops, General Rick Hillier, claimed that participation in Afghanistan 'established our credibility in the coalition. Canada has been tainted with an image of being blue-hatted peacekeepers, and I think . . . the aggressiveness and tenacity that the troops showed . . . dispelled the myth . . . [We] were like a pack of rabid pitbulls in satisfying the coalition's end state' (cited in Roach 2003: 153). Hillier emphasised the nature of the Afghanistan war as one that required warrior determination: 'Fighting a savage enemy in some of the harshest conditions and terrain any Canadian soldier has ever had to endure, [Canadian Forces soldiers] fought in close-quarter combat for days on end and overcame a determined and cunning enemy . . . Canadians demonstrated the justly earned reputation as fierce warriors' (cited in Horn 2010: 10). Defence elites were desperate to shed the peacekeeping myth and to signal the warrior or 'combat' ability of the Forces. Hillier asserted the image of the Canadian Forces as a combat institution that was capable of waging war, as opposed to the more passive image associated with peacekeeping. Other defence leaders, such as Colonel Bernd Horn, reinforced the assertion that Canadian peacekeeping was in the past: '[Afghanistan] signalled to allies and the Canadian public that the national peacekeeper myth was dead. Canada was once again prepared to deliberately send its sons and daughters into combat' (Horn 2010: 147–8).

It was not only military elites, but also academics like Jack Granatstein, who echoed these sentiments in national editorials. They wrote that Afghanistan was an opportunity to 'knock the powerful peacekeeping mythology right between the eyes' (Granatstein 2008) as the Forces 'have found their raison d'etre again. They are a military force; they are not a peacekeeping force . . . Peacekeeping has failed, except in the minds of the Canadian public' (Granatstein, cited in Blanchfield 2008). Foreign policy elites were eager to be rid of the peacekeeping myth and demonstrate to military allies (and the Canadian public) that the Forces were combat-capable. The media echoed these desires. The *Globe and Mail*, one of two national newspapers, reported that 'Canada decided to send its troops into a combat mission under US control in Afghanistan rather than participate in the British-led multinational force because it is "tired" of acting as mere peacekeepers' (Freeman 2002: A1).

Rejecting peacekeeping and justifying the Afghanistan conflict

The war in Afghanistan was positioned as a civilising mission, exemplified by racialised discourse about the threat of global terrorism. Violence in the war on terror, including the deployment of the Canadian Armed Forces (CAF) was justified through discursive logics about safe/unsafe masculinities and feminised populations in need of protection. As post-colonial feminists have theorised, the 'war on terror' functioned to reproduce cultural logics and statist racism through narratives that sought to justify violence, assumed to combat threatening 'differences of values, beliefs, and ways of life' (Bhattacharyya 2009: 102), embodied mainly in the figure of the 'dangerous brown man' (104).[8] Gender and race were inseparable in these discourses as narratives justified military action by representing Afghanistan and its 'unfree femininity and barbaric masculinity' (Bhattacharyya 2009: 73) as contrary to Western (and Canadian) 'free femininity and civilized masculinity' (73).

Race/gender logics underpinned the discourse that justified Canadian intervention in the war on terror but did so in nuanced ways across the war's time periods. In the early years of the war, Canadian discourse echoed what Iris Marion Young calls the 'logic of masculinist protection' (2003), whereby Canadian leaders justified military action as the masculine duty of the state to protect the nation's women and children, thereby 'constituting the state in relation to an outside enemy' (2003: 8). Early narratives emphasised that fighting terrorism in Afghanistan was for the benefit of protecting Canadians. Yet, representations in the latter half of the war pivoted the referent of security. Following 2008, the focus became on 'helping' Afghan feminised civilians (often women) in peacebuilding, thereby reproducing 'the triangular relationship . . . of a victim (brown women), a savage (brown men) and a saviour (white men/masculine states)' (Gentry 2015: 364; see also Spivak 1988; Mutua 2001; Cooke 2002). In this section, I consider the former representations in the early years of the conflict.

Post-9/11, political elites in Canada were concerned about terrorist threats to domestic security and used narratives of insecurity to support political claims that combat activity was required in Afghanistan. In a *Hamilton Spectator* article, Jack Granatstein mused: 'The Afghan War serves our national interests by helping to create a government there that will not support and shelter terrorists who can strike at us . . . Canada needs a military that can protect our people and protect our territory, the basic national interest of any nation-state' (Granatstein 2007a: A25). The threat posed by terrorism justified the need for militarisation according to logics that the military was inherently responsible for securing our national security interests.

The narrative that Canada was in Afghanistan to fight terrorism was a dominant discourse between 2001 and 2008. Initially (2001–2), narratives about fighting terrorist insurgents existed within a larger security discourse of shock and fear linked to the September 11, 2001 attacks on Washington and New York. As the war progressed, the Canadian government marketed the mission as a Whole of Government strategy, and the initial justifications for involvement (a response to 9/11) were replaced with narratives that fighting terrorism was a necessary tool for stabilisation in Afghanistan and *also* for preventing future attacks on Canadian soil. Therefore, the war was justified as a means to ensure both global and domestic security from the barbarism and savagery assumed to be inherent in Afghanistan's cultural environment.

The links between homeland security and the Canadian Forces' efforts abroad were reiterated frequently by political elites and evidenced officially in the Report on the Standing Committee on National Defence. The Report stated that the Afghanistan war was 'to protect the national security interests of Canada by helping to ensure that Afghanistan will not, once again, become a haven for international terrorists' (Parliament of Canada 2007: 6) Between 2001 and 2007, this messaging dominated elite discourse, and of significance was the representation of Canada/Afghanistan according to a civilised/savage dichotomy. During a 2006 House of Commons debate, Members of Parliament discussed the justifications for military contributions to Afghanistan:

> On September 11 an attack was launched against *innocent civilians* in our part of the world ... the war was against liberal, western, democratic values and the things we stand for. That was the motivating factor of that war, and it was a war. Where did the terrorists come from? They came from Afghanistan. Seventy thousand of them had been trained in a state that sponsored and protected this group against *civilized people* around the world and nothing was done about *these people*. I think the objective of our initial involvement in that war was to destroy those terrorist camps in Afghanistan and to remove the government in power that had sponsored and protected them, and, as has so rightly been put forward tonight, the role is to rebuild that country, to *bring back some civilization* and some badly needed things to their society. (Parliament of Canada 2006, emphasis added)

Throughout the debate, many speakers reproduced the message that 9/11 was carried out by dangerous, uncivilised Afghan terrorists who were a threat to 'innocent' Canadians.

In 2008, the Independent Panel on Canada's Future Role in Afghanistan released a report, which reinforced the dichotomy of civilised/uncivilised: 'Afghanistan is at war, and Canadians are combatants. It is a war fought between an elected, democratic government and a zealous insurgency of proven brutality' (Parliament of Canada 2008). Narratives like these represent the war as a struggle between good and evil, civility and brutality, a construction of the 'savages-victims-saviours' (SVS) metaphor outlined by Makua Mutua (2001). These metaphors, or representations, of a savage enemy who is 'cruel and unimaginable' (Mutua 2001: 202), 'a negation of humanity' (202), demonstrate the 'savagery inhere[nt] . . . of the one-party state, military junta or . . . theocracy' (203), and is held in contrast to the civilised, non-violent democracies who are 'saviours' to 'victims' who have been violated.

The narratives that describe 'us' (Canada as a nation who fights terrorism in order to provide order) and 'them' (terrorist members or groups of resistance that are disorderly) reproduce war as a masculine clash between white saviours and brown savages. Narratives by Canadian political elites describe terrorists as using fatal, vicious tactics to create bodily harm and fear, but it omits accounts of violence by Westernised forces. It reinforces and emphasises violence used by 'them', but does not make note of violence caused by 'us':

> There are bad people around who have killed and continue to kill, suppress and tear down the democratic process that is just starting to grow in Afghanistan. The truth of the matter is that there are people in this world who do not care for others apart from using them for their own purposes, which some of the Taliban and a few of the others are doing. (Parliament of Canada 2006)

The depiction of the enemy – 'bad people' – reinforced ideas that terrorists were incapable of civility and inherently driven by malice, rather than ideology or politics. These representations were also used to justify why NATO policies towards them could not follow the types of diplomatic means usually pursued when engaging with democratic (rational) foreign actors. Again, political elites debating the ongoing war in Afghanistan during a House of Commons debate explained:

> The Taliban may be in the habit of cutting people's heads off and making executive decisions about how to proceed, but we live in a democracy . . . our debate tonight demonstrated the strengths of a democracy

compared with the unspeakable tyranny of the Taliban. (Parliament of Canada 2006)

It was evident in elite political discourse, therefore, that the metaphor of savage–saviour dichotomy was a key part of early justifications for ongoing military commitments to Afghanistan. Media reproduced similar narratives:

> It isn't Canadian soldiers who have killed scores of ordinary Afghan civilians, women, and children, in suicide bombs and improvised explosive devices on the gutted roads of that country, who bomb schools and threaten teachers with death. It is the men like those my colleague interviewed [referring to Taliban interviewees] who do and who send in as cannon fodder any sufficiently poor, illiterate, desperate young Afghan men they can find. (Blatchford 2006)

Little political debate or media coverage included discussions of the historical imperial conditions of dispossession and violence by external actors in Afghanistan that led to contemporary Taliban political power. 'We', in these narratives, signals Canada's position in 'the West', a coded racialised reference common in international relations speak that plausibly conflates 'the West' as a 'racialized category indexed to Whiteness' (Sabaratnam 2020: 10). The conflation of whiteness to Westernness is reproduced by narratives that identify the West as 'progressive, endogenously developed, meritocratic, individualist and liberal spaces' (Sabaratnam 2020: 10). This in turn situates 'the West' as innocent and outside the politics that led to violent politics by 'dangerous brown men'. Early years of the Afghanistan war saw political discourse filled with Orientalist narratives. These representations have previously been observed in 'humanitarian' or human rights discourse (Ware 1992; Doty 1993; Razack 2004; Zine 2006) and were not exclusive to the Canadian context, as this racialised discourse was also observed in American political narratives legitimising the 'war on terror' (Nayak 2006; Shepherd 2006; Eisenstein 2007; Richter-Montpetit 2007).

Narratives about savagery and civilisation were dominant in the early years of the war (2001–7) but later shifted. While the gendered and racialised assumptions about Canada's non-peacekeeping mission in Afghanistan found resonance by certain stakeholders, these justifications were not wholly convincing to public audiences. I argue that it is because of the immutability of the peacekeeper myth, and the values reproduced in this myth to signal Canadian imaginaries about helpfulness, altruism, non-violence and paternalism, that discourse about the war in Afghanistan shifted in 2007. The 'shift' from war on terror rhetoric to helpful hero rhetoric permitted Afghanistan to be justified according to, rather than contrary to, the values of the peacekeeping myth. This will be outlined in greater detail below.

Failed manoeuvres and reclaiming the peacekeeping myth's values

Rejecting the peacekeeper myth was not a successful political branding exercise. While early years of the Afghanistan war saw political and military elites striving to 'rebrand' Canada's peacekeeping image and stoke political support for the war through racialised and fear-based narratives about 'dangerous brown men', these justifications did not resonate with public audiences. While defence officials positioned Afghanistan as an opportunity to 'shed' the peacekeeping myth, political elites became aware that public support for the war hinged upon the ability to retain elements of the peacekeeper image. Warrior masculinity, while popular within military cultures, was unpopular with civilian audiences. And while Canadians may have resonated with the construct of white saviours, public audiences were more concerned with how Canada could be represented as helpful rather than as global 'warrior' fighting terrorism – a trope associated with American nationalism and militarised masculinity.

Polling researchers in the early years of the war noted that a majority of respondents preferred 'traditional peacekeeping' – defined as the separation of two warring parties – to 'peacemaking' – defined as involving fighting alongside other United Nations (UN) troops to enforce peace (see Environics Research Group 2002, 2004).[9] After the election of Stephen Harper's Conservative Party government in 2006, the Department of Foreign Affairs undertook cross-country focus groups to understand Canadian attitude and feelings towards the mission and to test messaging about the mission based upon media coverage (Woods 2007). What the report found was that test audiences were uncomfortable with Prime Minister Harper's rhetoric that appeared to 'echo' President Bush's war on terror messaging, particularly in references about terrorism and the Taliban. The report listed terms that could be used to support the government's commitments to the war in Afghanistan, including 'rebuilding, restoring, reconstruction, hope, opportunity', and 'enhancing the lives of women and children' (Woods 2007: n.p.) The report also cautioned government elites about avoiding phrases like 'freedom, democracy, and liberty ... in combination this phrase comes across as sounding too American' (Woods 2007).

The test audiences were also used to consider the images and words that would be placed upon the federal government's main webpage (www.afghanistan.gc.ca) used to communicate to Canadians the purpose of the ongoing war, and participant feedback suggested 'pictures of children in schools, references to progress and development, and the explanation that Canada is in Afghanistan at the request of the democratically elected government' (Woods 2007: n.p.) Following these focus groups, an independent 2007 poll suggested that 'the best way for Mr. Harper to obtain [parliamentary consensus to extend the mission] would be to argue that Canada ha[d] a duty to safeguard the humanitarian gains of Afghan women and children' (Laghi and Freeman 2007). Of the 1,000 Canadians polled, 81 per cent listed the 'rights of women and children' as the most important factor in considering an extension (Laghi and Freeman 2007).

I suggest that the emergence of these studies, which demonstrated elite rhetoric justifying military activity due to a terrorist threat, was unpopular with public audiences and discouraged political elites from continuing to use this narrative to mobilise public support for the war post-2008. Canadians were more comfortable with the language of peacekeeping than they were with rhetoric of combat (Sjolander 2007: 328). The peacekeeping myth was deeply embedded in the national imaginary and despite more than five years of non-peacekeeping focus in foreign policy, the myth had not faded.[10]

It should not be surprising, then, that official discourse in the latter half of the mission shifted to focus less on counterterrorist rhetoric and more on how the military was *helping* Afghans. Narratives about humanitarian activities in Afghanistan by the CAF relied on the (re)framing of national identity according to values of helpfulness, altruism, paternalist care for Afghan 'womenandchildren', and non-violent strategies. Although the Harper government never fully abandoned its use of the 'fighting terrorism' combat rhetoric, there were increased government efforts to inform the public of humanitarian strategies in order to reinforce the values of the peacekeeping myth.

Nostalgia for the peacekeeping myth influenced discourse in the second half of the war. While earlier messaging in the war promoted Canadian civilised, white masculinity in contrast to barbaric, racialised masculinity of the 'enemy', exemplified by General Rick Hillier's infamous reference to Afghan insurgents as 'detestable murderers and scumbags' (Nickerson 2005), what discourse in later years of the war focused on was the *victims* of the insurgency: Afghan 'womenandchildren' (Enloe 1989: 1) and Canadian efforts to help these victims. Narratives by political elites reinforced the savage-victim-saviour (Mutua 2001) triad and positioned Afghan women as victims to be rescued (Jiwani 2004, 2005, 2009), reproducing what Gillian Youngs calls the warrior/maiden model of militarised national heroes – 'chivalrous knights' (Jiwani 2009) – who defend both actual and symbolic passive women and children (Youngs 2006: 8). These narratives contain a coded racialisation that 'reifies the West in a role of saviour to non-Western women which both deflects from problems of gendered violence within the supposedly more superior and progressive West' (Gentry 2015: 364). This chivalrous or helpful form of militarised masculinity justifies military violence as ethical and desired. As Patricia McFadden quipped, the 'politics of rescue lies at the heart of imperial intention' (McFadden 2008: 58).

Sensationalised media representations of Afghan women under Taliban oppression fail to present the historical entirety of the subordination and gloss over the new system of subordination of these same women, institutionalised through foreign intervention (Khan 2001, 2008). These representations aligned with government messaging about 'us' and 'them'. Consider an excerpt from a *Toronto Star* article:

> But when I hear [critics of the Afghanistan war] griping, I think of Afghan women like Nilab Zareen. The Taliban threw her out of the country's medical school. When I think of the NDP's [opposition political party] previous demands that we pull our troops immediately, I think of Zareen's struggle, and the girls who are no longer illiterate. (Cohn 2008)

Earlier narratives describing Afghanistan as a collapsed, dysfunctional society that required the assistance and firm guidance of our military forces made narrative shifts possible. Colleen Bell (2010) noted that viewing intervention in this manner – as a mission to civilise – presents the mission as an 'ethical move to emancipate distant populations from social inadequacy, corruption, and poverty' (65). In other words, earlier pejorative depictions of Afghanistan and of Afghans renders plausible the story that Canadians were helping Afghans to resolve these inadequacies and therefore conducting commendable work. This story centres upon the paternal helpfulness and altruism of the CAF, central tenets in the beloved peacekeeping myth. It is, therefore, re-mobilising elements of the peacekeeping myth by political elites and Canadian media that contributed to ongoing legitimisation of war efforts between 2007 and 2014.

The specificities of Canadian discourse, to be outlined below, echoed other national contexts where the gendered politics of rescue, for example in the US and UK contexts, have been part of justifications for the Afghanistan war (see Stabile and Kumar 2005; Shepherd 2006; Hunt and Rygiel 2008; Duncanson 2013; Welland 2015). While scholarship has attended to media representations portraying Afghan women as victims to be rescued (see Jiwani 2004, 2005, 2009), my analysis to follow centres upon the ways that militarised masculinity in representations of Canadian soldiers was used to signal a plausible, desirable role for the Forces that aligned with elements of the peacekeeping myth. Post 2007, discursive representations focused on Canadian soldiers as 'saviours' or heroes. This new idealisation – a novel militarised masculinity that came to represent the CAF in Afghanistan – functioned to reconcile defence elites' desire to 'show' the combat capability of the CAF with long-standing public desires for peacekeeping masculinity and the nostalgia of the peacekeeping myth.

Reinforcing the peacekeeper myth virtues

The fourth manoeuvre I explore involves the way that the 'helpful hero' soldier model and Support the Troops and soldier sacrifice discourses were used to resuscitate and sustain the peacekeeper myth in the later stages of the war in Afghanistan. I draw on a visual and discourse analysis of Department of Defence materials between 2006 and 2014 to show how elements of the peacekeeper myth were mobilised in official branding. The trope of Canadian soldiers as helpful heroes functioned to cast military activities in the war as helpful and therefore politically justifiable. The helpful hero signals ideals of the peacekeeping myth: casting the Canadian war efforts as paternally helpful, conducted with a spirit of altruism, and operating without the explicit deployment of lethal violence. These three elements of the myth were peppered throughout 'official' representations of the war issue by the Government of Canada and the Department of Defence, supported in media representations of the war.[11] This new 'helpful hero' idealised soldier helped amplify Support the Troops discourses, which became ubiquitous in the later stages of the war in Afghanistan.

Manoeuvring peacekeeping nostalgia

I argue that the helpful hero form of militarised masculinity rebranded Canadian peacekeepers as soldiers with the intentions of peacekeepers, but with the capacity of warriors. The virtues of altruism, paternal helpfulness and non-violence were infused in the representations of helpful heroes, drawing connection between the CAF in Afghanistan and the beloved peacekeeping myth. My analysis is based upon artefacts in multi-media formats, including recruitment campaigns, documents released by the Departments of Defence and Veterans Affairs, text and images from the Canadian government's quarterly reports on policies in Afghanistan (issued between 2008 and 2012), an informational brochure from the Department of Veterans Affairs about the Afghanistan war, and a gallery of '100 images from Afghanistan' compiled by the Canadian Joint Operations Command.

Between 2006 and 2008, the Department of National Defence (DND) released a series of video advertisements in a campaign called 'Fight with the Canadian Forces'. Ad #1, subtitled 'International Security and British Columbia search and rescue', showed images set in 'Afghanistan', the 'Gulf of Oman', as well as specialty rescue missions in 'British Columbia' (the locations were determined based upon the subtitles in the videos) where clips of soldiers carrying guns and moving stealthily in a submarine in fast-paced adventurous vignettes feature 'international' roles of the CAF.[12] Ad #2, subtitled 'Disaster Relief in Canada and Rescue at Sea', focused on soldiers assisting in national disasters, subtitled 'Forest Fires in British Columbia' and 'Flooding in Manitoba', signalling historical disaster scenarios in which the CAF have been deployed for domestic humanitarian relief. Ad #3, subtitled 'Drug Bust and Hard Landing', takes places in 'Canada's North' and 'Canada's East Coast' where soldiers confront drug smugglers and race across snowy landscapes on snowmobiles or parachute into a frozen plane cockpit to rescue frost-covered civilians. While the ads all clearly represent life in the CAF as fast paced and adventurous – jumping from a helicopter into the ocean, parachuting, rappelling down cliffs, racing snowmobiles, operating submarine technology – the 'story' of each advertisement primarily represents soldiers as heroes helping victimised groups of people. Values of the Canadian peacekeeping myth are embedded in the stories. Paternal helpfulness, in particular, is emphasised in the strategic geographic references (Goldie 2014) to Canadian crises such as forest fires and flooding. There are numerous historical deployments of the Forces to provide rescue and relief for Canadians facing acute national disasters (forest fires, capsized boats, flooding, ice storms). The ad use of Canadian geography creates a personal connection for Canadian citizens who may have experienced domestic relief by CAF assistance, reinforcing that the paternal nature of the Forces to help makes the institution a valued national treasure. In addition, in Ads #1 and #3, there are scenes where hunched groups of weary or terrified-looking civilians are ushered to safety by soldiers. In these representations, the actions of the Forces signal helpfulness and altruism: doing thrilling and at times dangerous work for the benefit of victimised Canadians.

The ads also signal a third component of the Canadian peacekeeping myth: non-violence. The videos do not depict the CAF inflicting violence upon others and avoid representing the gritty realities and traumas of war, rescue and disaster relief situations. In the scenes where 'enemies' lurk, the stories depict that the primary goal of soldiers is to rescue/save, and there is an explicit lack of violence. The recruitment ads demonstrate that CAF members fight – but the videos don't show killing, firing weapons, or other overt combat activities. The videos symbolise that soldiers help, but not in an overly feminised way. The depiction of military tasks in the Fight ads is euphemised: the soldiers carry guns, but do not fire them. There is little struggle shown in the interactions between the soldiers and other characters in the Fight Ad videos. In these scenes, CAF members conduct their tasks with great ease and no resistance. The ads suggest the presence of actualised dangers, but do not show the outcome of these dangers. (Wegner 2020).

The ads signal these components of the peacekeeper myth beloved by Canadians, but in a way that does not 'feminise' the activities of the Forces, a means to avoid ostracising the ads' 18–24 year target demographic. While the they indicate the technological and military prowess of the Forces, the focused stories illustrate that helpfulness is the key objective. Altruism and helpfulness, as indicated as desired elements associated with peacekeeping, make the ads appealing to a mixed audience. Consider Enloe's explanation for why peacekeeping is viewed so popularly by civilians: it 'inspires optimism because it seems to perform military duties without being militaristic' (1993: 33). The ads, while signalling the excitement and adrenaline of a career with the CAF, do so in ways that are not so militaristic that they detract from the optimistic sentiments of the peacekeeping myth's nostalgia.

The themes present in the DND recruitment ads were also present in the 'official' representations of the CAF in Afghanistan, featured on the government's website and in DND media and material releases. The novel form of militarised masculinity represented in these artefacts, *helpful hero masculinity*, signals the altruistic, paternally helpful and non-violent elements of the CAF missions in Afghanistan and is represented in visual discourse from the various 'official' sources. 'Helpful' activities in Afghanistan, which previously would have been cast as feminine 'peacekeeping' tasks, were re- masculinised in helpful hero representations through aesthetic depictions of the Canadian soldier as combat capable. The helpful hero trope contained an explicit warrior combat aesthetic, highlighting the modern technology and protective gear (for example, helmet, bulletproof vest, and automatic weapon) that Canadian soldiers utilised in Afghanistan. Photos from the Department of Defence's 'Combat Cam' show armoured vehicles operated by soldiers, personnel carrying heavy, automatic weapons, against a sandy, dusty backdrop, often illustrating dilapidated infrastructure like crumbling walls and buildings. While many of the photographs show personnel holding weaponry, most photos show soldiers carrying their gun in a safe 'muzzle controlled' position, with the barrel pointed at the ground or directly at the sky. The 'non-violence' of these soldiers is signalled through the overall lack of explicit imagery demonstrating lethal force. Notably, there are as many photos of personnel surveying landscapes through binoculars as there are of photos where artillery force is being deployed (an homage, perhaps to *The Reconciliation* statue's peacekeeper who looks through binoculars across the Ottawa memorial site, as described in Chapter 3).

Only four of the 100 featured Operation Athena portfolio photos show the deployment of firepower, illustrated in a single highly stylised image of a soldier firing a shoulder-positioned rock launcher while his colleague grips his ears and takes cover, as well as three photos of soldiers firing Howitzer cannons into the sky (respectively, images Ar2010-0320-78, KA2003-A331D, KA2003-A333D, KA2003-A334D, available on the Department of National Defence's Combat Cam repository[13]). There is also a featured photo, with blurry background, of what appears to be a shooting blind with a string of ammunition hanging over a handwritten message reading 'Warning! 2 Way Shooting Range' with the figure of a skull and crossbones underneath. While these photos signal and show the combat capacity of the Forces, they do not show who the target of this lethal force was nor the consequences of deploying the weaponry. The combat capability of the Forces in those select photos are offset by imagery of base life, including soldiers reading books, playing beach volleyball, playing hockey, lifting weights, doing step aerobics, and participating in a stationary cycling bicycle class. There are several photos of medic personnel, tending to colleagues in non-threatening scenarios such as monitoring blood pressure, fiddling with medical machinery, or dispensing pharmaceutical pills. Many of the subtitles on Combat Cam photos indicate that the photo is about 'mentorship' by the CAF members of an Afghan police or military officer.[14] These thematically align with paternal helpfulness, a desire by Canada and its military to altruistically assist Afghanistan despite 'tough' conflict conditions.

On the Department of Veteran Affairs landing webpage for Afghanistan, there was a digital pamphlet about the role of the Canadian Forces in Afghanistan (Veterans Affairs Canada 2019). The pamphlet briefly details the various missions and roles that the CAF performed between 2001 and 2014. In this discourse, illustrated by only two photos, the paternal helpfulness and altruism of the Forces is emphasised. One image in the pamphlet depicts two female soldiers assisting a young Afghan girl in need of burns treatment. A light-skinned female soldier, dressed in desert camouflage fatigues with a Canadian flag emblazoned on her sleeve, carries (coded as 'rescues' or 'helps') a young, brown-skinned girl with a head covering who has a visible wound on her left leg. A second, blonde-haired female soldier, wearing desert camouflage fatigues, bulletproof vest and helmet, reaches her arms out to assist the first soldier, who cradles the child. Despite being female, the soldiers signal a type of masculine protection – 'tough but tender' (Niva 1998) – that departs from gun-slinging sniper imagery but nonetheless still reflects a capacity for combat. As Masters (2005) notes, techno-militarised masculinity has come to signal idealised contemporary soldiers, reinscribing these bodies as masculinised. In the pamphlet photograph, the female soldiers exhibit their masculine qualities through their desert camouflage uniforms and protective vests, while their actions simultaneously signal that they are 'helping' the wounded child.

The use of this image presents two considerations for how the helpful heroes trope functioned to legitimise Canada's involvement in the war. First, there is racialised symbolism in the photo: two light-skinned Canadian heroes assisting a small, brown-skinned child in need of help. This imagery maps onto pre-existing understandings of Canadian peacekeepers as exemplifying white militarised masculinity (even read on female-embodied subjects) contrasted with dark threats (unseen but implied in existing discourse that sensationalised the 'foreignness' of brown insurgents in Afghanistan). It also maps to pre-existing fantasies of white saviours rescuing brown feminised victims (see Spivak 1994; Mutua 2001). The production of helpful hero masculinity in 'official' representations of the CAF in Afghanistan therefore reproduces gendered and racialised tropes symbolising elements of the peacekeeping myth.

Second, the helpful heroes depicted in this image obfuscate the relationship between humanitarianism and militarism (Terry 2009) present in the Afghanistan conflict. In other words, while the military personnel are depicted 'helping' a child with an urgent health need, the role that the Canadian military may have played in the destructive conditions that led to her wound is obscured. The photograph signals that the child is the recipient of help by Canadian soldiers but cannot capture the (potentially unhelpful) role that the presence of militarised forces had on the health and well-being of Afghan children in a broader context.

This type of visual symbolism, positioning soldiers as 'mimicking humanitarians in the lack of military significance and rapport with the innocent' (Pugh 2004: 47), was particularly stark in the Government of Canada's quarterly reports, which feature photos of dialogue between soldiers and community leaders in Afghanistan or smiling civilians. It was dominant throughout government messaging post-2008 that the objective of the CAF was to help, that they responded to a request from the elected government of Afghanistan for assistance (altruism), and that while the CAF had the capacity to use violence, it was done in the name of helpfulness. The virtues signalled in the representations of the CAF obscure the imperial nature of the Afghanistan conflict as well as Canada's own position in global colonialism.

Non-violence, therefore, in representations of Canada's military in Afghanistan, was not literally about non-violence, but about assumptions that some violence is principled and permitted while other forms are not: a central assumption in the broader peacekeeping myth.

Official representations told a 'war story' (Cooke 1996) about Afghanistan that highlighted the tough desert conditions of base life in Afghanistan, the ever-present threat of unseen dark threats, and the capacity of the CAF to wield lethal force with restraint for the purpose of paternally helping.

Solidifying legitimisation for the war through Support the Troops discourse

While government websites, media release, official reports and defence advertising sought to showcase the helpful heroes and the humanitarian objectives being fulfilled, such as the polio vaccination strategies or the construction of the Dahla Dam, the more explicit images showcasing the combat capacity of the Forces juxtaposed the 'innocence' of soldiers and the need to Support the Troops. In an inadvertent – yet effective – manoeuvre, the Government of Canada's official rhetoric began emphasising the 'sacrifice' of Canadian military personnel, which served to signal the 'innocence' element absent in depictions of war activities. This was influenced in two ways. The first was media attention to military fatalities, particularly between 2008 and 2010, when there was a prominence of obituary-style media articles that aimed to honour fallen soldiers. This media attention was encouraged by, and in turn encouraged, campaigns in Canada to Support the Troops through various fundraising and morale-boosting initiatives, such as Red Fridays Canada (Wegner 2017), the CANEX Yellow Ribbon Campaign (McCready 2013), and community memorialisation events like the Highway of Heroes and the Portraits of Honour tour (Wegner 2020).

The Support the Troops movement, exemplified by the iconic yellow ribbons sold to Canadians (and Americans) to affix to car bumpers, are symbols that 'affirm and exalt certain preferred national subjects: the masculinised, normative and morally unimpeachable young men (and to a lesser extent, women) whose sacrifice is not only the salvation of the national character, but retrospectively becomes its foundation and guarantor' (McCready 2013: 34). The use of yellow ribbons as a symbol for troop support has been described by A. L. McCready as a 'borrowed cultural practice' (2013: 40) related to heavy influences of US media in Canadian culture and the subsequent prominence of the symbol during Canada's involvement in Afghanistan. The official introduction of yellow ribbons into the Canadian cultural landscape happened through the Department of Defence's Support the Troops campaign, facilitated through the semi-private Canadian Forces Personnel Support Agency (CFPSA) that sold products through the Canadian Forces Exchange System (CANEX) discount stores and online forum (McCready 2013). Support the Troops rhetoric relied heavily upon the evocation of sacrifice and soldier fatalities to silence critics of policy in Afghanistan. The Harper government capitalised on this technique and conflated the Support the Troops messaging with support for the Afghan mission. When criticism of the mission was raised, the death of Canadian soldiers was often evoked to shame people into silence, noting that the moral altruism of Forces members who had lost their lives in Afghanistan should trump citizen concerns about the politics involved (Wegner 2017).

The emphasis on the altruism and sacrifice of Canadian soldiers was promoted in major media outlets featuring obituary-style articles about slain Canadian personnel. *The Canadian Press* reflected on the life of Yannick Scherrer: '[He] answered the call to service and dedicated himself to the cause of peace, security, and the rule of law in Afghanistan. He defended these principles with great courage and integrity' (Brautigam 2011). A majority of news coverage emphasised the courage and bravery of soldiers, and implied their altruistic motives. The *Calgary Herald* wrote of Cpl. Nathan Hornburg who 'went to support his fellow troops and friends, went because his country asked him to, and went because he felt, from the bottom of his heart, that it was the right thing to do' (Tetley 2007). The motivation to help others was reflected in the description of James McNeil as 'well liked and well respected by all his officers, peers and soldiers alike . . . he believed his deployments to Afghanistan would contribute to a better life for Afghan people' (Graveland 2010).

Judith Butler remarked that the extensive focus on sacrifice by 'us' positions the deaths of Canadians as grievable, while the deaths of Afghans went largely unnoticed (Butler 2004: 34). The lives of these deceased soldiers became not only noteworthy but a central part of discourse about the war in Afghanistan. The Support the Troops narratives focusing on deceased soldiers' sacrifices was the discursive element necessary to signal the innocence of the military in Afghanistan, the final virtue of the peacekeeping myth absent in official representations.

Race organises the logics of what Butler (2009) calls 'grievability'. The ways in which Canadian violence was obscured in the excessive focus on 'our' losses (or, in other discourse, as restrained and principled use of force) requires viewers to already be complicit in how colonial presents are reproduced: '[not] through geopolitics and geoeconomics alone . . . [but] set in motion through mundane cultural forms and cultural practices that mark other people as irredeemably "Other" and that license the unleashing of exemplary violence against them' (Derek Gregory 2004, cited in Welland 2015: 303).

As will be outlined in greater detail in Chapter 5, the summoning of 'innocence' in discourse about Support the Troops and military deaths was only possible due to long-standing national imaginaries that view historical and ongoing violence against colonised and racialised bodies as permissible. The 'co-mythologization' of whiteness and Western-ness through various epistemic practices (such as evolutionary and social sciences), which Sabaratnam has theorised, links epistemologies of innocence to white-subject positioning (2020: 10). It is this connection, the reproduction of 'innocence' in the excessive focus on Western military deaths at the expense of recognition of the wide-scale and enduring violence inflicted 'over there', that illustrates how dominant discourses on the war in Afghanistan – including Support the Troops rhetoric and the re-mobilisation of the peacekeeping myth – are legible only from a subject position of Western-ness and whiteness.

While the trope of 'innocence' was evoked through Support the Troops discourse, efforts to manoeuvre the peacekeeping myth's virtues to legitimise war in Afghanistan were, at best, partially successful. The four virtues of the peacekeeping myth – innocence, non-violence, altruism and paternal helpfulness – were mobilised, but not in holistically plausible ways. The power of the peacekeeping myth may have helped to sustain certain levels of legitimacy for Afghanistan, yet not enough for the desires of a foreign policy based on 'traditional peacekeeping' to wane. By 2010, an Ipsos Reid Corporation survey (2010) found that Canadians preferred the role of the Canadian Forces to be a 'friendly, helpful, provider of humanitarian assistance or peacekeeping services' (3). Traditional peacekeeping, stubbornly attached to the peacekeeping myth, was still promoted as an idealised role. This is best evidenced by post-war discourse, discussed in the final section of this chapter.

Post-war Visions: Canada – and the Peacekeeping Myth – Is Back

The war in Afghanistan *should have* destabilised the Canadian peacekeeping myth. Yet, it did not. In addition to the four manoeuvres outlined in this chapter, I argue that Canadian political leadership continues to sustain the peacekeeper myth, by claiming to be able to revive some 'true' version of it. In 2015, Canada's peacekeeping profile comprised only 111 peacekeepers out of 125,000 UN deployed personnel (Carroll 2016), no formal peacekeeping training had been institutionalised in CAF training (Dorn and Libben 2018), and there were political hesitations about whether Canada would deploy any personnel to the MUNISMA mission in Mali, or whether the country would simply provide equipment (Clark 2016). In addition to the overall decline in peacekeeping contributions by the CAF, surely Afghanistan should have been a foreign policy investment that finally myth-busted the peacekeeping myth. It did not: political elites continue to promote it.

In 2015, the Liberal Party of Canada and their leader Justin Trudeau campaigned actively on the phrase 'Canada is back', promising a renewed commitment to peacekeeping and promoting criticism of the Stephen Harper government (2006–15)'s active involvement in Afghanistan as contrary to Canada's long-standing commitment to good international citizenship and the peacekeeping ideal. The Trudeau election platform explicitly criticised Harper of 'turning his back' on the United Nations (Harper 2015) and stated, 'under Stephen Harper, [Canada's] influence and presence on the world stage has steadily diminished . . . our plan will restore Canada as a leader in the world . . . Canada can make a real and valuable contribution to a more peaceful and prosperous world' (quoted in Hillmer and Lagassé 2018). This sentiment was shared within government bureaucracy as well. In September 2015, a leaked document was obtained by *The Canadian Press*, which revealed that senior members of the Department of Foreign Affairs, Trade and Development (DFATD) felt that Canada's international reputation had been 'eroded' in key foreign policy areas (Blanchfield 2015). The document titled 'Canada's International Policy: Strategic Questions in a Changing Global Context' indicated that Canada's international clout was under threat and defined Canada's traditional role as a '"middle power", "honest broker", "principled actor". . . one ready to use soft power in tandem with other countries to "lead/shape/influence" on the global stage' (Chase and McCarthy 2015).

Other media outlets signalled the same sentiments: the *Montreal Gazette* reported how even former prime ministers such as Joe Clark and Jean Chretien have lamented Canada's loss of world standing, as exemplified by the decrease in peacekeeping troops and absence on UN subcouncils (Bruemmer 2015). Clark's 2013 book, *How We Lead: Canada in a Century of Change*, is sharply critical of Harper's foreign policies, noting that Canada's international reputation had been squandered due to an emphasis on the military and by turning away from diplomacy as a 'principal instrument [of foreign relations]' (Clark 2013). The narrative was not only present in domestic publications, but also found in international sources, such as the British *Guardian*'s coverage of the election. The August 2015 editorial explained that the Harper government had made 'the Canada that was a pillar of peacekeeping and the United Nations a distant memory' (Gurardian opinion 2015). The article concluded by stating 'but we may be permitted to hope there is now a chance that something of the old Canada, committed to moderation and multiculturalism at home and to multilateralism and cooperation abroad, will re-emerge from the fray' ('The Guardian view on Ca . . .', 2015). The desire to return to the idealised myth was heavily emphasised throughout the 2015 election and government transition in October 2015.

The call for a return to foreign policies rooted in the romanticised image of Canadian internationalism based in peacekeeping values was exemplified by an editorial by Sharanjeet Parmar, a war crimes prosecutor and Harvard lecturer, who wrote:

> Canada enjoys an illustrious history in international affairs that makes us proud: Lester B. Pearson won the Nobel Peace Prize for his role in the Suez Crisis, and invented the practice of peacekeeping . . . The next government and Parliament can continue this rich tradition and once again make us a valued and respected member of the international community. (Parmar 2015)

The nostalgic references and calls for principled foreign policy reflect the conflation of a 'real Canada' with peacekeeping mythology. Despite over a decade in the Afghanistan war, and no clear global peacekeeping presence at present, the peacekeeper myth remains deeply entrenched in the Canadian imagination. As I will outline in Chapter 5, this is because the peacekeeper myth also functions as a 'settler move to innocence' (Tuck and Yang 2012), whereby it obscures the ways that martial force has been instrumental in the maintenance of colonialism in Canadian 'domestic' politics, and the suppression of Indigenous rights movements over several decades.

Notes

1. While NGOs, aid organisations and partner countries contributed modest initiatives to support civilian aid and build infrastructures, and the Canadian government endorsed a Whole of Government approach that included defence, diplomacy and development strategies, the 'defence' components – counterinsurgency and stabilisation – were prioritised. This was partly due to ongoing

infrastructure destruction by insurgents, which leadership noted meant that diplomatic and development initiatives required defence support to carry out. Many ISAF 'development' projects utilised security by defence contracting companies that absorbed much of the trillion-dollar efforts by contributing states.

2. Recruitment levels dropped by 33 per cent between 1991 and 2001 and many members of the CAF were offered early release or early retirement compensation packages to reduce overall membership (Statistics Canada 2015).

3. Although the characteristics listed above have often been associated with idealised 'manliness' in and for military institutions, ideals can vary across time and space; consider Cohn's (1989) nuclear intellectual masculinity, Elshtain's (1995) chivalrous and protective 'Just Warrior' masculinity, Masters's (2005) techno-proficient cyborg soldier, or Higate's (2003) 'everyday' Royal Air Force (RAF) clerk, all variations of masculine ideals that differ across contexts.

4. Davis and McKee (2004) describe this as 'warrior creep', whereby the warrior ethos or warrior culture seeps into a broader range of non-combat environments and roles.

5. Marsha Henry (2017) explores the ways that intersectionality in scholarship on militarised masculinities is often done in problematic ways, particularly when it is applied to analytically show 'difference' within military settings (195), rather than its epistemological foundations as a framework for resisting patriarchy, racism and capitalism, and in particular, for understanding the oppressions of black women. While Henry does not necessarily support the 'origin narrative' (2017: 186) or seek to police where intersectionality can be used, she does caution the use of the term in scholarship that does not explicitly have anti-racist or anti-imperialist goals. My work here falls into a potentially troublesome 'grey area', whereby I am not using these frameworks to investigate, for example, poor black women in militaries. However, my use of the intersections of race/gender are intended to flesh out the 'complex relationship between identity, positionality, and power' (2017: 194), and I seek to make clear that it is because of the work of black feminists I can mobilise these important dimensions of the peacekeeping myth's power. As a white settler scholar, I am not sure I am able to judge if this is an 'appropriate' use of intersectionality frameworks, so I will leave it here that this may be an imperfect use of the construct, related to my own biases towards 'methodological whiteness' (Sabaratnam 2020). I shall leave the final assessment with you, dear reader.

6. Sherene Razack (2004) speaks to this in her discussion of the politics of race and colonialism in the 1993 Somalia torture scandal involving the now-defunct Canadian Airborne Regiment (CAR). She contemplates the racist training environment of two members of the CAR who were complicit in the torture of Somali teenager Shidane Arone in 1993. Two accused CAR members, Kyle Brown and Clayton Matchee, were of Indigenous/Aboriginal heritage. Razack discusses how these two men's actions were often measured against the stereotyping of men of colour as inherently violent throughout the National Inquiry, yet that, from testimonies, it was clear that race relations within the military units, including documented racist hazing, may indeed have affected how

and why the men acted as they did. The implicit racial hierarchies within the CAR unit positioned Matchee and Brown in a subordinate status to their non-Indigenous peers, and Razack suggests these racialised dynamics within the military unit may potentially help to understand their performance of extreme violence, exemplified by Matchee's announcement that the number of Somalis killed by the unit amounted to 'Indians two, white man nothing' (Razack 2004: 109) or the sharing of 'trophy photos' of themselves posing with Arone's brutalised body. Yet, the politics of the Somalia torture incident have been contested. Matchee's wife has asserted that it was a state of psychosis caused by anti-malarial drugs that resulted in her husband's violent actions. Matchee has a brain injury due to a suicide attempt following his second-degree murder conviction of Arone. As the Somalia Inquiry was cut short due to the Canadian 1997 election, the intricate politics of this violence – including the effects of colonialism and racism – remain unexamined.

7. As black feminists have long theorised, subject positioning is not only driven by gender. Race is also a vector of power (like sexuality, ability, class and age) that intersects with gender to produce and position subjects in relation to one another (Collins 1990; Crenshaw 1991). While militarised masculinities scholarship has detailed how masculinity impacts norms, behaviours and expectations for militaries and their members, it is worth noting that militarised masculinities in Western defence forces, specifically the forms of peacekeeper masculinity in Canada, have often assumed a white subject position for idealised referents.

8. I am grateful to Laura J. Shepherd for bringing Bhattacharyya's work to my attention through her own emerging research critiquing imperial and governance feminism in the realm of CVE (countering violent extremism). See Shepherd (2022).

9. A 2002 Focus Canada poll question read as follows (emphasis added): 'Some people say that Canadian Forces should adopt a traditional peacekeeping role, which means trying to keep the two conflicting sides apart. Others say that Canadian Forces should adopt a peace-making role, which might involve fighting alongside other UN troops to force peace in a disputed area. Which view is closer to your own?' (Environics Research Group 2002). Of the 2,021 adult Canadians polled, 52 per cent indicated that they preferred the 'traditional peacekeeping role'. In 2004, when Focus Canada posed the same question, the preference for 'traditional peacekeeping' had increased to 59 per cent (Environics Research Group 2004). Although polling numbers varied between regions, these studies confirm the prominence of Canadian support for the peacekeeper myth. In 2005, an Ekos Research Associates Inc. study asked: 'Should the Canadian Forces have a traditional peacekeeping role, which means trying to keep two conflicting sides apart? Or, should the CF have a peacemaking role, which might involve fighting alongside other UN troops to force peace in a disputed area?' The study found 57 per cent preferred 'traditional peacekeeping' (Ekos Research Associates 2005).

10. Part of the immutability of the peacekeeping myth is related to public ignorance about what the military actually does overseas. A study conducted by Ipsos-Reid/Dominion Institute/The Globe and Mail in 2003 asked respondents were asked

to name two CAF missions since 1990: only 41 per cent were able to provide two correct answers, 29 per cent were able to provide one correct answer, and 31 per cent were unable to provide any correct answers. This study did not differentiate between peacekeeping missions and non-peacekeeping assignments. In 2005, an Ipsos-Reid study found that 67 per cent of those polled knew 'very little' or 'nothing' about Canadian Forces operations in Afghanistan. Therefore, despite efforts by elites to dismantle the peacekeeping myth and summon a new gendered and racialised image for the nation/military, the peacekeeping myth endured. Some academics contributed to the confusion. One of Canada's leading peacekeeping scholars, Walter Dorn (2006), explained that in Afghanistan, 'some of the CF activities have been peacekeeping: support for elections, contributing to a secure environment in Kabul, and various forms of nation building' (105). Other academics disagreed with Dorn's description, noting that the Afghan mission '[was] not a UN mission; it was American-led and now NATO-led; it involves stabilisation and counterinsurgency, and not peacekeeping; it has a defined enemy; and Canada is not neutral in this engagement' (Maloney 2007: 101). The casual exchange of the terms 'peacekeeping' and 'humanitarianism' is part of how the peacekeeping myth's seductive power was used to legitimise the war in Afghanistan: even experts wanted to believe that Canada's war was normatively informed.

11. Media played an important role in promoting and controlling 'official' narratives about the war and providing visual and textual representations about what the CAF were doing in Afghanistan. Yet, bias towards government messaging was because media were not able to operate independently of defence activities. Many journalists required permission to embed with the Forces, otherwise forcing them to forgo security protection and take up independent travel arrangements. There was bureaucratic red tape and limitations placed on Canadian media reporting in Afghanistan. Colin Perkel with *The Canadian Press* explains: 'It's just one of the many restrictions that bind reporters who embed with the Canadian Forces in Afghanistan. Often, the military brands the most seemingly innocent detail as integral to operational security, which means an embedded journalist who discloses it faces the threat of expulsion from the base' (Perkel 2010). News reporters who were embedded with the Canadian Forces in Afghanistan were limited by 'security considerations' and were required to temper the ways they reported the war if they wished to have continued access to the front lines and the base. Instead of reporting military activity, the focus of embedded journalists often relied upon telling personalised stories about soldiers: their personalities, their hobbies and their bravery. Particularly after 2008, Canadian media coverage of the intervention in Afghanistan was saturated with biographical accounts of dead soldiers, and the Canadian military made a concerted effort to minimise discussion of non-lethal causalities. This is discussed in greater detail in the latter half of this chapter.

12. While Ad #1 was well received by marketing professionals and the target audience, political opponents criticised this imagery for being 'too American' (Goldie 2014: 424).

13. DND Combat repository available publicly at https://www.flickr.com/photos/ cfcombatcamera/albums/72157631895711034 (last accessed 10 October 2022).
14. As Julia Welland has explored in the context of the British army in Afghanistan, these partnering and advising roles that NATO forces have taken on may be positioned as distinct from empire or colonial ambition, but nonetheless, still 'largely uphold a hierarchical relationship between a superior white liberal warrior and inferior non-white "Other"' (2015: 302).

CHAPTER 5

Creating Martial Peace: Martial Politics and Militarised 'Peace' Enforcement in Canada

As I showed in Chapter 4, Canada's peacekeeping myth has sustained a romanticised and, in many instances, falsified account of what the Canadian military has done overseas in the name of peace. Yet the peacekeeper myth also relates to romanticised accounts of Canada's violent history of Indigenous–settler relations and facilitates political legitimisation of martial politics (Howell 2018) within the so-called peaceful Canadian state. Canada's peacekeeping myth has explicit neo-colonialist overtones, reproduced in romanticised accounts of the formation of the Canadian state with civil, just and orderly treaty-making processes with Indigenous nations. This account has been myth-busted by scholars who take aim at the 'myth of the peaceable kingdom' (Choquette 2019) or 'peace-making myth' (Regan 2011) as a problematic representation of Indigenous–settler relations in Canada that impede modern-day efforts for reconciliation. This chapter asks: What happens when Canada engages in violent 'peace-keeping' at home?

Canada's peacekeeper myth, and its implied political values of benevolent paternalism, innocence, altruism and non-violence, is contiguous with discourse about Canada's formation as a modern nation state and the history of 'peaceful' Indigenous–settler relations in this political project. Canada's peacekeeper myth has stood to legitimise foreign martial violence (as shown in Chapter 4 during the war in Afghanistan), but also stands to legitimise ongoing domestic deployments of militarised force against Indigenous populations. Martial violence and colonial violence have been mutually reinforcing in the state-making of contemporary Canada. Not unlike the mobilisation of the peacekeeper myth in gendered and racialised ways in the representation of the CAF in Afghanistan, mediated representations and accounts of martial force used against Indigenous nations also legitimise violence *within* the state, where violence has been justified because of a stated intent to produce peace and order. The relationship between martial violence and colonial violence becomes evident as the enforcement of 'peace' in Canada requires martial violence to enforce. *Martial peace* in Canada, therefore, involves repression of meaningful opportunities for justice that might address long-standing colonial violence. In the 'domestic' accounts of martial force, the state-led police force is positioned as legitimate, while grassroots and Indigenous-led resistance efforts have been positioned as threating, risky or uncivilised: antithetical to the presumed intrinsic peace and order of Canada.

This chapter therefore considers the forms of martial politics that the state has used in domestic 'peacekeeping' and what is at stake in the enforcement of martial peace. Canada's long-standing association of 'peace' with orderliness illustrates how martial, *war-like* politics often go unnoticed or even commended in the name of 'peacekeeping'. Alison Howell's (2018) martial politics defines the war-like (martial) relations that are a long-standing element of liberal politics, usually enacted on racialised, Indigenous, disabled and queer populations, who have been cast as a *threat to civil order* (2018: 118, emphasis added). I draw upon her framework, therefore, to show how the 'peace' sought in domestic settler–colonial relations in Canada is indeed part of broader martial politics.

As discussed in Chapter 1, martial politics and their attendant violence become obscured through the peacekeeping myth, whereby the use of militarist force is justified by its intentions, cast as apolitical and in the name of peace. This chapter explores how Canada's martial violence has been legitimised or condoned through the representations of militarised force as peaceful or in the name of peace. As earlier chapters have shown, certain violence has been legitimised through the peacekeeping myth, while political resistance has been criminalised and repressed. Resistance to contemporary 'peaceful' politics has been cast as an illegitimate form of violence. Understanding the symbolism of the peacekeeping myth is therefore not simply showing the ways Canada's militarised institutions have been violent, unhelpful, coercive and politically biased, but demonstrating that these institutions (and their violent actions) have been exalted and legitimised – both overseas and at home.

The Peacekeeping Myth Inside the State: Martial Politics and Canadian Indigenous–Settler Relations

This chapter explores the ways that martial force within the Canadian state has been represented as peaceful, paternal, non-violent and innocent. I consider the use of 'peacekeeping' against Indigenous-led protest and resistance movements. The 'domestic'[1] use of martial force has been far from peaceful and has repeatedly prioritised order over justice in 'managing' Indigenous–state conflict. I explore the ways that discourses of peacekeeping function alongside normative imaginaries (Millar 2021) of racism and colonialism to legitimise militarism and war-like relations within the Canadian polity.

Violence – in both martial and colonial forms – against Indigenous peoples has been endemic to the dispossession of North America (Turtle Island) by European imperialists that preceded the formation of the Canadian state in 1867. As Sunera Thobani explains, the claims to 'peaceful and orderly founding of a nation by Europeans anywhere on this continent, innocent and unconnected to orgiastic violence . . . [are] clearly an exercise in absurdity' (2010: 43). Yet the 'absurd' peacekeeping myth has dominated historical national discourses about the colonial encounter and has perpetuated narratives of white innocence in the face of 'hostile' Indigenous threats. In many historical accounts of the Canadian settler–colonial experience, Indigenous peoples were constituted as the very 'negation of [Canadian] values, ethics, and morality' (Thobani 2010: 38). The presumed values embedded in the peacekeeper myth (altruism, helpful paternalism, innocence and non-violence) have been contrasted with dichotomous representations of Othered subjects, found in representations of the self-serving, child-like or irrationally violent Indigenous protester. The peacekeeping myth draws from these discourses to reproduce state violence as legitimate and ethical, while Indigenous resistance has been represented in racialised and gendered framings as threatening, disorderly violence rather than legitimate political dissent. Essentially, Indigenous protest has been represented as a threat to peace while Canada's military and other martial institutions have been represented as the keepers of it.

While Chapters 3 and 4 have outlined the ways that Canada's peacekeeping myth is entangled with UN policy, discourse and practice of *international* military interventions, the myth's values have long been embedded in Canadian political consciousness as definitive of the state's moral composition and representative of the values in state-led martial force. The peacekeeper myth is therefore not only bound up in the imagination of the Canadian Armed Forces (CAF), but also in the Royal Canadian Mounted Police (RCMP), which for many Canadians represented 'the very essence of our national character – a respect for just authority' (Francis 1992: 61). National police forces have their own representational history of 'keepers of the Queen's peace' (Regan 2011: 101) and their modern participation in UN peacekeeping means they too are part and parcel of the Canadian peacekeeping myth.

I focus this chapter on contemporary use of martial force against Indigenous populations who sought to resist colonial exploitation through various protest mechanisms. I begin with a brief history of Canada's original peace and police force – the North-West Mounted Police (NWMP) – which would become the Royal Canadian Mounted Police, deployed to modern Canadian peacekeeping missions abroad and a fraternal organisation to the Canadian Armed Forces. This chapter considers how, while Canadian politicians were actively cultivating the peacekeeping myth as a component of Canada's international identity, martial politics were actively being mobilised through the force used against domestic Indigenous groups. While the actions of the police can be broadly understood as martial violence, I show how the deployment of force was also explicitly militarised, and often drew upon CAF expertise and equipment.

While the use of militarised police forces against Indigenous land defenders in Canadian history might seem far removed from the CAF's mythologised identity as peacekeepers, there are two important connections to note. The peacekeeping myth's founding story of Lester Pearson reiterates that Canada's vision of the original 1956 UNEF-1 mission was one of a 'peace and police' force. Peacekeeping and policing were understood as intertwined endeavours. Policing, and its representations in historical nostalgia, is therefore a key part of the establishment of the Canadian peacekeeping myth and institutions that benefit from mobilising the peacekeeping myth's legitimisation of violence and war-like relations. Like the 'peace and police vision' for international peacekeeping, the deployment of CAF personnel and resources against Canadian civilians has often been justified as keeping peace and/as order, with little attention paid to whether or not justice and rights were violated in the process. Not unlike United Nations missions, where the priority has been on ceasefires and control of lethal exchange, the lack of attention paid to justice in the 'creation' of peace in Canada leaves this vision of peace both shallow and martialised.

The second connection is that militarised force – as used by the NWMP and the RCMP – was intentionally created to dispossess Indigenous peoples of their lands and to control and subjugate Indigenous lives as a nation-building and empire-enforcing tool. While potentially derided as a 'domestic' institution, the RCMP, according to Colleen Bell and Kendra Schreiner (2018), has always been an *international* martial force, designed and implemented to 'pacify' and control Indigenous nations. The RCMP has not only deployed within Canada. Bell and Schreiner explain how the RCMP has been used as a source of inspiration for contemporary international policing projects, and integrated into 'counterinsurgency' missions, which they describe as an extension of the RCMP's original civilising mission mandate (Bell and Schreiner 2018). The RCMP and the CAF have co-operated on a number of tactical missions. In addition to the role that the CAF has played in assisting the RCMP in quelling Indigenous protests in Canada, the RCMP also has served an international role in UN peace missions. The RCMP is regularly used in United Nations missions, most notably several UN missions in Haiti since 1990, and has engaged in thirty-three other missions including Sudan, Kosovo and the West Bank (RCMP 2020).[2] RCMP personnel were deployed from 2007 to 2014 to the war in Afghanistan to work alongside the CAF in training the Afghan National Police. Known as the International Police Operations Program, RCMP officers participate as 'civilians' in overlapping peacekeeping mandates and missions with the Canadian Armed Forces. Their 'civilian' role includes conducting training, monitoring, mentoring, planning and evaluation of missions. Therefore, while distinct institutionally, the RCMP has benefited from long-standing mythologies about international peacekeeping *and* the 'peaceful' settlement of Canada, as well as ongoing training and equipment sharing by the CAF.

Therefore, while scholarship on militarism has only just begun to consider the significance and role of policing in issues of militarisation (Howell 2018; Manchanda and Rossdale 2021; Millar 2021), I wish to note that police, 'wear[ing] the same uniforms and us[ing] the same tools' (Newton, cited in Manchanda and Rossdale 2021: 12) as militaries, are not simply a 'boomerang effect of violent colonial governance' (Manchanda and Rossdale 2021: 12), but are rather a central tool in the formation and execution of colonial governance, imperative to how elites '"legitimated" their increasingly coercive imperial and colonial practices' (Peterson 2020:189) to internal and external stakeholders, and, importantly, fundamental to Canadian's international peacekeeping mandates, missions and myth.

Policing and its martial logics are central to early state-making which involved the consolidation of coercive and stratifying practices necessary in the creation of new political orders. Militarism and colonialism's mutually interdependent relationship is infused by racism and heteropatriarchal relations and exemplified by the ways that martial force by the Canadian settler state has been used to uphold colonial violence across centuries.

In the following section, I offer an overview of case examples of martial force used against Indigenous resistance movements. Indigenous resistance movements have not been exclusively pacifist, yet Indigenous martiality has been represented as threatening while excessive martial force by the RCMP and CAF have largely gone unquestioned. I do not seek to reify the idea that Indigenous communities have been unilaterally victimised by martial force. There is long-standing evidence that Indigenous communities have actively resisted colonialisation and militarised encroachments by the Canadian state over several centuries. It is impossible to offer a comprehensive account of this history in this short chapter alone.[3] Similarly, while I attempt to signal the political exploitations implemented by successive British and Canadian governments against Indigenous peoples that laid the foundation and impetus for Indigenous resistance in the form of land and rights protests, the complexity of many of these struggles is also beyond the scope of this overview (see instead Purich 1986; Alfred 1999, 2006; Knopf 2007; Balfour 2014; Coulthard 2014; Simpson 2014; Simpson 2017).

My modest intervention is to note that the ways political policies and strategies used to exploit First Nations and Indigenous communities throughout Canadian history would not have been possible without martial force to ensure compliance, and to illustrate how this martial force has been legitimised through the racialised logics of the peacekeeping myth. I examine how, during the development and creative mobilisations of the Canadian peacekeeping myth since 1956 (mapped in Chapters 3 and 4), this myth has also functioned to smooth over domestic martial politics and the positioning of these forms of violence as in the service of peace. Martial politics have been enabled through the conflation of the myth's values with state-initiated violence and by the contiguous reconstruction of the peacekeeping myth with colonialist logics. Colonisation requires martial force. Ongoing colonial relations and the thinly veiled construction of Canadian political society as demilitarised and peaceful requires the ever-present threat of, and mobilisation by, militarised force against those who seek to resist the status quo. I will return to this point at the end of the chapter.

Martial Violence and the Canadian Peacekeeper Myth from the NWMP to the RCMP (1867–Present)

Colonial institutions, such as the Hudson's Bay Company, had long used violent force in engagements with Indigenous populations during early decades of Indigenous–settler encounters (Katerberg 2003). This demonstrates that militarism should be understood not only through state-centric militarist endeavours, but also through political economies of imperial extraction and extractive enterprise (Manchanda and Rossdale 2021: 3). Nonetheless, the account I offer here begins in 1865 with the designation of the modern Canadian state and subsequent establishment of official martial institutions, specifically the North-West Mounted Police (NWMP). The 'official' justification for the establishment of martial forces centred upon the need to keep peace and order across geographically vast territories in what is modern-day Canada, thereby reinforcing 'peace' as a key mandate of these institutions and the frequent historical justification for violent police deployments. The formation of the North-West Mounted Police in 1873, designed by founding prime minister John A. MacDonald, was said to ensure 'the preservation of peace and the prevention of crime' (Gwyn 2012: 238). It was not long after the establishment and deployment of the NWMP that the institution would be mobilised to dampen political unrest and push forward an expanding imperialist project.

The first real 'crisis' faced by the newly established Canadian Confederation is historically understood to be the Red River Rebellion in Red River Colony (near modern-day Winnipeg, Manitoba on Treaty 1 territory). Indigenous occupants of the region were concerned about their entitlement to land rights after the territory had been 'sold' by the Hudson's Bay Company to the Canadian government. Local Metis residents (a culturally distinct First Nations population of mixed Indigenous and European ancestry) were concerned that their existing occupied lands would not be recognised by the Canadian government or that they would be dispossessed so the land could be 'sold' to settlers. A Métis leader, Louis Riel, negotiated the establishment of the province of Manitoba and a provisional government to retain political control over the lives of the Métis communities in the Red River Colony. In 1869, Riel's government executed a factionist who resisted the formation of his administration, and federal authorities sent a military expedition to Manitoba to detain Riel. Riel fled to exile in the United States.

Riel returned from exile in 1885 to lead what has been called the North-West Rebellion, a series of violent battles between Indigenous armed protestors and the NWMP in the district of Saskatchewan. The North-West Rebellion involved a resistance coalition comprised of Cree, Assiniboine and Métis nations who were frustrated by the Canadian government's negligence of their rights and lands and the growing food shortages in the territory. Small factions of the coalition began raiding settler communities. The Canadian government dispatched militarised force in response. An estimated 200 Métis and Indigenous warriors were confronted by thousands of state-led militia, including 500 NWMP officers, in a series of exchanges (Beal and Macleod 1984). After the deployment of martial force against the dissenting Indigenous-led coalition, with over 100 casualties on both sides, the state utilised further violence to deter future protests: Louis Riel and eight other Indigenous leaders

were executed in Canada's largest mass hanging at Battleford, Saskatchewan. Retellings of the uprising were not without explicit racialised
language. Historian A. L. Haydon commented in 1910 that 'both half-
breeds and Indians had been taught a severe lesson' (cited in Waiser
2011: 233) and that 'there had been war – red war, with its opportunities for fighting, for revenge, and for many other outlets of energy so
dear to the primitive mind. These instincts are hard to eradicate' (233).
Presumptions about 'Indianness' as primitive and instinctually violent
were reproduced while the politics of the rebellion – including failure to
uphold treaty duties by the government, went ignored.

Top officers in the original NWMP were those with military career
histories, including in the Royal Irish Constabulary, the Canadian Artillery and the Canadian Militia (Shantz 2016). The creation of the NWMP
and its role in the establishment of a peaceful, 'mild West' frontier in
Canada in historical accounts (Katerberg 2003) reified nostalgic imagery of the force as diplomatic or peaceful, with some historians describing the NWMP as a 'uniquely Canadian organization endeavoured
to accomplish what Macdonald had always wanted, the peaceful and
orderly settlement of western Canada' (Horrall 1972: 200). The establishment of the NWMP was described with the objective of a 'force of
soldier-policeman' (Horwall 1972: 199), characterised as a 'civil force
with a military organization but without military law' (199). Yet the
NWMP, designed to control activities in the vast Western lands beyond
Canadian state control, was also involved in vigilantism: Métis upris-
ings and the execution of Louis Riel 'were not marginal exceptions that
proved the rule, but central events in the region's development' (Katerberg 2003: 547).

Following the North-West Rebellion, the primary purpose of the
NWMP was to control and coerce Indigenous communities. Martial
force is central to the execution of various forms of oppressive colonial
violence (physical and epistemic) used to assimilate and exterminate
Indigenous peoples (Fanon 1961: 33). Police were used to uphold new
political orders and spatial relationships dictated by treaty 'agreements'
to share lands and under the new fiduciary relationship between the
state and Indigenous nations under the Indian Act, 1857.[4] Under the
Indian Act, Indigenous governance became subject to political regulations set by the federal government (known as the elected band council
system), rather than long-standing Indigenous governance conventions
(which, for many, involved clan-based, hereditary and consensus-based
systems of governing). Police were used to quell resistance by Indigenous communities who opposed newly established electoral band
council systems. Police enforced the new systems of governance, which

ensured that elected band council Chiefs would be held accountable to the Department of Indian Affairs regulations and budgets, often at the expense of the needs of the community. The RCMP would later continue these responsibilities, most famously in 1924, when they were deployed to ensure the transition of power at Six Nations in Ontario from the Haudenosaunee Confederacy Chiefs Council to the band council system by storming the council house, occupying the premises, and preventing members of the Confederacy from entering (Elliot 2015; Barrera 2020b).

Police were also used to force Indigenous populations onto the newly established reserve system. The reserve system was a political mechanism that dispossessed Indigenous communities of their traditional territories and sustenance practices; a way to 'legally' redistribute Indigenous territories to European migrants encouraged to settle in Canada's western territories. The reserve system utilised martial enforcement to contain Indigenous communities within reserve borders, through the establishment of the oppressive, apartheid-like pass system. Under the pass system, 'Indians' were only permitted to leave their reserve territories if granted a pass by a local government official, the 'Indian agent'. Pass holders had to return by the time the pass expired or face repercussions from the police. The martial enforcement of the pass system not only prohibited Indigenous mobilities on and off reserve territories, but also significantly impacted communities' access to traditional economic activities like trade or hunting. While a temporary measure enforced during the North-West Rebellion, the government of Canada found the system so useful they made it permanent after 1885 until 1951 (Storey 2022: 68). The 'successes' of the martially enforced pass system was said to be employed by South Africa as inspiration for their own apartheid system (Bourgeault 1988; Cambie 2007; Horwitz 2016).

The utilisation of the North-West Mounted Police as a martial tool for colonial politics is further evidenced through the overseas deployment of its members. Many officers were deployed for service in the Boer War in South Africa (1899–1902) under the British Army, an 'imperialist adventure involving British efforts to conquer southern Africa' (Shantz 2016: 14). Following the war in South Africa, the newly renamed Royal North West Mounted Police (RNWMP) was also deployed with the Canadian Siberian Expeditionary force to Siberia following the Russian Revolution (1918–19). After violent confrontations between the RNWMP and dissenting workers in the Winnipeg General Strike of 1919, the force was restructured to its modern iteration, the Royal Canadian Mounted Police (RCMP), in 1920.

The use of police force to coerce Indigenous populations to acquiesce to colonial structures and systems was a necessary tool in Canada's nation-building project. The removal of hundreds of thousands of Indigenous children from their communities and enforcement of attendance in mandatory boarding schools of the Indian Residential School System (IRSS) between 1886 and 1996 would not have been possible without martial threat from colonial and post-Confederation police forces. Yet, martial politics has extended beyond exploitative state policies and includes localised abuses of martial power. Contemporary examples (1976 to the present) include the practice of 'starlight tours' where police drive Indigenous individuals to the outskirts of a city and make them walk home in sub-zero temperatures, risking hypothermia and resulting in death (Campbell 2016). In addition, the disturbing number of Indigenous women and girls who have been reported as missing persons or murdered in Canada, well documented along the Highway of Tears (Highway 16) in British Columbia, has been attributed to police inaction on solving these crimes, as well as testimonies of Indigenous women and girls asserting that their violent encounters, including rape, were from police officers themselves (see Morin 2021).

Militarised and sexualised violence towards Indigenous women and girls is a national phenomenon. Most recently in 2015, a Radio Canada documentary inadvertently revealed a scandal in Quebec of the sexualised politics of contemporary martial and colonial violence. Local Indigenous women in the community of Val d'Or shared testimonies of frequent abuse and assault by police officers who would drive them out of town and sexually assault them. Many women expressed powerlessness at the hand of armed officials who would arrest them, abuse them, and then abandon them on isolated roads far from their homes (Ducas 2020). Despite the launch of an abuse hotline that logged over forty-five cases, and a subsequent formal investigation, there have been no charges laid against any of the officers. Instead, there has developed a culture of aggressive racist backlash against the women who came forward (Curtis 2020).

While these instances could be written off as a 'bad apples paradox' (Mackenzie et al. 2020) or the unfortunate actions of 'only select' unsavoury individuals (rather than the attitudes and protected privileges of those working in militarised security forces in general), I suggest this demonstrates how the peaceful, helpful, innocent or altruistic motivations of martial peacekeepers can clearly be contested (as in these examples), but yet the peacekeeping myth itself and the legitimacy it casts upon state-led martial force nevertheless remains intact and unscarred. The peacekeeping myth is intertwined and reinforcing of white supremacy in Canada, systems which require ongoing martial force to sustain them.

The peacekeeping myth and its associated legitimation of militarist force and powers cannot simply be dismantled through myth-busting. After all, the exploitation of Indigenous peoples has been widely mediated in Canada and even studied in national inquisitions such as the 1996 Royal Commission on Aboriginal Peoples (RCAP) or the 2015 Truth and Reconciliation Commission's final report. Exposing or revealing the falsity of the peacekeeping myth has not been enough to dismantle it or to call to question ongoing narratives that justify egregious violence by militarised institutions as legitimate ways to create or keep peace. I suggest this is because the peacekeeping myth and the vision of martial peace it espouses can only truly be dismantled when those who benefit from its logic begin to take responsibility for our complicity and privileges that the myth upholds. This will be expanded upon in the concluding chapter.

While this book has so far focused on the CAF as the militarised institution by which peacekeeping has legitimised violence, police institutions and the CAF are historically and institutionally entangled, specifically in processes to 'keep peace and order'. The RCMP 'has been and remains military in structure and purpose on an ongoing basis' (Shantz 2016: 2), central to the execution of colonial violence in Canada, and founded to 'ensure the negation of Indigenous sovereignty and to implement effective policies of containment and surveillance' (Nettelbeck and Smandych 2010: 356). In the following section, I therefore explore how the peacekeeper myth has been reproduced in discourse about the RCMP as a martial force and the ways this symbolism legitimises militarised violence by police. Like the Canadian Armed Forces, there is relatively stable public nostalgia about the institution as a beacon of Canadian values. For example, in a 2008 Ipsos Reid survey on the 'symbols that define Canada', the RCMP/'Mounties' were chosen as the fifth most iconic symbol of Canadian-ness, behind the 'maple leaf', 'hockey', 'the flag' and a 'beaver'. Canada's peacekeeper myth, and the fluidity and adaptability of this myth, extends to understandings of other forms of militarised and martial force, including by the RCMP in its engagements with Indigenous resistance movements in Canada.

Martial Peacekeeping and Indigenous Land Protests (1990–Present)

In 1990, Canada was the world's largest contributor of troops to UN peacekeeping missions globally. Following the award of the 1988 Nobel Peace

Prize to 'UN Peacekeepers', Canadian media and politicians celebrated the peacekeeper identity with frequent references to Lester Pearson's foundational role in the creation of peacekeeping, and, by extension of participation in many missions, Canadian peacekeepers' stake in the 1988 prize (Toronto Star 1988a). Canadian peacekeepers were commended for their restraint and willingness to 'take abuse and not los[e] patience' in missions (Korning 1988), exemplifying the paternal and non-violent nature of peacekeepers. Defence Minister Perrin Beatty told the House of Commons that Canada's contributions to UN peacekeeping 'ha[d] finally received their just recognition' (Toronto Star 1988b), while Prime Minister Brian Mulroney spoke to the United Nations in New York expressing pride in the CAF, 'who have made such a contribution to the cause of peace' (Toronto Star 1988b).

Yet within its domestic borders, this 'peak' period of Canadian peacekeeping saw the state utilise martial force to suppress several Indigenous land protests, most famously the 1990 Oka Crisis. From July to September 1990, there was a 78-day stand-off between Kanehsatà:ke (Mohawk) protestors, Quebec police, the Royal Canadian Mounted Police and the Canadian Army. The protest took place north of Montreal, sparked by the proposed expansion of a golf course and the development of condominiums on disputed Indigenous territory, specifically over the clear-cutting of Kanehsatà:ke ancestral burial grounds. Despite decades of attempting to reconcile land claims and confirm Aboriginal legal title to the disputed areas, the Kanehsatà:ke band council's extensive legal actions had been rejected by the federal government. The original golf course had been built in 1961 without consultation with Indigenous groups and infringed upon the community's ancestral territory (for full history, see Alfred 1995). To resist the proposed expansions, the Kanehsatà:ke constructed a barricade around the contested ancestral areas, known as the Pines. The coalition was supported by two neighbouring Indigenous nations, the Kahnawá:ke and Akwesasne, and by inter-national Indigenous supporters from across Canada and the United States. The federal government issued injunctions for the protestors to remove the roadblock, which activists ignored.

On 11 July 1990, the Sûreté du Québec (SQ) provincial police force used tear gas and concussion grenades on the barricaded protest area. A brief firefight followed, resulting in the death of an SQ member. Following a stand-down by the SQ, Indigenous supporters from other local areas joined the movement and blockaded Montreal's Mercier Bridge, cutting off access to central Montreal from surrounding suburbs. By August, the Canadian Armed Forces and RCMP were brought in under Operation Salon. The Canadian Army employed over 4,000 soldiers in armoured military vehicles with artillery to surround Mohawk protestors (Warrior Publications 2014), with reconnaissance aircraft providing feedback and armed naval elements on the nearby St Laurence River. Negotiations were tense and, on 18 September, another physical exchange occurred between soldiers and Mohawk protestors including tear gas and shots fired. The exchange ended with seventy-five injured Mohawk activists and twenty-two injured soldiers. Fourteen-year-old Waneek Horn-Miller was stabbed in the chest by a soldier's bayonet while carrying her four-year-old sister, an incident which was featured on national news cycles (CBC Unreserved 2016).

While both protestors and military personnel had access to heavily armed resources, the Oka Crisis has become well known for the moments of intense stand-off between the two sides, exemplified by an iconic photo of Indigenous protestor Brad Larocque, dressed in green camouflage fatigues, bucket hat and camouflage bandana, exchanging an intense stare with Canadian soldier Patrick Cloutier, also dressed in fatigues and helmet, their faces inches from one another. The photo – which was captured by Shaney Komulainen of *The Canadian Press* – was an iconic representation of the stand-off, with Komulainen herself later reflecting her admiration for Cloutier for showing restraint, 'hold[ing] his ground and not going crazy' (Baluja 2013). The subtext of this comment commended the officer for his rationality, benevolence and non-violence in the face of irrational, threatening and self-serving behaviour of the Indigenous protesters.

Following the crisis, political and media discourse contained contradictory themes, whereby there was some sympathy for the land disputes of the Kahnawá:ke, but there was widespread condemnation of the protest activities, including representation of the protests as a 'threat against public order' (Cahill 1990). Following the protests, the narratives about law and order continued, exemplified by a local disagreement about whether a fourteen-member Indigenous security force, ironically called the Mohawk Peacekeepers, was permitted to provide local security in place of the by now highly distrusted SQ. While the band council wished to use the Mohawk Peacekeepers, media called upon the 'legitimate police forces who must uphold the law and maintain peace and order' (Poirier 1990).

In this case, it appears that the utilisation of a popular concept – peacekeeper – was not easily mobilised to legitimise racialised, non-state militarised forces. Peacekeeping was distinctly relegated to state-sanctioned forces and bound within the subject position of whiteness. The association of peacekeeping with a white subject position in the beloved peacekeeping myth was not made explicitly, but has been underpinned by representations of the 'illegitimacy' of Indigenous grassroots police forces. Quebec's Public Security Minister, Claude Ryan, told the council that 'until a professional, competent native police force' was formed, the RCMP would continue to patrol the area (Toronto Star 1990). Prime Minister Mulroney, in the House of Commons, called for 'law and order' to be upheld in the face of Mohawk Warriors' use of weapons that were 'fundamentally hostile to Canadians' (Canadian Press 1990). Quebec minister André Bourbeau told Oka residents that 'Quebec is serious about re-establishing law and order everywhere, including native territories' (York and Picard 1990). Bourbeau's comments cast Indigenous reserves as places of anarchic threat. The casting of Indigenous dissidents and Indigenous communities as disorderly and a threat to peace weaved throughout discourse on the Oka crisis. Indigenous communities across Canada became represented as 'unreasonable, bent on hostility, and a threat to established order' (Grenier 1994: 328)

The following year, the 1991 *Citizen's Forum on Canada's Future* noted that

> activities as inciting to or participating in riot, rebellion, armed and unarmed blockades and other resorts to violence . . . have no rightful place in Canada. In my opinion, if the law and order and democratic processes which used to be so characteristic of Canada are to be restored and strengthened, all resort to anarchy and violence must be outlawed. (Canada, Privy Council Office 1991: 44)

This exemplifies the nostalgia for an imagined past peace, characterised by 'law and order and democratic processes', that existed only for white settlers. Law, order and justice were absent in the Indigenous political experience; the Indian Act and subsequent land right legislations had long been used to restrict and constrain, rather than empower Indigenous nations. For example, legally recognised Indians who wished to retain their 'entitlements' under the Indian Act were not permitted to organise politically, seek legal counsel or hire lawyers prior to 1951; they were also not permitted to vote at the federal level prior to 1960. The discourse about law, order and the fear of 'anarchy' contains a clear ignorance of all the ways that life for Indigenous peoples in Canada was not peaceful; it was martially repressed. Yet the mobilisation of discourse of law-upholding martial violence against illegitimate martial resistance stands to disguise the violence of Canada's law and 'order' throughout centuries proceeding this exchange. Popular discourse about Oka illuminates a key element of the kind of peace associated with the peacekeeping myth and Canadian 'values' – an emphasis on order rather than justice. As indicated by the Citizen's Forum, public opinion was wary about the use of protest to draw attention to long-standing Indigenous land claims.

It was assumed that *order* – martial peace – should be prioritised as a Canadian value.

The use of militarised state police force against Indigenous protest continued following Oka. In the 1995 Ipperwash Crisis, Anishinaabeg occupiers reclaimed traditional lands that had been appropriated from their community during the Second World War. The crisis occurred when martial force was used to disperse collective gathering of Indigenous occupiers on their reclaimed lands, gatherings that were viewed as threatening to neighbouring white communities. A long history informed the events that transpired.

In 1937, the Chief and Council of the Kettle and Stony Point First Nation had requested that the provincial government preserve an ancient burial ground at Ipperwash Beach and asked that the area be fenced in order to avoid future destruction of the site. Yet these efforts were derailed in 1942, when the Canadian government used the War Measures Act to force Kettle and Stony Point First Nation families off their land, later named Ipperwash Provincial Park. From 1942 onward, Ipperwash was used as a military base and training ground for military cadets and the land was controlled by the Department of National Defence (DND). The Stony Point Nation was told at the time of forced displacement in 1942 that the land would be returned after the war. By 1992, the land was still occupied by the DND. The Kettle and Stony Point First Nation filed an eviction notice but, by 1993, frustrated at the lack of legal progress, members of the Stony Point First Nation began to occupy portions of the land, and military employees slowly evacuated the area. Over two years, occupiers successfully seized the administrative buildings on the property and used the area for communal gatherings.

In September 1995, local police acquired incorrect 'intelligence' that a gathering of Indigenous occupiers in Ipperwash Park were acting aggressively towards passing traffic and potentially had rifles and AK 47s (Linden 2007: 447). Following concerns that the occupiers may cause damage to local cottages that would in turn diminish police credibility among (non-Indigenous) cottage owners whose 'confidence level was on edge' due to the recent occupation (Ipperwash Report 2007: 441), riot squads swarmed the park perimeter. The official report detailed that:

> The OPP dressed in riot gear. They stood shoulder-to-shoulder in rows and stretched across the road. This was a very intimidating sight for the Aboriginal occupiers. The police officers were equipped with bulletproof vests, shields, batons, helmets and guns. The Aboriginal people had no protective clothing and had simply stockpiled sticks and stones on the inside border of the park fence. The Aboriginal people had no body

armour or head protection. They also felt greatly outnumbered. As the police officers marched towards Ipperwash Park, the First Nations people were highly anxious and terrified. (Ipperwash Report 2007: 454–5)

When the riot forces approached the group of Indigenous occupiers, the occupiers shouted that those police were 'trespassing on our grandfathers' graves' (461), that the police were entering 'sacred ground' (460); they attempted to signal their unwillingness to leave the occupied lands. What police had failed to communicate to the protesters prior to their militarised descent was that the mandate of the injunction was to seize guns – the falsely assumed rifles or AK-47s speculated to be in possession of occupiers – not to remove the group from their occupied park (440). This communication shortcoming was highlighted as one of the biggest police failures of the September conflict.

The official inquiry report also noted that the Ontario Provincial Police (OPP) had not bothered to involve the local Anishinaabeg police force or First Nations mediators in attempts to resolve the occupation tensions (459–60). Rather, the deployment of three riot squads based on erroneous speculation about a potential firearms risk related to a gathering of Indigenous occupants around a bonfire at the edge of Ipperwash Park resulted in a violent confrontation. Ontario Provincial Police forces beat occupiers, shot at unarmed protestors wielding rocks and sticks, and killed an Indigenous occupier named Dudley George.

There are numerous references to the use of culturally insensitive language and assumptions by involved OPP officers, including the description of protestors yelling at police which 'sounded like war cries' (Ipperwash Report 2007: 458). Cultural and racist stereotypes by police also included the belief, by medics treating a protestor who had suffered head trauma following a 'punchout' (463) by eight officers, that the man was 'intoxicated' (468) rather than in shock, representative of long-standing racist stereotypes of Indigenous peoples in Canada as 'drunkard lawless brawlers' (Francis 1992: 81). Yet this was not simply an over-step of trigger-happy, individually racist police officers with inaccurate intel. Former Ontario premier Mike Harris was documented as remarking, 'I want the fucking Indians out of the park', just hours before George's death (Ipperwash Report 2007: 23). There was little political sympathy for the Anishinaabeg occupation and plenty of racialised fears about what the occupation meant for local peace and security.

Nonetheless, George's death drew national attention. The official inquiry report that was released in 2007 emphasised the need for better and more transparent procedural processes in the employment of police force, and improved training of officers in the requirements of 'peacekeeping' and the 'uniqueness' of Indigenous occupations and protests (Linden 2007). Once again, the use of police force was understood to be 'peacekeeping', and the subject of those activities was the surveillance and control of Indigenous populations coupled with the reproduction of racialised stereotypes about the 'threatening' nature of large groups of non-white men.

In the same year, across the country in British Columbia, the Gustafsen Lake stand-off between the RCMP, CAF and Indigenous-led protesters was unfolding. This 1995 'stand-off' involved heavy gunfire exchange and was the largest and most expensive RCMP operation to date in Canadian history (Lambertus 2016), estimated to cost CAD$5.5 million (Dembicki and Mackin 2009). The events took place near 100 Mile House, a small community surrounded by reserve lands, located halfway between Vancouver and Prince George, and halfway between Vancouver and Jasper National Park.

Gustafsen Lake is located between two reserves, Dog Creek and Canim Lake, and was incorporated under James Cattle Ranch. Despite James Cattle Ranch's occupation of Gustafsen Lake, as with much territory in British Columbia, the land is untreatied, meaning Indigenous nations have never agreed to cede the land. Complicated legal disputes between British Columbian First Nations and the federal government have played out for decades over land entitlements (Lambertus 2016). Residents of the two reserves had historically used Gustafsen Lake as a site to hold an annual Sundance ceremony.[5]

Disputes over the land and the Sundance gatherings began in the early 1990s when there were increasing complaints from local campers at a nearby campground about threatening militant behaviour and gunshot fire observed in the Sundance area (Lambertus 2016: 29). In response, Sundance participants said that tourists were not respecting their need for privacy during the ten-day rituals and that there were no weapons or injuries associated with the exchanges (34).

The James family and local Indigenous groups had a formal agreement to allow the Sundance ceremony on the land tract, without the erection of permanent structures, set to expire in 1993. In 1994, another Sundance was held. Indigenous participants were concerned that hundreds of cattle kept coming onto the sacred grounds and defecating where the ceremony was to take place. In July 1995, the year of the stand-off, the ceremony hosts erected a fence to keep the cattle out during their rituals. The erection of the fence, and the discovery by the James family that Indigenous leaders of the ceremony were living in a cabin at the lake, spurred tensions that the Sundancers were trying to establish a 'territorial imperative' (Lambertus 2016: 32). Indigenous participants openly questioned the James family land rights since the territory was not subject to a pre-existing treaty and they doubted the existence of a legitimate land deed.

In June 1995, the James family submitted a formal eviction notice to the local RCMP. The James family was told the dispute was a civil matter, to be settled in courts. Frustrated, Lyle James and several ranch employees carrying guns and a bullwhip confronted Sundance organisers, with one ranch hand allegedly stating 'this is a good day to burn down a goddamned cook house and to string up some red n*****s' (Lambertus 2016: 32). Despite this exchange, and the looming threat of racialised violence against Sundance participants, the 1995 Sundance ceremony continued. Following the rituals, a group of people remained on the land. The Indigenous occupiers reiterated that they had never wilfully ceded the lands to the crown, quoting the British Proclamation of 1763 which legally acknowledged unceded lands were to 'be left unmolested and undisturbed' (Lambertus 2016: 37). The occupation had begun.

Following the initial confrontation with Lyle James and his group of employees, the Indigenous occupants surrounded the camp with hundreds of logs as a barrier wall. Occupants of the Sundance site called themselves Ts'peten Defenders and released media briefs declaring they were trying to defend their rights to occupy traditional and sacred lands of unceded Secwépemc (Shuswap) territory. Mediation attempts were made to broker a deal between the James ranch and Indigenous camp occupants but they were ultimately unsuccessful. In August, when two of the Ts'peten camp residents were caught fishing salmon upstream (deemed illegal as it was outside sanctioned fishing season), police arrested the individuals for possession of rifles and small guns, escalating the matter as a security concern for the RCMP.

Following the initial RCMP seizure of weapons, the situation was considered criminal and more than 400 RCMP officers and many media outlets flooded the area. The RCMP Emergency Response Team (ERT) was deployed covertly to the encampment's perimeter. On 18 August 1995, fearing the camouflage-covered, automatic rifle-bearing men crawling outside the perimeter were 'the rednecks coming back [to] kill us' (Dembicki and Mackin 2009: n.p.), a Ts'peten occupant shot at the ERT. The ERT retreated, but this triggered the deployment of military helicopters circling the encampment and nine armoured personnel carriers (APCs) patrolling the perimeter. Head inspector of a local RCMP subdivision explained to the media, 'there has been an escalation; the threat is serious. We see this as an act of terrorism' (Dembicki and Mackin 2009: n.p.). A spokesperson for the Defenders, 'Wolverine' Jones Ignace, told the RCMP that if they moved into the camp, it would be 'clearly war . . . we're not going to go peaceful . . . nobody is going to tell you to put your weapons down' (Smith 2016). Tensions were high.

On 10 September, the RCMP, aided by the CAF under Operation Wallaby, set up a base camp called Camp Zulu, which included a field hospital, communications centre, APCs and helicopters on loan from the CAF, and tactical units with heavily armed kits. Operation Wallaby's team deployed explosive devices buried in an access road to the contested site camp. The RCMP waited to deploy the explosives until a red pickup carrying a truck bed full of water bottles approached the camp border. Following the explosion, an APC rammed the disabled pickup (Dembicki and Mackin 2009) and gunfire exchange continued between ERT and the Defenders in the heavily wooded and grassy perimeter. There were hours of intense gunfire exchange, and on 17 September, the Defenders' camp surrendered. The stand-off was estimated to have exchanged 77,000 rounds of ammunition (Smith 2016).

Following the stand-off, eighteen individuals were arrested for various offences and there was a media flurry surrounding the trial. Local Indigenous communities and the National Assembly of First Nations demanded an inquiry on the RCMP's excessive use of force at the stand-off, but no inquiry has yet been initiated (Lambertus 2016: 199). Sandra Lambertus's comprehensive media analysis of the events at Gustafsen Lake argues that the media were heavily biased towards police actions; an interview with the editor of the *Vancouver Sun* suggests that journalists themselves understood the stand-off as war-like:

> Basically, the more this thing dragged on, the more we really felt-it was-almost like the B.C. version of the Kuwait war . . . the RCMP . . . control[ed] where the media could go, exactly the information they were going to get on a daily basis, making sure they didn't have access to the opposing forces. (Lambertus 2016: 192)

In her analysis of the trial, Lambertus notes that police represented the stand-off as a life-and-death matter, thereby justifying 'several departures from standard police procedures [as] necessary' (2016: 196).

This messaging was replicated in media coverage that again positioned the Indigenous protest as illegitimate, threatening to local order, and excessively militant. Lambertus explains that media coverage of the Oka, Ipperwash and Gustafsen Lake protests evoked wartime characterisations and clear 'us against them narratives' to describe the political nature of the conflict (2016: 200), reinforcing public understandings of Indigenous peoples as threatening and depoliticising the circumstances that led to the mediated conflicts. The reproduction of police as benevolent and helpful peacekeepers was present in media coverage, particularly when Indigenous occupation and protest was cast as disorderly, violent, petulant and self-serving.

While these three case studies did involve asymmetrical reciprocal Indigenous use of martial force, it is the representation of this force as illegitimate and threating to order, and the representation of RCMP or CAF force as legitimate and order-enforcing that perpetuates racialised stereotypes and political bias against long-standing Indigenous claims for justice. These representations are contiguous with the long-standing mythology that police force against Indigenous resistance in the 'founding' of Canada and the implementation of the modern treaty system was peaceful, orderly and done in the name of good government. Oka, Ipperwash and Gustafsen Lake included mediated accounts depicting police actions as helpful, altruistic or paternal. Many representations of these conflicts lacked a historical understanding of the nature of the protest or blockade and fail to account for the levels of disempowerment and frustration experienced by Indigenous nations who were failed by 'official' mechanisms like Canada's land claim processes or other legal avenues.

A long-standing dispute in the Grand River region of Ontario, commonly called the Caledonia land dispute, is an example of how Indigenous blockades and protests have been represented dominantly as disorderly or threatening to (local) peace. In this region, the Haldimand Tract, a piece of territories granted to Indigenous allies of the British government in the eighteenth century, is the land in question. In 1841, the government convinced the Six Nations of the Grand River to lease their lands beyond the allocated reserve territory as a means to prevent illegal squatters. The Six Nations claim this permission involved unfair coercion and, despite several petitions to challenge the decision, the land claims went unacknowledged. Throughout the 1970s, 1980s and 1990s there were twenty-nine land claims submitted by the Six Nations, including a single settlement by Indigenous people, and Northern Affairs Canada's unauthorised use of reserve land for a tract of railway. The Six Nations of the Grand River therefore have a long-standing dispute with subsequent Canadian governments who have improperly sold, leased or given away their original Haldimand Tract lands, and who owe the Six Nations capital from historical and ongoing land leases.

In 1992, a development company called Henco Industries Ltd. purchased 40 hectares of land with the intention of building a development called the Douglas Creek Estates. This land was part of territories under land claim by the Six Nations, and, in 1995, the Six Nations sued the government and province over the developers' purchase of the land. Henco held that they held legitimate rights, ensured by their purchase from the federal government; the Six Nations held that they never ceded the title to these lands. In 2006, members of the Six Nations occupied the development site. Media coverage of this event represented the Ontario Provincial Police not as altruistic heroes, or benevolent helpers, but as inept and passive.

Local residents were represented as subjects that were 'innocent' and 'non-violent' and failed by police who did not adequately control the 'reign of terror' (Blatchford 2009). Exemplified by journalist Christie Blatchford's national bestseller *Helpless: Caledonia's Nightmare of Fear and Anarchy and How the Law Failed All of Us* (2011), the occupation was expressly represented as illegal, criminal and threatening to residents. Blatchford claims that the book was not about Aboriginal land claims, but about the 'failure of government to govern and protect its citizens equally' (2011: xiv), as if they could be heuristically separated for narrative simplicity. While a martial police force was not employed to suppress the Caledonia protests, this dispute contained mediated representations about the use of Indigenous protest as illegitimate and threatening to peace and order.

The use of militarised personnel and technology against Indigenous land claims protests would continue into the new millennium. Indigenous–settler relations across Canada have also been fraught with tensions, and, in Eastern Canada, this is true particularly following the 1999 Supreme Court of Canada ruling (*R. v. Marshall*) that granted Indigenous rights to fish out of season. In New Brunswick, non-Indigenous fisheries expressed concern that this new ruling would permit Indigenous fishers to deplete lobster stocks that the broader economic community relied upon. The Department of Fisheries and Oceans signed moratoriums with several Esgenoôpetitj First Nations bands that agreed to restrict trapping outside regular seasons, but two First Nations, the Burnt Church and Indian Brook, rejected this. Non-Indigenous groups reacted by destroying Mi'kmaq lobster traps. A series of shouting matches between Indigenous and non-Indigenous boats followed. Tensions escalated to a confrontation in Yarmouth, NB where 600 non-Indigenous fishermen with rifles and shotguns blocked the harbour to prevent Indigenous fishers gaining access. In response, there was an establishment of an armed encampment in Burnt Church, NB to permit Indigenous fishers access to the water.

The Department of Fisheries and Oceans (DFO) responded by appealing to the Supreme Court who clarified the decision by initiating limits on the number of traps that the Mi'kmaq fishers could use. The band councils defied lobster trap restrictions and the DFO engaged in 'trap raiding' to empty the now 'illegal' Mi'kmaq traps. When Mi'kmaq warriors took to patrolling their dropped lines in fishing boats, there was a series of confrontations between the Mi'kmaq fishers, non-Indigenous fishers, and the DFO and RCMP. National news headlines amplified the militant and threatening nature of Mi'kmaq fishers in headlines such as 'N.S. natives get combat training for lobster wars' (Lambie 2000), articles detailing federal fishery officers being shot at by the Mi'kmaq reserve (Hamilton 2000), and reporting that the RCMP had issued a secret report that classified 'aboriginal criminal extremism' and 'aboriginal militancy' as threatening (Bell 2000) to local communities. These mediated representations of Indigenous protests as threatening to local economies and security further reified the actions of Indigenous communities as selfish, disorderly and violent.

The RCMP's role in this conflict was to support the DFO. Representations of the Mi'kmaq by state officials were continuous with the notion of the irrational, selfish and threatening Indigenous community that refused to be peaceful by creating disorder. The idea of peace as the absence of sustained political resistance was central to 'official' narratives about the Burnt Church conflict. DFO Minister Herb Dhaliwal was quoted as saying:

> Confrontation on the water is not the way to resolve this situation. I will not tolerate any action by any users of the resource which would jeopardize a peaceful and prosperous fishery. I'm calling on all Canadians for calm, for restraint, and for a real commitment to peace. (Hamilton and Hunter 2000)

Mi'kmaq attempts to fish for sustenance, which they believed was their legal entitlement under the Marshall Decision, was deemed 'not peaceful'. Months later, as tensions continued, Minister Dhaliwal, through the media, 'spoke' to the Burnt Church band council and said, 'you cannot say you accept the rule of law [the Marshall decision] when it's in your favour and not accept the rule of law when it's not [Dhaliwal's ministerial seizure of unsanctioned traps]' (CBC News 2000), further positioning Indigenous protest as illegal, unlawful and unjustified. The tensions at Burnt Church would continue to simmer over the next decades, laying the background for future martial politics between the RCMP and Mi'kmaq communities on Canada's East coast.

In 2013, heavily armed RCMP officers in full camouflage surrounded and arrested Mi'kmaq anti-fracking protesters of the Mi'kmaq Warrior Society. The Indigenous protesters had barricaded construction equipment of a shale gas company in New Brunswick. The Chief of Elsipotog

First Nation expressed deep concern about the risks of water contamination in the expansion of the shale gas project. A reporter documented the heavily armed officers shouting 'Crown land belongs to the government, not to fucking natives' (Blackburn 2013) while firing rubber bullets in the wooded area around the barricade. However, dominant media news coverage of the Elsipotog blockade featured an image of a burning police car, summoning the image of law-breaking, disorder-causing Indigenous protests. The media representation inadequately covered the months-long peaceful protest that had preceded the RCMP raid. The response to the peaceful blockage was heavily militarised: it involved an early dawn raid of police snipers crawling through the forest with assault rifles, dogs, tear gas and rubber bullets (Lukacs 2013). Premier David Alward, when commenting on the protesters, claimed, 'clearly there are those who do not have the same values we share as New Brunswickers' and asserted 'in no way can we as a country of laws condone the breaking of laws and violence' (Luckacs 2013). Canada at this time had objected to the United Nations Universal Declaration of the Rights of Indigenous Peoples (UNDRIP), and narratives of militarised police violence against peaceful protest in Canada were still centred upon the legitimacy of these martial deployments because they were done in the name of *order*.

Following the exchange, the commissioner of the Civilian Review and Complaints Commission (CRSS) launched an investigation into the RCMP's handling of the demonstrations. The commission was launched after twenty-one complaints alleging improper arrest and excessive use of force were filed, and complainants also noted the racially charged statements used by officers during the raids. Despite complaints, media described the RCMP's involvement as 'efforts that [had not been successful . . . [following] the RCMP [efforts to] work diligently with all parties involved in hopes for a peaceful resolution' (Pattern 2013). The Commissioner expressed regret that the inquiry was stalled after the RCMP took three years to transfer records to the watchdog in a 'disorganized fashion that was unsearchable' (Barrera 2020a).

The use of military and police force to subdue Indigenous land protesters in Canada is an ongoing phenomenon, exemplified by police raids on the Wet'suwet'en Unis'ot'en camp in North-Central British Columbia. Like the other historical cases detailed so far, the Gitksan Wet'suwet'en have failed to have their lands recognised through formal processes, despite living on untreatied British Columbia territory. In their 1991 land claim that was dismissed in the Courts, the ruling judge infamously made explicitly ethnocentric claims about pre-colonial conditions, calling the lives of Indigenous peoples 'nasty, brutish, and short' where 'they had no written language, no horses or wheeled vehicles, slavery and starvation was not uncommon, wars with neighbouring peoples were common' (Gordon 2005). This narrative, expressed in official capacity by a ruling land claims judge, exemplifies the ways in which Indigenous people and their protests have been delegitimised due to long-standing statements about the 'benefits' of colonisation and treaty-making. These bigoted assumptions fail to recognise the devastating exploitation Indigenous communities and cultures have endured in colonial history. Imperialistic logics pervade Canadian understanding of Indigenous resistance, whereby Indigenous groups have been understood as having inferior cultural and moral capacities that have been used to justify violence as 'simply the extension of the West's enlightened reason upon the "savage" Indian occupied frontiers of the New World' (Williams Jr. 1997, cited in Regan 2011: 81). Despite this ruling and its paternalist undertones, the Wet'suwet'en heredity chiefs have held firm that they never signed a title, and therefore hold claim to the land based on their pre-Confederation occupation (Ducklow 2019).

In 2010, the Unis'ot'en clan, one of five in the Wet'suwet'en nation, erected a blockade to their traditional lands in northern British Columbia. The hereditary chiefs of the Wet'suwet'en First Nation set up a camp on lands where several planned energy pipelines were meant to cross. The camp includes a checkpoint, enforced by camp members who live, year round, on the territory. Coastal GasLink, one of the pipeline developers, applied for an injunction in November 2018 when their workers were prevented from entering the checkpoint area to clear the pipeline route. The RCMP were mobilised to enforce the injunction to remove the bridge blockage to the contested area. In 2019, there was approval of 'lethal overwatch' (deployment of officers permitted to use lethal force) against Wet'suwet'en protesters and a major operation in January was estimated to cost the RCMP CAD$1,464,691 over a three-month period (Madsen 2020: 120). By 2020, there had been widespread arrest of protestors by RCMP officers dressed in military-green fatigues, armed with assault rifles (Dhillon and Parrish 2019). The RCMP raid of the Wet'suwet'en First Nation in February 2020 involved police helicopters equipped with sensors and cameras, and dog service teams; it worked for a week to dismantle winter encampments along a 60 km logging road and enforced an exclusion zone, prohibiting Indigenous people access to use of their own land (Madsen 2020: 114). In response, in 2020, many solidarity protests across Canada were staged, including rail and port blockades. The Tyendinaga Mohawk successfully halted traffic between Toronto and Montreal but was eventually removed by the Ontario Provincial Police.

While media have represented Wet'suwet'en politics with greater sensitivity than past land protests, many headlines depicting the nationwide rail blockades represent these as 'Indigenous anti-pipeline activists' (Cecco 2020) or a failure of the federal government to ensure its 'duty to consult on resource development projects' (Heidenreich 2020). Popular support for the Wet'suwet'en protests, therefore, is not necessarily based upon recognising Indigenous sovereignty over unceded lands, but because there is modest but growing intolerance for climate-threatening oil and gas industries in Canada (Uguen-Csenge 2019). The representation of Wet'suwet'en as an anti-pipeline protest (rather than an Indigenous nation embracing its long-standing political sovereignty over territory), reinforced through Greenpeace's 2018 statement of solidarity with the Wet'suwet'en Camp (Cornwell 2018), may inadvertently represent another stereotypical trope about Indigenous Canadians, one Hames (2007) calls the ecologically 'noble savage'. While Indigenous communities have long expressed concerns about ecological damage and the need to care for land rather than exploit it through extraction, these concerns have gone unattended by media and mainstream activist attention for decades. Ongoing protests, for example, at the British Columbia Fairy Creek site in addition to Wet'suwet'ens' ongoing road blockages against Coastal GasLink expansions, seek to represent acts of environmental civil disobedience as exemplary of Indigenous and settler solidarity against pipeline development, yet there is risk that Indigenous communities' priorities and desire for political sovereignty, or even 'land back' (Tuck and Yang 2012) visions of decolonisation, get set aside while anti-pipeline politics take precedent over decolonisation.

It is important to recognise that the militarisation and martial force used against Indigenous land protests is troublesome, not only because these communities are taking welcome action to resist extractivist and ecologically damaging activities in an era of climate catastrophe, but primarily because there has been widespread failure to uphold these nations' sovereignty, both the spirits of treaty-making (in many treatied areas across Canada), and, in the case of British Columbian nations, recognition of the unceded lands upon which these nations are entitled to control as they see fit. The violation of this sovereignty has been condemned by international organisations, with scant attention paid to these abuses in Canadian news cycles.

In November 2021, after heavily armed RCMP officers, including snipers with high-calibre rifles, used an axe and chainsaw to force their way into the home of Wet'suwet'en land defences, the United Nations Committee for the Elimination of Racial Discrimination expressed concerns over these human rights violations (Cunningham 2022; Palmater 2022).

In addition to martial force used against land defenders at Wet'suwet'en, there has also been force used on the Site C dam site in Peace River, British Columbia, and against the Tiny House Warriors, a group of Secwépemc land defenders protesting against Trans Mountain pipeline extension on their territories. Indigenous peoples from these nations have reported constant monitoring, recording, harassment and intimidation by pipeline security forces and the RCMP, including drone surveillance, installation of razor wire fencing around encampments, and physical assaults (Palmater 2022). Alarmingly, a lot of this violence has been attributed to actions by the Community-Industry Response Group (C-IRG), a 'secretive arm of the RCMP in BC' (Forester 2022) created in 2017 to 'provide strategic oversight addressing energy industry incidents and related public order, national security and crime issues' (Forrester 2022). The mandate of the C-IRG involves a three-stage mandate, in which during the second stage, a massive show of force involving a Tactical Troop team, a paramilitary SWAT unit called the Emergency Response Team (ERT), with a dog unit, liaison team and other logistical support units, would support the Tactical Troop team with lethal overwatch and 'pain compliance techniques' (Clarke 2022).[6] The background and experience of leading figures in the C-IRG include former veterans of the Afghanistan war, and contains close networks with private security forces that have been used against environmental protesters other pipeline sites, such as at Fairy Creek, BC (Clarke 2022). The mobilisation of these police resources demonstrates not simply that Canada's police institutions are highly militarised (Madsen 2020), but that there are active and strategic state efforts to suppress legitimate Indigenous claims to sovereignty, conducted by martial institutions represented as peace-oriented.

The legitimation of martial force against Indigenous protests stems from, first, wide-scale denial of Indigenous sovereignty, and, second, individual Canadians' intolerance for the inconvenience associated with Indigenous protests which, in several instances, have relied upon shutting down railroads, roads and bridges. The legitimation of martial force against these protests is made in the name of 'economic necessity'. A 2020 Ipsos Reid poll indicated that 61 per cent of Canadians disagreed with protestors shutting down roads and rail corridors and over half of those polled wanted to use the police to end protests (Bricker 2020). These attitudes suggest how militarised or martial force can be legitimised when it is used as a tool to preserve the 'status quo' – to martial peace. Discourses of martial peace are reinforced by the representations of Indigenous protest as disorderly, threatening and self-serving. When state-led martial force is used against Indigenous protestors to maintain 'peace' or 'order, it might better be understood as protecting a particular political order – one in which non-Indigenous Canadians have benefited in extraordinary ways over centuries. Martialling peace through the suppression of Indigenous protest therefore reinforces long-standing colonial exploitation, often through explicitly violent means.

Martialling Peace, the Peace-Keeping Myth and the Endurance of Empire

I am not the only scholar who has theorised the connection between domestic and international martial violence. Sherene Razack observed how Canada's role as peacekeeper in the world replicated the colonial models of military activities used in the 'settlement' of the nation. David Bercuson and Jack Granatstein – both prominent academics who have written on Canadian peacekeeping – declared that the Canadian army's actions in putting an end to Mohawk protests at Oka was a 'classic example of peacekeeping' (Granatstein and Bercuson 1991: 232), of which the irony Razack explains is academic promotion of peacekeeping as an 'imperial fantasy' (2004: 35). Razack explains how the 'self-effacing, cooperative, peace-loving Canadian is the heart of the national mythology' (2004: 36) where Canada is a 'hero of conscience and spirit' (Davies 1980, cited in Razack 2004: 36).

Razack has noted that most of the writing on Canada's peacekeeping history and mythology has largely omitted the colonial contexts of peacekeeping: how peacekeeping discourse serves to reinforce Du Bois's 'colour line'. The peacekeeping myth therefore functions to uphold whiteness as the epistemic position on which peace and order are understood, which in turn have reinforced white supremacy in Canada.

For Razack (2004), peacekeeping is an activity where 'white Northern states secure their identities and positions' (33) through the colour line whereby 'participation in aggressive interventions [reproduces] the argument that the natives will understand little else but force' (39). Frantz Fanon, too, discussed how colonial relations are upheld through martial force: 'The policeman and the soldier, by their immediate presence and their frequent and direct action maintain contact with the native and advise him by means of rifle butts and napalm not to budge. It is obvious here that the agents of government speak the language of pure force' (Fanon 1961: 37).

Despite the crude or excessive use of violence by 'peacekeeping' martial forces, the intent or goal of preserving peace continues to justify these means, particularly when reinforced by 'us versus them' narratives. Indigenous, racialised dissidents are represented as threats to the security or 'peace' of white Canadians, sustained through the peacekeeping myth's reproduction of gendered and racialised logics about security, nationhood and violence. The peacekeeping myth, and the martial peace it purports to keep, is sustained through discourse that has little to do with peace, but a strong continuity with insecurity, an 'ontology of liberal individuals who see themselves as having the capacity to liberate others' (Härting and Kamboureli 2009: 662). Peacekeeping, Razack explains, 'provides a way for both settler colonies and ex-colonial powers to perform themselves as members of an international brotherhood of civilized states' (2004: 45).

The peacekeeping myth casts some actors as civilised with the right to instil 'discipline', and others as uncivilised, rogue and violent. This assessment is particularly relevant to the ways that Indigenous protest in Canada has been cast as disruptive or threatening to profitable resource economies. Militarised violence 'out there' is intimately connected to the structural and colonial violence 'at home', a continuum of violence that feminists have long stressed is integral to understanding militarist conflicts (Cockburn 2004). The peacekeeper myth, as examined through various discourses, heuristically demonstrates the work that racism, colonialism and gender 'do' in sustaining and legitimising militarist ideology and practice through the legitimisation of state martial force. This will be considered in the concluding chapter to follow.

Notes

1. To affirm the sovereignty of Indigenous nations, as was the 'spirit and intent' of treaty land-sharing agreements, relations between the Canadian state and Indigenous nations might better be understood as 'inter-national'. Critical scholars have sought to problematise Westphalian state 'national' divisions, artificially reproduced through international relations scholarship, and seek to politicise the cartographies established through centuries of colonialism. Indigenous polities and their inter-national politics have long been part of political relations in pre-contact North America, despite IR's epistemic exclusion of these long-standing frameworks (Beier 2007, 2009).
2. More information on peace operations is available on the RCMP webpage. Available at https://www.rcmp-grc.gc.ca/en/peace-operations (last accessed 10 October 2022).
3. However, particularly in light of the thousands of graves of IRSS (Indian Residential School Sysem) attendees being unearthed in Canada, it is worth noting that when some of these children sought to run away from the abusive and exploitative constraints of the residential schools, their parents, grandparents and other kin camped outside schools as a means of protest, and actively hid their children from the police-supported round-ups that forcibly removed these children from their communities and placed them into state coercive care. The Truth and Reconciliation Commission (TRC)'s final report (2015), a part of

the Indian Residential School System's (IRSS) class action lawsuit against the Canadian government, details some of the endurance of Indigenous peoples in the face of genocidal and oppressive political and martial force.

4. The term 'Indian' describes a legal classification of Indigenous peoples entitled to treaty rights in Canada. The Indian Act, and its many iterations, has been used to regulate and administer the daily lives and political affairs of registered 'Indians' and their reserve communities. The Indian Act has proved incredibly controversial, as its roots were in the 1857 Gradual Civilization Act that sought to assimilate Indigenous peoples into Eurocentric political and cultural ways. It outlawed cultural and spiritually significant Indigenous practices such as potlatch ceremonies (designed for wealth redistribution and reproducing community lineages through oral recordings). It also eventually sought to more aggressively assimilate 'Indians' into mainstream Canadian culture (and in turn, cease legal and fiscal entitlements to these peoples) through the passing of Bill C-31 that created gender-based exclusions for who could claim Indian Act rights and entitlements: specifically, women who married non-Indigenous men would lose their status, although men who married non-Indigenous women would keep theirs (see Lawrence 2003). Despite the overt assimilationist and gendered colonial politics enabled by the Indian Act, it is one of few legal and historical documents that Indigenous communities have had to ensure their rights and treaty entitlements (see RCAP 1996: 235–308).

5. The Sundance is a spiritually significant Indigenous ceremony, practised primarily by Plains Cree cultures in Canada. The Sundance was one of many culturally prohibited ceremonies under the Indian Act, restricted until 1951. For Gustafsen Lake Indigenous communities, the Sundance ritual had been held since 1989 on the land tract occupied by James Cattle Ranch.

6. The RCMP, as a paramilitary organisation, has increasingly focused on specialised units to manage various events by the Emergency Response Term (ERT), in particular protest policing (Madsen 2020)

Conclusion Myths, Militarism and Martial(ed) Peace

The peacekeeping myth – the widely held belief that peacekeeping is a softer, non-violent, ethically justifiable use of militarised force – legitimises warfare and martial violence. This central claim I've made throughout the book requires an understanding of the connection between militarism and martial politics; it requires attention to how peace has been martialled to justify warfare and violence. Martial politics describes the war-like relations that have always existed within liberal societies, and the martial violences that have been inflicted upon Indigenous, black, queer and disabled populations. In Howell's (2018) articulation of martial politics, her framework was positioned as an alternative to militarisation frameworks that dominate critical and feminist international relations scholarship. As Howell astutely notes, militarisation is often under-theorised and frameworks that employ militarisation often fail to recognise the violent nature of liberal politics within and outside assumedly 'peaceful' states.

Yet in Howell's framework, what is left unspoken is how 'peace' has been used to justify these martial politics. Despite the extensive peace theorisations by international relations and peace studies scholars, peace is significantly under-theorised. There is need for greater attention to how peace has been discursively manoeuvred – martialled – to justify military violence. We must pay closer attention to how we envision peace and how we justify the means to its (imagined) end. 'Martial peace', therefore, refers to the fantasies and nostalgic myth making about the nature of liberal societies that is used to justify the violent and war-like relations Howell labels 'martial politics'. Martial peace is the aspirational end-goal, the fantasy about orderliness in liberal politics that fails to capture the injustices that are side-swept in discourses about war, peace and peacekeeping. Nostalgic fantasies in myths about peacekeeping – captured in nuanced ways across national contexts in versions of the peacekeeping myth – sustain martial politics/violence through the reproduction of militarist logics. The peacekeeping myth, used to heuristically illustrate how discourses about peace and peacekeeping are deeply infused with militarist ideology, underpins how current visions of peace legitimise and perpetuate warfare.

Militarist ideology *within the peacekeeping myth* perpetuates and legitimises war. Militarism is not simply the glorification of war and military institutions and does not only lurk at the margins of defence institutions and arms industries; it is upheld by dominant global desires for peace – negative or martial peace. Militarism circulates within discourses about peace and permeates institutions tasked with 'keeping' peace.[1] It is deeply embedded across national imaginaries – national mythscapes – in discourses about peace and peacekeeping. And deep emotional attachments to these myths make the militarist logics difficult to dismantle. I will return to this at the end of the chapter.

The peacekeeping myth illustrates the way that war is legitimised, not simply by the glorification of military power or through the social and political prestige associated with military values but through the assumptions we have about peace – what it is, and how we 'keep' or 'make' it. Myths about peacekeeping reproduce ontological assumptions that peace is only possible through international norms like state sovereignty that 'protects' citizens (Young 2003), and through the elimination of violence with more violence. Resisting militarism requires challenging these norms. bell hooks (1995) reminds us that 'to fight militarism we must resist the socialization and brainwashing in our culture that teaches passive acceptance of violence in daily life, that teaches us we can eliminate violence with violence' (1995: 63).

The unproblematised acceptance of international peacekeeping as a desirable and normatively 'good' military practice has fed into the peacekeeping myth. Peacekeeping is not an antithesis to war. Aside from the obvious connections that many 'peacekeeping' dominant nations justify military expenditure to uphold UN peacekeeping commitments, the ways that militarised violence is justified in peacekeeping myths extend beyond UN peacekeeping missions to other uses of martial force conducted in the name of 'peace'. In Chapter 4, I consider how militarised force in the multi-decade war in Afghanistan was justified according to discourses about bringing 'peace' to Afghanistan and having Canada's helpful heroes – Peacekeeper 2.0s – embody the altruism, paternal helpfulness, non-violence and innocence beloved in the national version of the peacekeeper myth. Chapter 5 considers how those same attributes and desires for negative peace (even at the expense of justice for Indigenous nations) present in Canada's peacekeeper myth have been mobilised to justify martial force 'at home' against Indigenous populations.

To understand the connections between peacekeeping and warfare or violence, therefore, requires not positioning them dichotomously. Rather than the painstaking work done to differentiate peacekeeping from other forms of militarised force, largely through United Nations policy and scholarly taxonomies (discussed in Chapter 2), we must therefore consider the ontological continuities between discourses of peacekeeping and 'other' militarised violence. Not unlike counterinsurgency warfare or traditional state-directed wars, peacekeeping is militarised force executed to secure or establish a political vision: peacekeeping enables global norms and structures and upholds distinct political visions for the world.

Therefore, in conclusion, I wish to emphasise the three significant ways that the peacekeeper myth matters for scholars critical of military power, war and violence in global politics. First, understanding peacekeeping as myth helps to broaden scholarly theorisations about militarism, including its nebulous connections with IR's normative practices that reproduce martial violence as an anticipated and expected part of global relations. Second, the exaltation of military activities, whether combat or peacekeeping, imbues defence institutions with power and obscures the role of these institutions in upholding existing politics that perpetuate colonial and imperial violence. And third, the peacekeeping myth matters because we – and reader, I mean myself personally – are complicit in its ongoing reproduction. The seductive and emotional attachments that we have to the peacekeeping myth allow us to remove ourselves from the complicity, privilege and benefits of the current world order we live in. I'll discuss each in turn.

Celebrating Peacekeeping, Perpetuating Military Exaltation

Feminist and critical IR scholarship has extensively considered militarisation, stemming from important work done by early scholarship (Enloe 1983, 1989, 2000; Lutz 2002; Cowen and Gilbert 2007; Bernazzoli and Flint 2009) and extending to a robust set of literature that connects gender and militarisation on militarised masculinities (Niva 1998; Sasson-Levy 2003; Whitworth 2004; Masters 2005; Sion 2007; Woodward and Winter 2007; Belkin and Carver 2012; Bevan and MacKenzie 2012; Conway 2012; Eichler 2012; Duncanson 2013; Bulmer and Eichler 2017; Henry 2017; Wegner 2021a). One key element of these analyses that utilise militarisation frameworks is the valorisation of combat and warrior aesthetics and ethos, central to meaning making and value derision in military institutions (MacKenzie 2015). This has been a long-standing assumption about how militarism operates within social, cultural and political realms: that militarism (as linked to militarisation) is about social endorsement and excitement for war preparation and war making. The celebration of militarised violence, it has been theorised, hinges upon reverence for combat, 'a key term in a lexicon that perpetuates the epistemic normalisation and – indeed – celebration of state violence' (Millar and Tidy 2017: 157).

While this may be true in nations where military combat history has been celebrated, what the peacekeeper myth stands to demonstrate is that military exaltation is not strictly tied to combat. In fact, as Chapter 3 takes care to illustrate, militarisation in the name of peace (for example in the Canadian context), is another mechanism by which military personnel and militaries as institutions are valorised, necessary or essential.

The valorisation of militaries (and militarisation) is intimately related to other broad myths in international relations, articulated by Cynthia Weber (2014), such as 'international anarchy is the permissive cause of war'. Weber's use of myth interrogates IR theory as a cultural practice, rather than a set of observed, apolitical theoretical frameworks that are reproduced across many sites: classic IR texts, films, art, television and classroom lectures. (2014: 272). It is through these deeply embedded myths in IR that our understanding of the world is shaped, including our understandings of the necessity of military force to secure global peace. And peacekeeping, rather than an apolitical practice, or a morally desirable use of military force, has also been mythologised according to beliefs about the world and the need for militaries to secure peace. Celebrating peacekeeping uncritically through the myth's reproduction, therefore perpetuates global consciousness that peace must be martialled through militarised force.

The Value of the Peacekeeping Myth for Anti-Militarist Scholarship

The peacekeeper myth, as examined through various discourses, heuristically demonstrates the work that racism, colonialism and gender 'do' in sustaining and legitimising militarist ideology and practice through the legitimisation of state martial force. Narratives about martial violence in the name of peace are powerful and seductive stories: in international settings they narrate stories about the West bringing human rights and democracy to non-Western countries (Razack 2004: 48), and in domestic settings they have been justified as restoring order and protecting the 'peace' of non-Indigenous political economies. Therefore, when I suggest the peacekeeping myth is beloved (and in my case examples, I mean specifically by Canadians), I mean that it is loved by elite, white and politically powerful people who benefit from the status quo and feel threatened by challenges to existing 'peace and order'. The peacekeeping myth legitimises violence through discourses that exalt and preserve white settler dominance. These structural forms of violence 'keep people impoverished, debilitated and disempowered [and are] also methods of warfare that sustain the same white masculinist power elites that benefit from today's endless armed conflicts' (Otto 2020: 28). Yet as bell hooks (1995) notes, it is not only elites who benefit from the peacekeeping myth and the status quo it ensures: many individuals possess value systems and cling 'to a perspective on human relationships that embraces social domination in all its forms. Imperialism and not patriarchy is the core foundation of militarism' (1995: 61).

The peacekeeping myth therefore is a means to investigate how various vectors of power (gender, race, nationality) are upheld through visions of peace – visions of negative or partial peace that do not account for the broad politics in which peace is 'kept' or enforced. Within the halls of global governance, academic classrooms and policy-making circles, the belief in the necessity of armed force to guarantee peace is rarely questioned. Although not one of Cynthia Weber's 'core myths' in IR (2014), the assumption about the inevitability of violent conflict and need for militarised force is ubiquitous in many circles. This is not due to naivety, but largely because UN governance, mainstream academic theorisations, and government policy making are all primarily reactive. For the world to look different, for true anti-militarist and anti-imperialist challenges to social domination to succeed, more radical and visionary thinking is required. Dismantling myths about peace and peacekeeping would be a first step in revisioning global futures in anti-militarist and anti-oppressive ways.

Emotional Attachments to the Peacekeeping Myth: The Politics, Research Priorities and Privileges Enabled by the Myth

Within my discussion of the Canadian version of the peacekeeping myth, one under-explored component of the myth is its anti-American sentiments. Evident in public fears that Afghanistan war discourse sounded 'too American', and the need to position Canadian martial violence as not only civilising but helpful (rather than explicitly imperial), the mobilisation of the peacekeeping myth virtues is part of a desire to allow Canadians 'to imagine themselves playing a secondary, more innocent role in world affairs' (Razack 2004: 33). The virtues of the peacekeeping myth represent martial force as civilising, and distinct from American use of militarised force (understood to be more brash and aggressive than the non-violence and altruistic Canadian gendered ideal). How quintessentially Canadian to assume that other nations use militarised violence 'wrong', but that Canadian use of militarised force – done in the name of peace and order – is ethically justifiable. Anti-American sentiments in the peacekeeping myth reproduce a unique form of militarism: one not centred on the glorification of combat, but one that nonetheless justifies the deployment of military force as a beneficial public good. Narratives about Mounties and peacekeepers 'brand Canada as a boy scout and a non-colonial power. Ironically, both myths mask the history of "internal colonisation" and a coercive power used by the Canadian state against First Nations' (Ozguc 2011: 48)

Yet emotional attachments to the peacekeeping myth are not simply a way to reassure Canadians that their national identity is somehow morally superior to their southern neighbours; they are also the personal attachments to, and the beliefs that, the characteristics of the peacekeeping myth apply to them personally. Conceptualising the world as an arena where military force is required to keep 'bad apples' at bay allows individuals to turn away from their own benefits and their own complicity in the world that is created. As bell hooks reminds us:

> Ideologically, most of us have been raised to believe war is necessary and inevitable. In our daily lives, individuals who have passively accepted this socialization reinforce value systems that support, encourage, and accept violence as a means of social control. (hooks 1995: 63)

Therefore, understanding the peacekeeping myth matters for those interested in challenging existing violent means of social control that uphold various vectors of oppression: gender, race, coloniality, class and so on. For Canadians, this means that the peacekeeping myth stands to reconstitute our own political realities as non-violent and oppressive, when in fact, as a settler colonial nation, settler Canadians are direct beneficiaries of the colonial project. The colonial project has been whitewashed through existing global conventions and practices that instil Canada as a normative voice in international politics. As Whitworth (2004: 185) reminds us, 'peacekeeping is part of the subject-constituting project of the colonial encounter', thereby making the peacekeeping myth a seductive distraction from the work required to rectify existing violence and oppression in Canada and beyond. The peacekeeping myth in Canada, is an example of what Tuck and Yang (2012: 1) refer to as 'settler moves to innocence', because within this myth, settler Canadians understand themselves to be not immigrants on (stolen) Indigenous lands they have migrated to, but global ambassadors for peace and order. The peacekeeping myth and the self-affirming characteristics it signals about 'Canadian values' helps to reconcile settler guilt and complicity, ensuring settler futurity as the dominant way of life.

As a settler, I have benefited immensely from the 'peaceful' political order in Canadian life where I grew up on Treaty 4 territory with little conscious awareness of the structural violence that permeated the reserve communities and Indigenous populations surrounding me (a testament to the power of the reserve system that literally removes the suffering and exploitation from the daily world-view of settler communities). My deeply steeped consciousness about Canada's 'peaceful' history and peacekeeping reputation would go on to professionally impact my scholarly work and selection of PhD research topic. The origins of this research project began in my doctoral studies, where I sought to examine the impacts of the global 'war on terror' and the war in Afghanistan on Canada's peacekeeping legacy. As an academic, I've been asked to make my work 'speak' to many literatures who engage in this issue: middle power theorists, feminist international relations scholars, critical military studies, humanitarian militarisation analyses. Relating Canada's role in Afghanistan was simple enough to 'fit' into these various frameworks. But as the project has proceeded, it has become more difficult to 'speak' to these literatures, which take for granted the necessity of global peacekeeping and assume the urgency of military action to rectify global disorderliness without looking closely at the politics of imagining peace and order. It has also become starkly evident that I needed to confront my own privileges that have come from these narrow political constellations. While the project was originally conceived in response to how elites manipulated the peacekeeping myth to justify militarised foreign policy priorities, I am now concerned that the scholarly frameworks I've sought to contribute are short-sighted: many have failed to critically consider the politics of peace and order that inadvertently distract from and contribute to global violence, violence happening within my own communities.

Reimagining peace requires more than anti-militarism. It also requires we reimagine order and justice. It requires careful listening to voices that have long challenged the legitimacy, justice and longevity of current political orders, but whose voices have been ignored and overshadowed by serious academic frameworks. For Canadians, I envision this as moving beyond calls for reconciliation and taking seriously calls for decolonisation that centre Indigenous-led futurities. It means forfeiting the emotional attachments to global peacekeeping as a celebrated use of military force. It means a commitment to rethinking the political structures we have upheld through ongoing martial violence. My humble contribution to this cause has been laid out in the chapters that precede this: a critical examination of the ways that visions of peace have been used to distract from the politics of peacekeeping and inattention to justice in the policing and keeping of global order(s). The work left to be done, particularly by scholars like myself, is careful listening and collaboration with the voices for whom justice has been bypassed, and in particular those whose lands and extracted resources continue to fund scholarly research on peace, militarism and security (my own included). Anti-militarist politics therefore requires not only myth-busting but also collectively revisioning the world – and what we imagine peace to be – in alternative ways. We must pay careful attention to the politics that our research enables and the injustices we uphold in the name of keeping peace.

Notes

1. To pre-empt accusations that this means we should just 'do away with the UN' or 'abandon UN peacekeeping altogether', I'd like to suggest that it is possible to be critical of the political configurations of current global governance structures without demanding that we 'throw the baby out with the bathwater'. There is excellent critical scholarship that calls for UN reform, such as Jasmine-Kim Westendorf's *Violating Peace* (2020), that critically challenges how UN peacekeeping activities are conducted while still recognising the potential and importance of global governance that can take us from (politically) where we are to where we want to be.

2. I am wary of the ways that critical IR scholarship often conflates militarism and militarisation, something that disciplines like anthropology and geography have been more cautious about teasing out (Lutz 2002; MacLeish 2013; Rech et al. 2015). While militarisation processes – whether the gross accumulation of small arms or weapons of mass destruction, exorbitant defence budgets, or the use of militaries to conduct non-combat tasks and purposes for national interests – are indeed worthy of political contestation, these processes cannot be challenged without attention to militarism and efforts to critique militarist ideology that lurks as common sense in many 'everyday' and academic discourses. As Chris Rossdale reminds us, militarism is a 'social system of values and practices which promote and underpin the use of military approaches to a vast range of situations' (2019a: 67). Recent advancements in critical military studies demonstrate how envisioning militarism as ideology does not relegate it to a simple cognitive process but recognises that militarism as ideology derives power and endurance through emotional aspects, articulated by scholarship that theorises militarism as affect (Burridge and McSorley 2013; McSorley 2016; Chisholm and Ketola 2020; Welland 2021; Wegner 2021b). These emerging approaches seek to challenge the pervasive legitimisation of military violence in global politics (Eastwood 2018) by considering the spatial, temporal and culturally specific

and affective manifestations of militarism (Rech et al. 2015) that make it so insidious. This book considers some of these specificities.

3. The deployment of martial force and the ongoing legitimisation of military violence in discourses of peace to some extent overlaps with observed shifts in the 'militarization of humanitarianism' (McCormack and Gilbert 2022), whereby claims to ethical or 'virtuous' use of military violence have been made (Chandler 2006; Jabri 2007; Der Derian 2009; DeLauri 2019; Zolo 2001). This work seeks specifically to consider how 'peace' and 'peacekeeping', which capitalise on the 'virtuous' humanitarian tropes, legitimise military violence.

REFERENCES

Åhäll, Linda. 2015. *Sexing War/Policing Gender: Motherhood, Myth and Women's Political Violence.* London and New York: Routledge.

Åhäll, Linda. 2016. 'The Dance of Militarisation: A Feminist Security Studies Take on "the Political"'. *Critical Studies on Security* 4 (2): 154–68.

Alfred, Taiaiake. 1995. *Heeding the Voices of Our Ancestors: Kahnawake Mohawk Politics and the Rise of Native Nationalism.* Don Mills, ON: Oxford University Press.

Alfred, Taiaiake. 1999. *Peace, Power, Righteousness: An Indigenous Manifesto.* Don Mills, ON: Oxford University Press.

Alfred, Taiaiake. 2006. 'A Young Warrior's Perspective on the Conflict at Six Nations'. *New Socialist* 58 (Sept–Oct): 23–5.

Anderson, Benedict. 1991. *Imagined Communities: Reflections on the Origin and Spread of Nationalism.* London: Verso.

Anker, Lane. 2005. 'Peacekeeping and Public Opinion'. *Canadian Military Journal* (Summer): 23–32.

Annan, Kofi. 1998. 'Peacekeeping, Military Intervention and National Sovereignty in Internal Armed Conflicts'. In *Hard Choices: Moral Dilemmas in Humanitarian Intervention*, edited by Jonathan Moore, 55–69. Lanham, MD: Rowman & Littlefield.

Annan, Kofi. 2005. *In Larger Freedom: Towards Development, Security and Human Rights for All.* Report of the Secretary General, A/58/323, 2 September 2005.

Applebaum, A. I. 2007. 'Forcing a People to Be Free'. *Philosophy and Public Affairs* 35: 371.

Arendt, Hannah. 1970. *On Violence.* New York: Harcourt.

Astor, Hilary. 2007. 'Mediator Neutrality: Making Sense of Theory and Practice'. *Social and Legal Studies* 16 (2): 221–39.

Autesserre, Severine. 2019. 'The Crisis of Peacekeeping: Why the UN Can't End Wars'. *Foreign Affairs* 98, 101.

Ayoob, M. 2004. 'Third World Perspectives on Humanitarian Intervention and International Administration'. *Global Governance* 10 (1): 99–118.

Ayhan, Kadir Jun. 2019. 'Rethinking Korea's Middle Power Diplomacy as a Nation Branding Project'. *Korea Observer* 50 (1): 1–24.

Bacevich, Andrew J. 2013. *The New American Militarism: How Americans Are Seduced by War*. New York: Oxford University Press.

Balfour, Lindsay. 2014. 'Framing Redress after 9/11: Protest, Reconcilation and Canada's War on Terror Against Indigenous Peoples'. *The Canadian Journal of Native Studies* 34 (1): 25–41.

Baluja, T. 2013. 'Catching Up with the Photographer Behind the Iconic Oka Standoff Photo'. *J Source: The Canadian Journalism Project*. Available at https://j-source.ca/article/catching-up-with-the-photographer-behind-the-iconic-oka-standoff-photo/#:~:text=Canadian%20soldier%20Patrick%20Cloutier%20and,1%2C%201990 (accessed 16 November 2022).

Barkawi, Tarak. 2016. 'Decolonizing War'. *European Journal of International Security* 1 (2): 199–214.

Barkawi, Tarak, and Shane Brighton. 2011. 'Powers of War: Fighting, Knowledge and Critique'. *International Political Sociology* 5: 126–43.

Barkawi, Tarak, and Shane Brighton. 2019. 'Concepts and Histories of War'. *Millennium: Journal of International Studies* 48 (1): 99–104.

Barkawi, Tarak, and Mark Laffey, 2006. 'The Postcolonial Moment in Security Studies'. *Review of International Studies* 32 (2): 329–52.

Barnett, Michael. 2005. 'Humanitarianism Transformed'. *Perspectives on Politics* 3 (4): 723–40.

Barnett, Michael. 2012. 'International Paternalism and Humanitarian Governance'. *Global Constitutionalism* 1 (3): 485–521.

Barnett, Michael. 2016. 'Peacebuilding and Paternalism'. In *Peacebuilding in Crisis: Rethinking Paradigms and Practices of Transnational Cooperation*, edited by Tobias Debial, Thomas Held and Ulrich Schneckener. London: Routledge.

Barrera, Jorge. 2020a. 'Watchdog Memos Show RCMP Was Slow in Turning Over 2013 Mi'kmaw Demonstration Documents'. *CBC News*, 14 October 2020. Available at https://www.cbc.ca/news/indigenous/rcmp-nb-shale-gas-records-report-1.5760849 (accessed 12 October 2022).

Barrera, Jose. 2020b. 'Neither Liberals nor Conservatives Took Action on Report on Six Nations Land Conflict, Says Former Chief'. *CBC News*, 5 October. Available at https://www.cbc.ca/news/indigenous/

coyle-report-recommendations-six-nations-1.5749012 (accessed 16 November 2022).

Barrett, Frank J. 2001. 'The Organizational Construction of Hegemonic Masculinity: The Case of the US Navy'. In *The Masculinities Reader*, edited by Stephen M. Whitehead and Frank J. Barrett, 77–9. Cambridge: Polity Press.

Barthes, Roland. 1972. *Mythologies*. Translated by Annette Lavers. London: Hill & Wang.

Basham, Victoria M. 2013. *War, Identity and the Liberal State: Everyday Experiences of the Geopolitical in the Armed Force*. London: Routledge.

Basham, Victoria M. 2016. 'Gender, Race, Militarism, and Remembrance: The Everyday Geopolitics of the Poppy'. *Gender, Place & Culture* 23 (6): 883–96.

Basham, Victoria M. 2018. 'Liberal Militarism as Insecurity, Desire and Ambivalence: Gender, Race and the Everyday Geopolitics of War'. *Security Dialogue* 49 (1–2): 32–43.

Basham, Victoria M., Aaron Belkin and Jess Gifkins. 2015. 'What Is Critical Military Studies?' *Critical Military Studies* 1 (1): 1–2.

BBC Bitsize, n.d. 'Reasons for westward expansion'. Available at https://www.bbc.co.uk/bitesize/guides/znhkpg8/revision/2 (accessed 12 October 2022).

Beal, B., and Roy Macleod. 1984. *Prairie Fire: The 1885 North-West Rebellion*. Edmonton, AB: Hurtig.

Beeson, Mark. 2011. 'Can Australia Save the World? The Limits and Possibilities of Middle Power Diplomacy'. *Australian Journal of International Affairs* 65 (5): 563–77.

Behringer, Ronald M. 2012. *The Human Security Agenda: How Middle Power Leadership Defined US Hegemony*. London: Continuum.

Beier, J. Marshall. 2007. 'Inter-national Affairs: Indigeneity, Globality and the Canadian State'. *Canadian Foreign Policy Journal* 13 (3): 121–31.

Beier, J. Marshall. 2009. 'Forgetting, Remembering, and Finding Indigenous Peoples in International Relations'. In *Indigenous Diplomacies*, edited by J. M. Beier. New York: Palgrave Macmillan.

Beier, J. Marshall, and Jana Tabak. 2020. 'Children, Childhoods, and Everyday Militarisms'. *Childhood* 27 (3): 281–93.

Belkin, Aaron. 2012. *Bring Me Men: Military Masculinity and the Benign Façade of American Empire 1898–2001*. London: Columbia University Press.

Belkin, Aaron, and Terrell Carver. 2012. 'Militarized Masculinities and the Erasure of Violence'. *International Feminist Journal of Politics* 14 (4): 558–67.

Bell, Colleen. 2010. 'Fighting the War and Winning the Peace'. In *Canadian Foreign Policy in Critical Perspectives*, edited by J. Marshall Beier and Lana Wylie, 58–71. Don Mills, ON: Oxford University Press Canada.

Bell, Colleen, and Kendra Schreiner. 2018. 'The International Relations of Police Power in Settler Colonialism: The "Civilizing" Mission of Canada's Mounties'. *International Journal* 73 (1): 111–28. DOI: 10.1177/0020702018768480.

Bell, Duncan. 2003. 'Mythscapes: Memory, Mythology, and National Identity'. *British Journal of Sociology* 54 (1): 63–81.

Bell, Stewart. 2000. 'Native Militancy Blamed on Courts in RCMP Report'. *National Post*, 23 September 2000. A01/front.

Bellamy, Alex J. 2014. 'The "Next Stage" in Peace Operations Theory?' In *Peace Operations and Global Order*, 17–38. London: Routledge.

Bellamy, Alex J., Paul D. Williams, and Stuart Griffin. 2010. *Understanding Peacekeeping*. Cambridge: Polity Press.

Bengtsson, Richard. 2000. 'The Cognitive Dimension of Stable Peace'. In *Stable Peace Among Nations*, edited by Arie Kacowitz, Yaacov Bar-Siman-Tov, Ole Elgstrom and Meganus Jerneck, pp. 92–107. New York: Rowman & Littlefield.

Bercuson, David J. 2009. 'Up from the Ashes: The Re-professionalization of the Canadian Forces after the Somalia Affair'. *Canadian Military Journal* 9 (3). Available at http://www.journal.forces.gc.ca/vo9/no3/06-bercuson-eng.asp (accessed 12 October 2022).

Berdal, Mats, and David H. Ucko. 2015. 'The Use of Force in UN Peacekeeping Operations: Problems and Prospects'. *The RUSI Journal* 160 (1): 6–12.

Bernazzoli, Richelle M., and Colin Flint. 2009. 'Power, Place and Militarism: Toward a Comparative Geographic Analysis of Militarization'. *Geography Compass* 3 (1): 393–411.

Berthiaume, Lee. 2013. 'Harper Government's Defence Spending Cuts Raise Spectre of Another "Decade Of Darkness"'. *National Post*, 20 March.

Bevan, Marianne, and Megan H. MacKenzie. 2012. '"Cowboy" Policing versus "the Softer Stuff"'. *International Feminist Journal of Politics* 14 (4): 508–28.

Bhattacharyya, G. 2009. *Dangerous Brown Men: Exploiting Sex, Violence and Feminism in the 'War on Terror'*. London: Bloomsbury.

Blackburn, Mark. 2013. 'Crown Land Belongs to the Government, Not to F*Cking Natives'. *APTN National News*, 17 October.

Blanchard, Eric M. 2003. 'Gender, International Relations, and the Development of Feminist Security Theory'. *Signs* 28 (4): 1289–312.

Blanchfield, M. 2008. 'A Difficult Question'. *Ottawa Citizen*, 6 December, A5.

Blanchfield, M. 2015. 'Foreign Affairs Officials Urge New Directions for Canada in "Secret" Transition Memo'. *Toronto Star*, 29 September.

Bland, Douglas. 1998. 'A Sow's Ear from a Silk Purse: Abandoning Canada's Military Capabilities'. *International Journal* 54 (1): 143–74.

Blatchford, Christie. 2006. 'Our Soldiers Aren't Trying to "Kill Everybody"'. *The Globe and Mail*, 28 November.

Blatchford, Christie. 2008. *Fifteen Days: Stories of Bravery, Friendship, Life and Death from Inside the New Canadian Army*. Anchor Canada.

Blatchford, Christie. 2009. 'A Reign of Terror, a Trail of OPP Inaction'. *Globe and Mail*, 20 November. Available at https://www.theglobeandmail.com/news/national/a-reign-of-terror-a-trail-of-opp-inaction/article4313192/ (accessed 12 October 2022).

Blatchford, Christie. 2011. *Helpless: Caledonia's Nightmare of Fear and Anarchy and How the Law Failed All of Us*. Anchor Canada.

Bliesemann de Guevara, Berit (ed.) 2016. *Myth and Narrative in International Politics*. London: Palgrave Macmillan.

Boucher, Jean-Christophe, and Kim Richard Nossal. 2015. 'Lessons Learned? Public Opinion and the Afghanistan Mission'. In *Canada Among Nations, 2015: Elusive Pursuits*, edited by F. O. Hampson and S. Saideman, 73–93. Waterloo, ON: Centre for International Governance Innovation.

Bouka, Yolande. 2021. 'Make Foreign Policies as if Black and Brown Lives Mattered'. In *Feminist Solutions for Ending War*, edited by Megan Mackenzie and Nicole Wegner. London: Pluto Press.

Boulding, Elise. 2000. *Cultures of Peace: The Hidden Side of History*. Syracuse, NY: Syracuse University Press.

Boulding, Kenneth. 1978. *Stable Peace*. Austin, TX: University of Texas Press.

Bourgeault, Ron. 1988. 'Canada Indians: the South African Connection'. *Canadian Dimension* 21 (8): 6–10.

Bratt, Duane. 1998. 'Canada's Peacekeeping Mission to Eastern Zaire, A Failed Attempt at Rehabilitating the Military'. *The Canadian Journal of Peace and Conflict Studies* 30 (4): 21–33.

Brauer, Kinley. 1999. 'Manifest Destiny Revisited'. *Diplomatic History* 23 (2): 379–384.

Brautigam, T. 2011. 'Canadian Soldier, Cpl. Yannick Scherrer, 24, Killed in Afghanistan'. *The Canadian Press*, 28 March.

Bricker, Darrell. 2020. 'Majority of Canadians (61%) Disagree with Protestors Shutting Down Roads and Rail Corridors; Half (53%) Want Police to End It'. *Ipsos Reid News Report*, 19 February 2020. Available at https://

www.ipsos.com/en-ca/news-polls/Majority-Canadians-Disagree-With-Protestors-Shutting-Down-Roads-And-Rail-Corridors-And-Half-Want-Police-To-End-It (accessed 12 October 2022).

Brighton, Shane. 2011. 'Three Propositions on the Phenomenology of War'. *International Political Sociology* 5 (1): 101–5.

Bromfield, Nicholas. 2018. 'The Genre of Prime Ministerial Anzac Day Addresses, 1973–2016'. *Australian Journal of Politics and History* 64 (1): 81–97.

Bromfield, Nicholas, and Alex Page. 2020. 'How Is Australianness Represented by Prime Ministers?: Prime Ministerial and Party Rhetoric of Race, Class, and Gender on Australia Day and Anzac Day, 1990–2017'. *Australian Journal of Political Science* 55 (2): 191–210

Brown, Drew. 2017. 'Justin Trudeau Is Taking His Time with Peacekeeping Promises, Too'. *Vice News*, 15 May 2017. Available at https://www.vice.com/en/article/bmw5q3/justin-trudeau-is-taking-his-time-with-peacekeeping-promises-too (retrieved 12 October 2022).

Brown, James. 2014. *Anzac's Long Shadow: The Cost of Our National Obsession*. Collingwood, VIC: Redback.

Bruemmer, R. 2015. 'Has Canada's Reputation Dimmed – and Does It Matter?' *Montreal Gazette*, 26 September.

Bulmer, Sarah, and Maya Eichler. 2017. 'Unmaking Militarized Masculinity: Veterans and the Project of Military-to-Civilian Transition'. *Critical Military Studies* 3 (2): 161–81.

Burke, Anthony. 2007. 'Ontologies of War: Violence, Existence, and Reason'. *Theory and Event* 10 (2).

Burridge, Joseph, and Kevin McSorley. 2013. *War and the Body: Militarisation, Practice and Experience*. London: Routledge.

Butler, Judith. 2004. *Precarious Life: The Powers of Mourning and Violence*. London: Verso.

Butler, Judith. 2009. *Frames of War*. London: Verso.

Cahill, Jack. 1990. 'How the War Measures Act Was Tamed'. *Toronto Star*, 4 November, B4.

Cambre, Maria-Carolina. 2007. 'Terminologies of Control: Tracing the Canadian-South African Connection in a Word'. *Politikon* 34 (1): 19–34.

Campbell, Meagan. 2016. 'New Light on Saskatoon's "Starlight Tours"'. *Macleans'*, 8 April. Available at https://www.macleans.ca/news/canada/new-light-on-saskatoons-starlight-tours/ (accessed 12 October 2022).

Canada, Privy Council Office. 1991. Citizens' Forum on Canada's Future: Report to the People and Government of Canada / Keith Spicer, chairman. Available at https://publications.gc.ca/site/eng/9.699760/publication.html.

Canadian Press. 1990. 'Dialogue, Not Guns, Way to Settle Grievances of Natives, Siddon Says'. *Toronto Star*, 25 September, A3.

Canadian War Museum. 2021. 'Izzy Doll'. Available at https://www.warmuseum.ca/learn/izzy-doll/ (accessed 12 October 2022).

Carr, Andrew. 2014. 'Is Australia a Middle Power? A Systemic Impact Approach'. *Australian Journal of International Affairs* 68 (1): 70–84.

Carroll, Michael K. 2016. 'Peacekeeping: Canada's Past, but Not Its Present and Future?' *International Journal* 71 (1): 167–76.

CBC News. 2000. 'Dhaliwal Takes Tough Line with Burnt Church Protesters'. *CBC News*, 16 August.

CBC Unreserved. 2016. 'Sisters Recall the Brutal Last Day of Oka Crisis'. *CBC News*, 18 September. Available at https://www.cbc.ca/radio/unreserved/reflections-of-oka-stories-of-the-mohawk-standoff-25-years-later-1.3232368/sisters-recall-the-brutal-last-day-of-oka-crisis-1.3234550 (accessed 16 November 2022).

Cecco, Leyland. 2020. 'Canada: Police Clear Rail Blockage by Indigenous Anti-Pipeline Activists'. *The Guardian*, 25 February. Available at https://www.theguardian.com/world/2020/feb/24/canada-police-indigenous-anti-pipeline-activists-rail-blockade (accessed 12 October 2022).

Champion, Christian Paul. 2010. *The Strange Demise of British Canada: The Liberals and Canadian Nationalism, 1964–68*. Montreal: McGill-Queen's University Press.

Chandler, David. 2005. 'Introduction: Peace without Politics?' *International Peacekeeping* 12 (3): 307–21.

Chandler, David. 2006. *Empire in Denial: The Politics of State-Building*. London: Pluto Press.

Chapnick, Adam. 1999. 'The Middle Power'. *Canadian Foreign Policy* 7 (2): 73–82.

Chapnick, Adam. 2000. 'The Canadian Middle Power Myth'. *International Journal* (Spring) 55 (20): 188–206.

Chase, Steven, and Shawn McCarthy. 2015. 'Leaked Internal Report Warns of Canada's Declining World Influence'. *The Globe and Mail*, 27 September.

Chisholm, Amanda, and Hanna Ketola. 2020. 'The Cruel Optimism of Militarism: Feminist Curiosity, Affect, and Global Security'. *International Political Sociology* 14 (3): 270–85. DOI: 10.1093/ips/olaa005.

Choquette, Elena. 2019. 'The Making of a 'Peaceable Kingdom': Land, Peopling and Progress in an Expanding Canada'. Unpublished manuscript. Available at https://open.library.ubc.ca/cIRcle/collections/ubctheses/24/items/1.0379725.

Clapham, C. 1998. 'Rwanda: The Perils of Peacemaking'. *Journal of Peace Research* 35 (2): 193–210.

Clark, C. 2013. 'Joe Clark's New Book: Canada Is the Country that "Lectures and Leaves"'. *The Globe and Mail*, 1 November.

Clark, Campbell. 2016. 'Sending Canadian Peacekeepers to Mali Should Be an Obvious Choice'. *The Globe and Mail*, 20 November.

Clarke, John. 2022. 'Canada's Brutal and Dangerous "Pipeline Police"'. *Counterfire*, 27 June. Available at https://www.counterfire.org/articles/opinion/23288-canada-s-brutal-and-dangerous-pipeline-police (accessed 12 October 2022).

Citizens' Inquiry into Peace and Security. 1992. *Transformation Moment: A Canadian Vision of Common Security*. Waterloo, ON.

Cockburn, Cynthia. 2004. 'The Continuum of Violence: A Gender Perspective on War and Peace'. In *Site of Violence*, edited by Wenona Giles and Jennifer Hyndman, 24–44. Berkeley: University of California Press.

Cockburn, Cynthia. 2009. 'Militarism and War'. In *Gender Matters in Global Politics*, edited by Laura J. Shepherd. London: Routledge.

Cockburn, Cynthia, and Dubravka Žarkov. 2002. *The Postwar Moment: Militaries, Masculinities and International Peacekeeping, Bosnia and the Netherlands*. London: Lawrence & Wishart.

Cohen, Andrew. 2008. *The Unfinished Canadian: The People We Are*. Toronto: Emblem.

Cohn, Carol. 1989. 'Sex and Death in the Rational World of Defense Intellectuals'. *Signs: Journal of Women in Culture and Society* 12 (4): 687–718.

Cohn, Carol. 2008. 'Mainstreaming Gender in UN Security Policy: A Path to Political Transformation?' In *Global Governance*, edited by S. M. Rai and G. Waylen. London: Palgrave Macmillan.

Cohn, Carol, and Sara Ruddick. 2004. 'A Feminist Ethical Perspective on Weapons of Mass Destruction'. In *Ethics and Weapons of Mass Destruction*, edited by Steven Lee and Sohail Hasmi. Cambridge: Cambridge University Press.

Collins, Patricia Hill. 1990. *Black Feminist Thought: Knowledge, Consciousness, and the Politics of Empowerment*. New York and London: Routledge.

Comte, M. 2009. 'Afghanistan Will Unravel NATO, Says Canadian General'. *Agence France Presse*, 22 October.

Confortini, Catia C. 2006. 'Galtung, Violence and Gender: The Case for a Peace Studies/Feminism Alliance'. *Peace and Change* 31 (3): 333–67.

Constanze Schellhaas, and Annette Seegers. 2009. 'Peacebuilding: Imperialism's New Disguise?' *African Security Review* 18 (2): 1–15.

Conway, Daniel. 2012. *Masculinities, Militarization and the End Conscription Campaign: War Resistance in Apartheid South Africa*. Manchester: Manchester University Press.

Cook, Ramsay. 1986. *Canada, Quebec, and the Uses of Nationalism*. Toronto: McClelland and Stewart.

Cooke, Miriam. 1996. *Women and the War Story*. Berkeley: University of California Press.

Cooke, Miriam. 2002. 'Saving Brown Women'. *Signs: Journal of Women in Culture and Society* 28 (1): 468–70.

Cooke, R. 2016. 'The Precipice of Myth: Mythology/Epistemology'. In *Myth and Narrative in International Politics*, edited by Berit Bliesemann de Guevara, pp. 67–85. London: Palgrave Macmillan.

Cooper, Andrew F. 1997. *Canadian Foreign Policy: Old Habits and New Directions*. Scarborough, ON: Prentice Hall Canada.

Cooper, Andrew F., Richard A. Higgott and Kim Nossal. 1994. *Relocating Middle Powers: Australia and Canada in a Changing World Order*. Vancouver: UBC Press.

Cornwell, Steve. 2018. 'Greenpeace Canada Open Letter of Support for the Unist'ot'ten Camp'. Greenpeace.org, 21 December. https://www.greenpeace.org/canada/en/press-release/6895/greenpeace-canada-open-letter-of-support-for-the-unistoten-camp/.

Costs of War Project. 2021. 'Afghan Civilians'. Watson Institute of International and Public Affairs, Brown University. Available at https://watson.brown.edu/costsofwar/costs/human/civilians/afghan (accessed 12 October 2022).

Coulthard, Glen Sean. 2014. *Red Skin, White Masks: Rejecting the Colonial Politics of Recognition*. Minneapolis: University of Minnesota Press.

Cowen, Deborah, and Gilbert, Elizabeth (eds). 2007. *War, Citizenship, Territory*. London: Routledge.

Cox, Robert W. 1981. 'Social Forces, States and World Orders: Beyond International Relations Theory'. *Millennium: Journal of International Studies* 10 (2): 126–55.

Cox, Wayne, and Claire Turenne Sjolander. 1998. 'Damage Control: The Politics of National Defence'. In *How Ottawa Spends, 1998–99: Balancing Act: The Post-Deficit Mandate*, edited by Leslie Pal, 217–42. Toronto: Oxford University Press.

Crenshaw, Kimberlé. 1991. 'Mapping the Margins: Intersectionality, Identity Politics, and Violence against Women of Color'. *Stanford Law Review* 43 (6): 1241–99.

Cunningham, Nick. 2022. 'Canada Steps Up Surveillance of Indigenous Peoples to Push Fossil Fuel Pipelines Forward'. *DeSmog*. 17 June. Available at https://www.desmog.com/2022/06/17/canada-rcmp-surveillance-indigenous-peoples-fossil-fuel-pipelines-undrip-human-rights/ (accessed 12 October 2022).

Curtis, Christopher. 2020. 'Indigenous Women Have 'Unfinished Business' Years after Val d'Or Police Abuse Scandal'. *Ricochet Media*, 7

October. Available at https://ricochet.media/en/3316/indigenous-women-have-unfinished-business-years-after-val-dor-police-abuse-scandal (accessed 12 October 2022).

Davenport, Christian, Erik Melander, and Patrick M. Regan. 2018. *The Peace Continuum: What It Is and How to Study It.* Oxford: Oxford University Press.

Davis, Karen D., and Brian McKee. 2004. 'Women in the Military: Facing the Warrior Framework'. In *Challenge and Change in the Military: Gender and Diversity Issues*, edited by Franklin C. Pinch, Allister T. MacIntyre, Phillis Browne and Alan C. Okros, 52–75. Winnipeg, MB: Canadian Defence Academy Press.

Dawson, Graham. 1994. *Soldier Heroes: British Adventure, Empire and the Imagining of Masculinity.* London: Routledge.

De Carvalho, Benjamin, and Iver B. Neumann. 2015. *Small State Status Seeking: Norway's Quest for International Standing.* New York: Routledge.

Decima Research Group. 2007. *Key Findings of Qualitative Research for the Canadian Forces Recruitment Advertising Campaign 'Fight'.* Canada: Department of Defence.

Decker, Alicia C., Summer Forester and Eliot Blackburn. (2016). 'Rethinking Everyday Militarism on Campus: Feminist Reflections on the Fatal Shooting at Purdue University'. *Feminist Studies* 42 (1): 194–216.

De Lauri, Antonio. 2019. 'Humanitarian Militarism and the Production of Humanity'. *Social Anthropology/Anthropologie Sociale* 27 (1): 84–99.

Dembicki, Geoff, and Bob Mackin. 2009. 'Olympics' Top Cop Helped Blow up Truck at Gustafson Lake Stand-off'. *The Tyee*, 20 October. Available at https://thetyee.ca/News/2009/10/20/GustafsenStandOff/ (accessed 12 October 2022).

Demurenko, Andre, and Alexander Nikitin. 1997. 'Concepts in International Peacekeeping'. *Military Review* 77: 67–71.

Department of Canadian Heritage 2014. 'Reconciliation: The Peacekeeping Monument'. Available at http://www.pch.gc.ca.

Der Derian, James. 2009. *Virtuous War: Mapping the Military- Industrial-Media-Entertainment Network*, 2nd edn. New York: Routledge.

Dewitt, David B., and John J. Kirton. 1983. *Canada as a Principal Power: A Study in Foreign Policy and International Relations.* Toronto: John Wiley & Sons.

Dhillon, Jaskiran, and Will Parrish. 2019. 'Exclusive: Canada Police Prepared to Shoot Indigenous Activists, Documents Show'. *The Guardian*, 20 December. Available at https://www.theguardian.com/world/2019/dec/20/canada-indigenous-land-defenders-police-documents (accessed 16 November 2022).

Diehl, Paul F. 2016. 'Exploring Peace: Looking Beyond War and Negative Peace'. *International Studies Quarterly* 60: 1–10.

Diehl, Paul F., and Alexandru Balas. 2014. *Peace Operations*. Toronto: John Wiley & Sons.

Diehl, Paul F., Daniel Druckman and James Wall. 1998. 'International Peacekeeping and Conflict Resolution: A Taxonomic Analysis with Implications'. *Journal of Conflict Resolution* 42 (1): 33–55. DOI: 10.1177/0022002798042001002.

Donald, Dominick. 2002. 'Neutrality, Impartiality, and UN Peacekeeping at the Beginning of the 21st Century'. *International Peacekeeping* 9 (4): 21–38.

Donoghue, Jed, and Bruce Tranter. 2015. 'The Anzacs: Military influences of Australian Identity'. *Journal of Sociology* 51 (3): 449–63.

Dorn, Walter A. 2005. 'Canadian Peacekeeping: Proud Tradition, Strong Future?' *Canadian Foreign Policy Journal* 12 (2): 7–32.

Dorn, Walter A. 2006. 'Peacekeeping Then, Now, and Always'. *Canadian Military Journal* (Winter): 105–6.

Dorn, A. Walter. 2007. 'Canadian Peacekeeping: No Myth, But Not What It Once Was'. *SITREP* 67 (2): 5–16.

Dorn, Walter A. 2009. 'Canada's Honourable Role as a Peacekeeping Nation'. In *Afghanistan and Canada: Is There an Alternative to War?* edited by Lucia Kowaluk and Steven Staples, 275–83. Montreal: Black Rose Books.

Dorn, Walter A., and Joshua Libben. 2018. 'Preparing for Peace: Myths and Realities of Canadian Peacekeeping Training'. *International Journal* 73 (2): 257–81.

Doty, Roxanne L. 1993. 'Foreign Policy as Social Construction: A Post-Positivist Analysis of U.S. Counterinsurgency policy in the Philippines'. *International Studies Quarterly* 37 (3): 297–320.

Doyle, Michael W. 2001. 'The New Interventionism'. *Metaphilosophy* 32 (1–2): 212–35.

DPKO Office of Military Affairs. 2009. *Concept Note on Robust Peacekeeping*. New York.

Ducas, Michel. 2020. 'Five Years Later, Val-d'Or's Long Road to Reconciliation with Indigenous Neighbours'. *Montreal Gazette* 23 December. Available at https://montrealgazette.com/news/quebec/five-years-later-val-dors-long-road-to-reconciliation-with-indigenous-neighbours (accessed 12 October 2022).

Ducklow, Zoe. 2019. 'Nine Things You Need to Know about the Unist'ot'en Blockage'. 8 January. *The Tyee*. Available at https://thetyee.ca/Analysis/2019/01/08/LNG-Pipeline-Unistoten-Blockade/ (accessed 12 October 2022).

Duffield, Mark. 2001. *Global Governance and the New Wars: The Merging of Development and Security*. London: Zed Books.

Duncanson, Claire. 2009. 'Forces for Good? Narratives of Military Masculinity in Peacekeeping Operations'. *International Feminist Journal of Politics* 11 (1): 63–80.

Duncanson, Claire. 2013. *Forces for Good? Military Masculinities and Peacebuilding in Afghanistan and Iraq*. London: Springer.

Duncanson, Claire. 2015. 'Hegemonic Masculinity and the Possibility of Change in Gender Relations'. *Men and Masculinities* 18 (2): 231–48.

Dworkin, G. 1972. 'Paternalism'. *Monist* 56 (1): 64–84.

Dyvik, Synne L., and Lauren Greenwood. 2016. 'Embodying Militarism: Exploring the Spaces and Bodies In-Between'. *Critical Military Studies* 2 (1–2): 1–6.

Easley, Leif-Eric, and Kyuri Park. 2018. 'South Korea's Mismatched Diplomacy in Asia: Middle Power Identity, Interests, and Foreign Policy'. *International Politics* 55: 242–63.

Eastwood, James. 2018. 'Rethinking Militarism as Ideology: The Critique of Violence after Security'. *Security Dialogue* 49 (1–2): 44–56.

Eichler, Maya. 2012. *Militarizing Men: Gender, Conscription and War in Post-Soviet Russia*. Stanford, CA: Stanford University Press.

Eisenstein, Zillah. 2007. *Sexual Decoys*. London: Zed Books.

Ekos Research Associates Inc. 2005. 'Canadian Attitudes Towards the CF'. 9–17 February.

Elliot, Alice. 2015. 'The Meaning of Elections for Six Nations'. *Briarpatch*. 21 May. Available at https://briarpatchmagazine.com/articles/view/the-meaning-of-elections-for-six-nations (accessed 12 October 2022).

Elshtain, J. 1995. *Women and War*, 2nd edn. Chicago: University of Chicago Press.

English, John. 2003. *Canadian Peacekeeping Is Not What It Used To Be*. Ottawa: Canadian Defence and Foreign Affairs Institute.

Enloe, Cynthia. 1983. *Does Khaki Become You? The Militarization of Women's Lives*. Boston, MA: South End Press.

Enloe, Cynthia. 1989. *Bananas, Beaches, and Bases*. London: Pandora Press.

Enloe, Cynthia. 1993. *The Mourning After: Sexual Politics at the End of the Cold War*. Berkeley: University of California Press.

Enloe, Cynthia. 2000. *Maneuvers: The International Politics of Militarizing Women's Lives*. Berkeley: University of California Press.

Enloe, Cynthia. 2004. *The Curious Feminist: Searching for Women in a New Age of Empire*. Berkeley: University of California Press.

Enloe, Cynthia. 2007. *Globalization and Militarism: Feminists Make the Link*. Lanham, MD: Rowman & Littlefield.

Enloe, Cynthia. 2013. 'Combat and "Combat": A Feminist Reflection'. *Critical Studies on Security* 1 (2): 260–3.

Environics Institute. 2012. Focus Canada surveys 2012. Available at https://www.environicsinstitute.org/docs/default-source/project-documents/focus-canada-2012/canada's-role-in-the-world.pdf?sfvrsn=b9ede752_4 (accessed 12 October 2022).

Environics Institute. 2018. Canada's World Survey 2018. Available at https://www.environicsinstitute.org/docs/default-source/project-documents/canada's-world-2018-survey/canada's-world-survey-2018---final-report.pdf?sfvrsn=17208306_2 (accessed 12 October 2022).

Environics Research Group Limited. 2002. Focus Canada 2002.

Environics Research Group Limited. 2004. Focus Canada 2004.

Environics Research Group. 2007 (March). *Advertising Post-Test: Prepared for DND*. Canada: Department of Defence.

Fabian, L L. 1971. *Soldiers Without Enemies: Preparing the United Nations for Peacekeeping*. Washington, DC: Brookings Institution.

Fairclough, Norman; Jane Mulderrig and Ruth Wodak. 2011. 'Critical Discourse Analysis'. In *Discourse Studies: A Multidisciplinary Introduction*, 2nd edn, edited by Teun A. Van Dijk. London: Sage.

Fanon, Frantz. 1961. *The Wretched of the Earth*. New York: Grove Press.

Fisher, Peter. 2011. *Highway of Heroes: True Patriot Love*. Toronto: Dundurn Press.

Forester, Brett. 2022. 'Behind the Thin Blue Line: Meet a Secretive Arm of the RCMP in B.C'. *APTN News*, 16 June. Available at https://www.aptnnews.ca/ourstories/cirg/.

Fortna, Virginia P. 2008. *Does Peacekeeping Work?* Princeton, NJ: Princeton University Press.

Foucault, Michel. 1972. *Archaeology of Knowledge and the Discourse on Language*, translated by A. M. Sheridan Smith. New York: Vintage.

Francis, Daniel. 1992. *The Imaginary Indian: The Image of the Indian in Canadian Culture*. Toronto: Arsenal Pulp Press.

Francis, Daniel. 1997. *National Dreams: Myth, Memory, and Canadian History*. Vancouver: Arsenal Pulp Press.

Fraser, Graham. 2002. 'Military Muscle Needed to Back Good Intentions'. *Toronto Star*, 10 November.

Frazer, Elizabeth, and Kimberly Hutchings. 2019. *Can Political Violence Ever Be Justified?* Cambridge: Polity Press.

Freeman, A. 2002. 'Canadians Sought War, Insider Says: British Officials Who Offered Passive Role Says Armed Forces Wanted to Face Combat'. *The Globe and Mail*, 11 January, A1.

Galtung, Johan. 1969. 'Violence, Peace, and Peace Research'. *Journal of Peace Research* 6 (3): 167–91.

Galtung, Johan. 1971. 'A Structural Theory of Imperialism'. *Journal of Peace Research* 8 (2): 81–117. DOI: 10.1177/002234337100800201.

Galtung, Johan. 1985. 'Twenty-five Years of Peace Research: Ten Challenges and Some Responses'. *Journal of Peace Research* 22 (2): 141–58.

Gelber, Lionel. 1945. 'Canada's New Stature'. *Foreign Affairs* 24 (October 1945–July 1946): 280–1.

Gentry, Caron E. (2015) 'Epistemological Failures: Everyday Terrorism in the West", *Critical Studies on Terrorism* 8 (3): 362–82.

George, Alexander. 2000. 'Foreword'. In *Stable Peace among Nations*, edited by Arie Kacowitz, Yaacov Bar-Siman-Tov, Ole Elgstrom and Meganus Jerneck, xi–xviii. Lanham, MD: Rowman & Littlefield.

Gibler, Douglas M. 2012. *The Territorial Peace: States, Development and International Conflict*. Cambridge: Cambridge University Press.

Gilligan, M. J., and E. J. Sergenti. 2007. 'Does Peacekeeping Keep Peace? Using Matching to Improve Causal Inference'. Working paper, Department of Politics, New York University and Harvard University.

Gleditsch, Nils Petter, Jonas Nordkavelle and Havard Strand. 2014. 'Peace Research – Just the Study of War?' *Journal of Peace Research* 51 (2): 145–58.

Goldie, J. L. 2014. 'Fighting Change: Representing the Canadian Forces in the 2006–2008 Fight Recruitment Campaign'. *Canadian Journal of Communications* 39 (3): 413–30.

Goldstein, Joshua. 2001. *War and Gender*. Cambridge: Cambridge University Press.

Gordon, J. King. 1966. *Canada's Role as a Middle Power*. Toronto: The Canadian Institute of International Affairs.

Gordon, James. 2005. 'Judge Quits Panel Hours after Critic Demands It: Cites Personal Reasons'. *National Post*, 18 October, A7.

Gough, Paul. 2002. '"Invicta Pax" Monuments, Memorials and Peace: An Analysis of the Canadian Peacekeeping Monument, Ottawa'. *International Journal of Heritage Studies* 8 (3): 201–23.

Goulding, M. 1993. 'The Evolution of United Nations Peacekeeping'. *International Affairs* 69 (3): 451–64.

Government of Canada. 2005. *Canada's International Policy Statement: A Role of Pride and Influence in the World*. Ottawa, ON.

Government of Canada. 2008a. *Canada's Engagement in Afghanistan: Quarterly Report to Parliament*. Archived www.gc.afghanistan.ca.

Government of Canada. 2008b. *Canada's Engagement in Afghanistan: Quarterly Report to Parliament*. Archived www.gc.afghanistan.ca.

Government of Canada. 2008c. *Canada's Engagement in Afghanistan: Quarterly Report to Parliament*. Archived www.gc.afghanistan.ca.

Government of Canada. 2008d. *Canada's Engagement in Afghanistan: Quarterly Report to Parliament*. Archived www.gc.afghanistan.ca.

Government of Canada. 2009a. *Canada's Engagement in Afghanistan: Quarterly Report to Parliament*. Archived www.gc.afghanistan.ca.

Government of Canada. 2009b. *Canada's Engagement in Afghanistan: Quarterly Report to Parliament*. Archived www.gc.afghanistan.ca.

Government of Canada. 2009c. *Canada's Engagement in Afghanistan: Quarterly Report to Parliament*. Archived www.gc.afghanistan.ca.

Government of Canada. 2009d. *Canada's Engagement in Afghanistan: Quarterly Report to Parliament*. Archived www.gc.afghanistan.ca.

Government of Canada. 2010a. *Canada's Engagement in Afghanistan: Quarterly Report to Parliament*. Archived www.gc.afghanistan.ca.

Government of Canada. 2010b. *Canada's Engagement in Afghanistan: Quarterly Report to Parliament*. Archived www.gc.afghanistan.ca.

Government of Canada. 2010c. *Canada's Engagement in Afghanistan: Quarterly Report to Parliament*. Archived www.gc.afghanistan.ca.

Government of Canada. 2010d. *Canada's Engagement in Afghanistan: Quarterly Report to Parliament*. Archived www.gc.afghanistan.ca.

Government of Canada. 2011a. *Canada's Engagement in Afghanistan: Quarterly Report to Parliament*. Archived www.gc.afghanistan.ca.

Government of Canada. 2011b. *Canada's Engagement in Afghanistan: Quarterly Report to Parliament*. Archived www.gc.afghanistan.ca.

Government of Canada. 2011c. *Canada's Engagement in Afghanistan: Quarterly Report to Parliament*. Archived www.gc.afghanistan.ca.

Government of Canada. 2011d. *Canada's Engagement in Afghanistan: Quarterly Report to Parliament*. Archived www.gc.afghanistan.ca.

Gow, James 1995. 'Strategic Peacekeeping: UNPROFOR and International Diplomatic Assertion'. In *Peacekeeping in Europe*, edited by Espen Barthe Eide. Peacekeeping and Multinational Operations series, no. 5. Oslo: NUPI.

Granatstein, Jack L. 1998. *Who Killed Canadian History?* Toronto: HarperCollins.

Granatstein, Jack L. 2002a. *Canada's Army: Waging War and Keeping the Peace*. Toronto: University of Toronto Press.

Granatstein, J. L. 2002b. *A Friendly Agreement in Advance: Canada–US Defense Relations Past, Present, and Future*. C.D. Howe Institute, June 1. Available at https://www.cdhowe.org/public-policy-research/friendly-agreement-advance-canada-us-defense-relations-past-present-and-future (accessed 12 October 2022).

Granatstein, J. L. 2004a. 'Brush Up on our "Proud History"'. *National Post*, 3 February.

Granatstein, J. L. 2004b. 'Fatal Distraction: Lester Pearson and the Unwarranted Primacy of Peacekeeping'. *Policy Options*, May 2004, 67–73.

Granatstein, Jack L. 2007a. 'Hurrah to Rebuilding Canadian Forces: New Study Using Cold War Spending for Comparison Does Nothing to Advance Real Debate on Defence'. *Hamilton Spectator*, 17 November, A25.

Granatstein, J. L. 2007b. 'Defence Spending Still Inadequate'. *Guelph Mercury*, 26 October, A13.

Granatstein, Jack L. 2007c. *Whose War Is It? How Canada Can Survive in the Post-9-11 World*. Ottawa, ON: Phyllis Bruce Books.

Granatstein, J. L. 2008. 'The End of The Hillier Era'. *Ottawa Citizen*, 16 April.

Granatstein, Jack L., and David J. Bercuson. 1991. *War and Peacekeeping*. Toronto: Key Porter Books.

Graveland, B. 2010. 'Early Morning Ramp Ceremony for Canadian Sergeant Killed by IED Blast'. *The Canadian Press*, 22 June.

Gray, Harriet. 2016. 'The Geopolitics of Intimacy and the Intimacies of Geopolitics: Combat Deployment, Post-Traumatic Stress Disorder, and Domestic Abuse in the British Military'. *Feminist Studies* 42 (1): 138–65.

Greener, Beth K. (2013) 'Providing Peacekeepers: The Politics, Challenges and Future of United Nations Peacekeeping Contributions'. *International Peacekeeping* 20 (5): 636–8. DOI: 10.1080/ 13533312.2013.864007.

Grenier, Marc. 1994. 'Native Indians in the English-Canadian Press: The Case of the "Oka Crisis"'. *Media, Culture and Society* 16: 313–36.

Grewal, Inderpal. 2003) 'Transnational America: Race, Gender and Citizenship after 9/11'. *Social Identities* 9 (4): 535–61.

Greig, J. Michael, and Paul F. Diehl. 2005. 'The Peacekeeping–Peacemaking Dilemma'. *International Studies Quarterly* 49 (4): 621–45.

Guardian opinion. 2015. 'The Guardian View on Canada's Elections: Is the Stephen Harper Era Over?' *The Guardian*, 4 August.

Gunnarsson, Hanna. 2015. 'Accountability of the UN and Peacekeepers: Focus Study on Sexual Exploitation and Abuse'. *SOAS Law Journal* 2 (1): 207–29.

Gwyn, Richard. 2012. *Nation Maker Sir John A. Macdonald: His Life, Our Times*. Toronto: Vintage Canada.

Haan, W.D., 2008. 'Violence as an Essentially Contested Concept'. In *Violence in Europe*, edited by Sophie Body-Gendrot and Pieter Spierenburg, 27–40. New York: Springer.

Haigh, Joseph. 2020. 'Vicarious Militarism: Ontological (In)Security and the Politics of Vicarious Subjectivity in British War Commemorations'. Unpublished manuscript. Available at http://wrap.warwick. ac.uk/153852/.

Hall, Katharine. 2021. 'Martial Politics, MOVE and the Racial Violence of Policing'. *Politics*. DOI: 10.1177/02633957211042732.

Hall, Stuart. 1997. *Representation: Cultural Representations and Signifying Practices*. London: Sage.

Hames, Raymond. 2007. 'The Ecologically Noble Savage Debate'. *Annual Review of Anthropology* (36): 177–90.

Hamilton, Graeme. 2000. 'Trap Raid Aborted as Gunfire Heard: Fisheries Officers Say Shots Came from Burnt Church Reserve'. *National Post*, 26 September, A04.

Hamilton, Graeme, and Justine Hunter. 2000. 'Tension Rises at Burnt Church as Deadline Nears; Warriors Vow to Take 'Counter Action' If Ottawa Removes Traps'. *National Post*, 22 September, A04.

Harper, Tim. 2015. 'Trudeau Can Reset the Canadian Global Image: Tim Harper'. *Toronto Star*, 23 October.

Härting, Heike, and Smaro Kamboureli. 2009. 'Introduction: Discourses of Security, Peace-keeping Narratives, and the Cultural Imagination in Canada'. *University of Toronto Quarterly* 78 (2).

Hayes G. 1997. 'Canada as a Middle Power: The Case of Peacekeeping'. In *Niche Diplomacy. Studies in Diplomacy*, edited by Andrew F. Cooper. London: Palgrave Macmillan.

Heidenreich, Phil. 2020. '61% of Canadians Oppose Wet'suwet'en Solidarity Blockages, 75% Back Action to Help Indigenous People: Poll'. *Global News*, 19 February. Available at https://globalnews.ca/news/6567463/wetsuweten-rail-port-blockades-coastal-gaslink-pipe-line-poll-canada/ (accessed 12 October 2022).

Henry, Marsha. 2012. 'Peacexploitation? Interrogating Labor Hierarchies and Global Sisterhood Among Indian and Uruguayan Female Peace-keepers'. *Globalizations* 9 (1): 15–33.

Henry, Marsha. 2017. 'Problematizing Military Masculinity, Intersectionality And Male Vulnerability in Feminist Critical Military Studies'. *Critical Military Studies* 3 (2): 182–99.

Higate, Paul. 2003. *Military Masculinities: Identity and the State*. London: Praeger.

Higate, Paul. 2007 'Peacekeepers, Masculinities, and Sexual Exploitation'. *Men and Masculinities* 10 (1): 99–119.

Higate, Paul R., and Marsha Henry. 2004. 'Engendering (In)Security in Peace Support Operations'. *Security Dialogue* 35 (4): 481–98.

Higate, Paul, and Marsha Henry. 2009. *Insecure Spaces: Peacekeeping, Power and Performance in Haiti, Kosovo and Liberia*. London: Zed Books.

Hillmer, Norman, and Granatstein, J. L. 1994. *Empire to Umpire*. Toronto: Irwin.

Hillmer, Norman, and Lagassé, Philippe (eds) 2018. *Justin Trudeau and Canadian Foreign Policy*. Basingstoke: Palgrave Macmillan.

Historica Canada. 2016a. 'Heritage Minutes: Dextraze in the Congo'. YouTube video, uploaded 5 August. Available at https://www.youtube.com/watch?v=-xGV3s6suh4 (accessed 12 October 2022).

Historica Canada. 2016b. 'The Lost Heritage Minute: Lester B. Pearson'. YouTube video, uploaded 30 March. Available at https://www.youtube.com/watch?v=-lD3c--x1Qs (accessed 12 October 2022).

Hobsbawm, Eric, and Terence Ranger (eds) 1992. *The Invention of Tradition*. Cambridge: Cambridge University Press.

Hocking, B. 1997. 'Finding Your Niche: Australia and the Trials of Middle-Powerdom'. In *Niche Diplomacy: Studies in Diplomacy*, edited by Andrew F. Cooper. London: Palgrave Macmillan.

Holmes, John W. 1982. *The Shaping of Peace: Canada and the Search for World Order, 1943–1957*, vol. 2. Toronto: University of Toronto Press.

hooks, bell. 1995. 'Feminism and Militarism: A Comment'. *Women's Studies Quarterly* 23 (3/4): 58–64.

Horn, Bernd. 2006. *The Canadian Way of War: Serving the National Interest*. Toronto: Dundurn Press.

Horn, Col. Bernd. 2010. *No Lack of Courage: Operation Medusa, Afghanistan*. Toronto: Dundurn Press.

Horrall, S. W. 1972. 'Sir John A Macdonald and the Mounted Police Force for the Northwest Territories'. *The Canadian Historical Review* 53 (2): 179–200.

Horwitz, Simonne. 2016. '"Apartheid in a Parka"? Roots and Longevity of the Canada–South Africa Comparison'. *Safundi* 17 (4): 460–78.

Howard, Lise Morje. 2008. *UN Peacekeeping in Civil Wars*. Cambridge: Cambridge University Press.

Howard, Lise Morje, and Anjali Kaushlesh Dayal. 2018. 'The Use of Force in UN Peacekeeping'. *International Organization* 72 (1): 71–103.

Howell, Alison. 2005. 'Peaceful, Tolerant and Orderly? A Feminist Analysis of Discourse of "Canadian Values" in Canadian Foreign Policy'. *Canadian Foreign Policy Journal* 12 (1): 45–69.

Howell, Alison. 2018. 'Forget "Militarization": Race, Disability and the "Martial Politics" of the Police and of the University'. *International Journal of Feminist Politics* 20 (2):117–36.

Hunt, Krista, and Kim Rygiel. 2008. *(En)Gendering the War on Terror*. London: Routledge.

Huntington, Samuel P. 1957. *The Soldier and the State: The Theory and Politics of Civil-Military Relations*. Cambridge, MA: Belknap Press.

Ingebritsen, Christine. 2002. 'Norm Entrepreneurs: Scandinavia's Role in World Politics'. *Cooperation and Conflict* 37 (1): 11–23.

Institute for Peace and Economics. 2022. *Global Peace Index.* Available at https://www.economicsandpeace.org/wp-content/uploads/2022/06/ GPI-2022-web.pdf (accessed 16 November 2022).

Ipsos Reid. 2008. *Defining Canada: A Nation Choose the 101 Things That Best Define their Country.* 30 June 2008. Report: The Dominion Institute.

Ipsos Reid Corporation 2010. *Qualitative & Quantitative Research: Views of the Canadian Forces—2010 Tracking Study.* (March). Ottawa, ON: Department of National Defence. Available at http://epe.lac-bac. gc.ca/100/200/301/ pwgsc-tpsgc/por-ef/national_defence/2010/078-09/ summary.pdf.

Jabri V. 2007. *War and the Transformation of Global Politics.* New York: Palgrave Macmillan.

Jackson, Susan T. 2013. 'The National Security Exception, the Global Political Economy and militarization'. In *The Marketing of War in the Age of Neo-militarism,* edited by Kosgas Gouliamos and Christos Kassimeris, 214–35. London: Routledge.

James, Alan. 1990. *Peacekeeping and International Politics.* Basingstoke: Macmillan and IISS.

James, Alan. 1995. 'Peacekeeping, Peace-Enforcement and National Sovereignty'. In *A Crisis of Expectations: UN Peacekeeping in the 1990s,* edited by Ramesh Thakur and Carlyle A. Thayer. Boulder, CO: Westview Press.

Janowitz, Morris. 1971. *The Professional Soldier.* London: Collier Macmillan.

Jefferess, David. 2009. 'Responsibility, Nostalgia, and the Mythology of Canada as a Peacekeeper'. *University of Toronto Quarterly* 78 (2): 709–27.

Jiwani, Yasmine. 2004. 'Gendering Terror: Representations of the Orientalized Body in Quebec's Post-September 11 English-Language Press'. *Critique: Critical Middle Eastern Studies* 13 (3): 265–91.

Jiwani, Yasmine. 2005. 'The Great White North Encounters September 11: Race, Gender, and Nation in Canada's National Daily, The Globe and Mail'. *Social Justice* 32 (4): 50–68.

Jiwani, Yasmine. 2009. 'Helpless Maidens and Chivalrous Knights: Afghan Women in the Canadian Press'. *University of Toronto Quarterly* 78 (2): 728–44.

Jockel, Joseph T. 1994. *Canada and International Peacekeeping.* Washington, DC: Center for Strategic and International Studies.

John, Jojin V. 2014. 'Becoming and Being a Middle Power: Exploring a New Dimension of South Korea's Foreign Policy'. *China Report* 50 (4): 325–41.

Jordaan, Eduard. 2003. 'The Concept of a Middle Power in International Relations: Distinguishing between Emerging and Traditional Middle Powers'. *Politikon* 30 (1): 165–81.

Kagan, Robert W. 2002. 'Power and Weakness'. *Policy Review*, 1 June. Available at https://www.hoover.org/research/power-and-weakness (accessed 14 October 2022).

Karim, Sabrina, and Kyle Beardsley. 2016. 'Explaining Sexual Exploitation and Abuse in Peacekeeping Missions: The Role of Female Peacekeepers and Gender Equality in Contributing Countries'. *Journal of Peace Research* 53 (1): 100–15. DOI: 10.1177/0022343315615506.

Karlsrud, John. 2015. 'The UN at War: Examining the Consequences of Peace-Enforcement Mandates for the UN Peacekeeping Operations in the CAR, the DRC, and Mali'. *Third World Quarterly* 36 (1): 40–54.

Karlsrud, John. 2019. 'From Liberal Peacebuilding to Stabilization and Counterterrorism'. *International Peacekeeping* 26 (1): 1–21.

Katerberg, William H. 2003. 'A Northern Vision: Frontiers and the West in the Canadian and American Imagination'. *The American Review of Canadian Studies* 33 (4): 543–63.

Keating, Tom. 1993. *Canada and World Order: The Multilateralist Tradition in Canadian Foreign Policy*. Don Mills, ON: Oxford University Press.

Keating, Tom. 2002. *Canada and World Order: The Multilateralist Tradition in Canadian Foreign Policy*, 2nd edn. Toronto: Oxford University Press.

Keohane, Robert O. 1969. 'Lilliputians' Dilemmas: Small States in International Politics'. *International Organization* 23: 296.

Kerr, Benjamin, Peter Godfrey-Smith and Marcus W. Feldman. 2004. 'What Is Altruism?' *Trends in Ecology & Evolution* 19 (3): 135–40.

Kershner, Seth, and Scott Harding. 2019. 'Militarism Goes to School'. *Critical Military Studies* 5 (3): 191–4.

Khan, Sharnaz. 2001. 'Between Here and There: Feminist Solidarity and Afghan Women'. *Genders* (Spring): 33.

Khan, Sharnaz. 2008. 'Afghan Women: The Limits of Colonial Rescue'. In *Feminism and War: Confronting US Imperialism*, edited by Robin L. Riley, Chandra T. Mohanty, and Minnie B. Pratt, 161–78. New York: Zed Books.

Kitchen, Veronica. 2002. 'From Rhetoric to Reality: Canada, the United States, and the Ottawa Process to Ban Landmines'. *International Journal* 57 (1): 37–55.

Klem, Bart. 2018. 'The Problem of Peace and the Meaning of Post-war'. *Conflict, Security & Development* 18 (3): 233–55.

Klep, Chris, and Donna Winslow. 1999. 'Learning Lessons the Hard Way – Somalia and Srebrenica Compared'. *Small Wars & Insurgencies* 10 (2): 93–137.

Knopf, Kerstin. 2007. 'Terra-Terror-Terrorism?: Land, Colonization and Protest in Canadian Aboriginal Literature'. *The Canadian Journal of Native Studies* 2: 293–329.

Ko, Sangtu. 2012. 'Korea's Middle Power Activism and Peacekeeping'. *Asia Europe Journal* 10: 287–329.

Korning, Paul. 1988. 'Report on Defence: It's the Boys in Borrowed Blue Berets'. *The Globe and Mail*, 10 October, B13.

Krishna, Sankaran. 2001. 'Race, Amnesia, and the Education of International Relations'. *Alternatives: Global, Local, Political* 26 (4): 401–24.

Krishnasamy, K. 2001. 'Recognition for Third World Peacekeepers: Indian and Pakistan'. *International Peacekeeping* 8 (4): 56–76.

Krosnell, Annica, and Erika Svedberg (eds) 2011. *Making Gender, Making War: Violence, Military and Peacekeeping Practices*. London: Routledge.

Krystalli, Roxani C. 2021. 'Narrating Victimhood: Dilemmas and (In)dignities'. *International Feminist Journal of Politics* 23 (1): 125–46.

Laghi, Brian, and Alan Freeman. 2007. 'Canadians Cool to Extending Mission'. *The Globe and Mail*, 19 July, A13.

Lake, Marilyn, Joy Damousi, Mark McKenna and Henry Reynolds. 2010. *What's Wrong with ANZAC?: The Militarisation of Australian History*. Sydney: University of New South Wales Press.

Lambertus, Sandra. 2016. *Wartime Images, Peacetime Wounds: The Media and the Gustafsen Lake Standoff*. Toronto: University of Toronto Press. E-publication.

Lambie, Chris. 2000. 'N.S. Natives Get Combat Training for Lobster Wars: 'Tire of being the victims''. *National Post*, 21 December, A02.

Lawrence, Bonita. 2003. 'Gender, Race, and the Regulation of Native Identity in Canada and the United States: An Overview'. *Hypatia* 18 (2).

Lederer, Edith M. 2020. 'Fraud and Sex Abuse Probes in UN Peace Operations Increase'. *ABCNews*, 21 March. Available at https://abcnews.go.com/US/wireStory/fraud-sex-abuse-probes-peace-operations-increase-69722819 (accessed 14 October 2022).

Lee, Sabine, and Susan Bartels. 2020. '"They Put a Few Coins in Your Hand to Drop a Baby in You": A Study of Peacekeeper-fathered Children in Haiti'. *International Peacekeeping* 27 (2): 177–209.

Leira, Halvard. 2013. '"Our Entire People are Natural Born Friends of Peace": The Norwegian Foreign Policy of Peace'. *Swiss Political Science Review* 19 (3): 338–56.

Levine, Daniel H. 2014. *The Morality of Peacekeeping*. Edinburgh: Edinburgh University Press.

Linden, Sidney B. 2007. *The Ipperwash Inquiry*. Available at https://wayback.archive-it.org/16312/20211208091140/https://www.attorneygeneral.jus.gov.on.ca/inquiries/ipperwash/report/index.html.

Lukacs, Martin. 2013. 'New Brunswick Fracking Protests Are the Frontline for a Democratic Fight'. *The Guardian*, 22 October.

Lutz, Catherine. 2002. 'Making War at Home in the United States: Militarization and the Current Crisis'. *American Anthropologist* 104 (3): 723–35.

Lyon, Peyton V., and Brian W. Tomlin. 1979. *Canada as an International Actor*. Toronto: Macmillan.

Mabee, Bryan. 2016. 'From "Liberal War" to "Liberal Militarism": United States Security Policy As the Promotion of Military Modernity'. *Critical Military Studies* 2 (3): 242–61.

McCormack, Killian, and Emily Gilbert. 2022. 'The Geopolitics of Militarism and Humanitarianism'. *Progress in Human Geography* 46 (1): 179–97. DOI: 10.1177/03091325211032267.

McCready, A. L. 2013. *Yellow Ribbons*. Winnipeg: Fernwood Publishing.

McCullough, Colin. 2016. *Creating Canada's Peacekeeping Past*. Vancouver, BC: UBC Press.

McFadden, Patricia. 2008. 'Interrogating Americana: An African Feminist Critique'. In *Feminism and War: Confronting US Imperialism*, edited by Robin L. Riley, Chandra T. Mohanty and Minnie B. Pratt, 56–67. New York: Zed Books.

Mac Ginty, Roger. 2014. 'Everyday Peace: Bottom-Up and Local Agency in Conflict-Affected Societies'. *Security Dialogue* 45 (6): 548–64. DOI: 10.1177/0967010614550899.

McKay, Ian, and Jamie Swift. 2012. *Warrior Nation: Rebranding Canada in an Age of Anxiety*. Toronto: Between the Lines Publishing.

MacKenzie, Megan. 2015. *Beyond the Band of Brothers: The US Military and the Myth that Women Can't Fight*. Cambridge: Cambridge University Press.

MacKenzie, Megan, and Alanna Foster. 2017. 'Masculinity Nostalgia: How War and Occupation Inspire a Yearning for Gender Order'. *Security Dialogue* 48 (3): 206–23.

MacKenzie, Megan, Eda Gunaydin and Umeya Chaudhuri. 2020. 'Illicit Military Behaviour as Exceptional and Inevitable: Media Coverage of Military Sexual Violence and the "Bad Apples" Paradox'. *International Studies Quarterly* 64 (1): 45–56.

MacKenzie, Megan, and Nicole Wegner 2021. *Feminist Solutions For Ending War*. London: Pluto Press.

MacLeish, Kenneth. 2013. *Making War at Fort Hood*. Princeton, NJ: Princeton University Press.

McPhedran, Taline. 2016. Majority Supports Peacekeeping Missions in Active Fighting Areas: Nanos Survey. *CTV News*, 13 October. Available at https://www.ctvnews.ca/politics/majority-supports-peacekeeping-missions-in-active-fighting-areas-nanos-survey-1.3114666 (accessed 14 October 2022).

McSorley, Kevin. 2016. 'Doing Military Fitness: Physical Culture, Civilian Leisure, and Militarism'. *Critical Military Studies* 2 (1-2): 103–19. DOI: 10.1080/23337486.2016.1148292.

Madsen, Chris. 2020. 'Green is the New Black: The Royal Canadian Mounted Police and Militarisation of Policing in Canada'. *Scandinavian Journal of Military Studies* 3 (1): 114–31.

Malito, Debora V. 2017. 'Neutral in Favour of Whom? The UN Intervention in Somalia and the Somaliland Peace Process'. *International Peacekeeping* 24 (2): 280–303.

Maloney, Sean. 2007. 'Why Keep the Myth Alive?' *Canadian Military Journal* (Spring): 100–2.

Manchanda, Nivi, and Chris Rossdale. 2021. 'Resisting Racial Militarism: War, Policing and the Black Panther Party'. *Security Dialogue* 52 (6): 473–92.

Martin, Pierre, and Michel Fortmann. 1995. 'Canadian Public Opinion and Peacekeeping in a Turbulent World'. *International Journal* (Spring): 370–400.

Masters, Cristina. 2005. 'Bodies of Technology: Cyborg Soldiers and Militarized Masculinities'. *International Feminist Journal of Politics* 7 (1): 112–32.

Mazurana, Dyan, Angela Raven-Roberts and Jane Parpart. 2005. *Gender, Conflict, and Peacekeeping*. Lanham, MD: Rowman & Littlefield.

Melakopides, Costas. 1998. *Pragmatic Idealism: Canadian Foreign Policy, 1945–1995*. Montreal and Kingston: McGill-Queen's University Press.

Middlemiss, Dan W., and Joel J. Sokolsky. 1983. *Canadian Defence: Decisions and Determinants*. San Diego, CA: Harcourt Brace.

Millar Katharine M., and Joana Tidy. 2017. 'Combat as a Moving Target: Masculinities, the Heroic Soldier Myth, and Normative Martial Violence'. *Critical Military Studies* 3 (2): 142–60.

Millar Katherine M. 2016. 'Mutually Implicated Myths: The Democratic Control of the Armed Forces and Militarism'. In *Myth and Narrative in International Politics*, edited by B. Bliesemann de Guevara. London: Palgrave Macmillan.

Millar, Katharine M. 2021. 'What Makes Violence Martial? Adopt A Sniper and Normative Imaginaries of Violence in the Contemporary United States'. *Security Dialogue* 52 (6): 493–511.

Miller, Benjamin. 2001. 'The Global Sources of Regional Transitions from War to Peace'. *Journal of Peace Research* 38 (3): 199–225.

Milliken, Jennifer. 1999. 'The Study of Discourse in International Relations: A Critique of Research and Methods'. *European Journal of International Relations* 5 (2): 225–54.

Molloy, Patricia. 1995. 'Subversive Strategies or Subverting Strategy? Toward a Feminist Pedagogy for Peace'. *Alternatives* 20 (2): 225–42.

Monnakgotla, K. 1996. 'From Ambivalence and Diversity to Stability in Southern Africa'. *New Partners in Peace: Towards a Southern African Peacekeeping Capacity, IDP Monograph Series,* 5, 7.

Montgomery, Adam. 2017. *Invisible Injured: Psychological Trauma in the Canadian Military from the First World War to Afghanistan.* Montreal: McGill-Queen's University Press.

Morgan, David H. J. 1994. 'Theater of War: Combat, the Military, and Masculinities'. In *Theorizing Masculinities,* edited by Harry Brod and Michael Kaufman, 165–82. London: Sage.

Morin, Brandi. 2021. '"No one is going to believe you": When the RCMP Abuses Indigenous Women and Girls'. *Al Jazeera,* 29 December. Available at https://www.aljazeera.com/features/longform/2021/12/29/no-one-will-believe-you-when-the-rcmp-abuses-indigenous-girls (accessed 14 October 2022).

Mueller, Harald. 1992. 'The Internalization of Principles, Norms and Rules by Governments: The Case of Security Regimes. In *Regime Theory and International Relations,* edited by Volker Rittberger. Oxford: Clarendon Press.

Mueller, John. 2007. *The Remnants of War.* Ithaca, NY: Cornell University Press.

Murray, R. W., and McCoy, J. 2010. 'From Middle Power to Peacebuilder: The Use of the Canadian Forces in Modern Canadian Foreign Policy'. *American Review of Canadian Studies* 40 (2): 171–88.

Mutimer, David. 2016. 'The Road to Afghanada: Militarization in Canadian Popular Culture during the War in Afghanistan'. *Critical Military Studies* 2 (3): 210–25.

Mutua, M. 2001. 'Savages, Victims, and Saviors: The Metaphor of Human Rights'. *Harvard International Law Journal* 42 (1): 201–45.

Narayan, Uma. 1995. 'Colonialism and Its Others: Considerations on Rights and Care Discourses'. *Hypatia* 10 (2): 133–40.

Nayak, Meghana. 2006. 'Orientalism and "Saving" US State Identity after 9/11'. *International Feminist Journal of Politics* 8 (1): 42–61.

Ndulo, Muna. 2009. 'The United Nations Responses to the Sexual Abuse and Exploitation of Women and Girls by Peacekeepers during Peacekeeping Missions'. *Berkeley Journal of International Law* 27 (1): 127–61.

Nettelbeck, Amanda, and Russell Smandych. 2010. 'Policing Indigenous Peoples on Two Colonial Frontiers: Australia's Mounted Police and Canada's North-West Mounted Police'. *Australian & New Zealand Journal of Criminology* 43 (2): 356–75.

Neumann, Iver B. 2011. 'Peace and Reconciliation Efforts and Systems-Maintaining Diplomacy'. *International Journal* (Summer) 66 (3): 563–79.

Nickerson, Michael. 2005. 'The Not-so-civil Servant and the "Scumbags" Who Hate Us'. *The Globe and Mail*, 20 July.

Niva, Steve. 1998. 'Tough and Tender: New World Order, Masculinity and the Gulf War'. In *The "Man Question" in International Relations*, edited by Marysia Zalewski and Jane Parpart, 109–28. Boulder, CO: Westview Press.

Nordstrom, Carolyn. 2004. *Shadows of War*. Berkeley: University of California Press.

Nossal, Kim Richard. 1997. *The Politics of Canadian Foreign Policy*, 3rd edition. Scarborough, ON: Prentice Hall.

Notar, Susan A. 2006. 'Peacekeepers as Perpetrators: Sexual Exploitation and Abuse of Women and Children in the Democratic Republic of the Congo'. *American University Journal of Gender, Social Policy & the Law* 14 (2): 413–30.

Off, Carol. 2000. *The Lion, the Fox and the Eagle: A Story of Generals and Justice in Yugoslavia and Rwanda*. Toronto, ON: Vintage.

Otto, Diane. 2020. 'Rethinking "Peace" in International Law and Politics From a Queer Feminist Perspective'. *Feminist Review* 126 (1): 19–38. DOI: 10.1177/0141778920948081.

Ozguc, Umut. 2011. 'Remaking Canadian Identity: A Critical Analysis of Canada's Human Security Discourse'. *Journal of Human Security* 7 (3): 37–59.

Palmater, Pamela. 2022. 'Breaches of Indigenous Human Rights Condemned by UN'. *The Lawyer's Daily*, 17 May. Available at https://www.thelawyersdaily.ca/articles/36369/breaches-of-indigenous-human-rights-condemned-by-un-pamela-palmater (accessed 14 October 2022).

Paris, Roland. 2002. 'International Peacebuilding and the "Mission Civilatrice"'. *Review of International Studies* 28 (4): 637–56.

Paris, Roland. 2010. 'Saving Liberal Peacebuilding'. *Review of International Studies* 36 (2): 337–65.

Parliament of Canada 1993. *Minutes of Proceedings and Evidence*. Standing Committee on National Defence and Veterans Affairs. 34th Parliament, 3rd Session. 10 April.

Parliament of Canada. 2005. *Canada's Military and the Legacy of Neglect: Our Disappearing Options for Defending the Nation Abroad and at Home*. Senate Committee on National Security and Defence. (September). Retrieved from http://www.parl.gc.ca.

Parliament of Canada. 2006. House of Commons Debate. 39th Parliament, 1st Session. 10 April.

Parliament of Canada. 2007. *Canadian Forces in Afghanistan. Report of the Standing Committee on National Defence*. House of Commons. Standing Committee on National Defence. 1st Session.

Parliament of Canada. 2008. *Independent Panel on Canada's Future Role in Afghanistan. Final Report*. Available at https://publications.gc.ca/collections/collection_2008/dfait-maeci/FR5-20-1-2008E.pdf.

Parmar, Sharanjeet. 2015. 'How Canada Can Repair Its International Reputation?' *Toronto Star*, 26 October.

Parpart, Jane, and Kevin Partridge. 2014. 'Soldiering On: Pushing Militarized Masculinities into New Territory'. In *The Sage Handbook of Feminist Theory*, edited by Mary Evans, Clare Hemmings, Marsha Henry, Hazel Johnstone, Sumi Madhok, Ania Plomien and Sadie Wearing, 550–65. London: Sage.

Partis-Jennings, Hannah. 2020. 'A Pint to Remember: The Pub as Community Militarism'. *Critical Military Studies* 8 (2): 119–38.

Patience, Allan. 2014. 'Imagining Middle Powers'. *Australian Journal of International Affairs* 68 (2): 210–22.

Pattern, Melanie. 2013. 'RCMP Arrest 40 at Shale Protest; Five Police Vehicles Set Ablaze in Clashes'. *National Post*, 18 October, A4.

Patterson, Kevin, and Jane Warren. 2008. *Outside the Wire: The War in Afghanistan in the Words of Its Participants*. Toronto: Vintage Canada.

Pelaez, A. 2007. 'Country Survey XX: Defence Spending and Peacekeeping in Uruguay'. *Defence & Peace Economics* 18 (3): 281–302.

Perkel, Colin. 2010. 'One Bomb, Many Lives: A Look Back At Last Year's Tragic Blast in Afghanistan'. *The Canadian Press*, 30 December.

Peterson, V. 2020. 'Family Matters in Racial Logics: Tracing Intimacies, Inequalities, and Ideologies'. *Review of International Studies* 46 (2): 177–96. DOI: 10.1017/S0260210519000433.

Poirier, Patricia. 1990. 'Quebec Sending Police to Reserve "Incidents" Likely, Mohawks Say'. 16 October, A6.

Potter, E. H. 2009. *Branding Canada: Projecting Canada's Soft Power through Public Diplomacy*. Montreal and Kingston: McGill-Queen's University Press.

Pratt, C. (ed.) 1990. *Middle Power Internationalism: The North–South Dimension*. Montreal and Kingston: McGill-Queen's University Press.

Preece, Jonathan Caskie. 2010. 'The Canadian Peacekeeping Narrative: Myth, Legend, and Canadian Foreign Policy Beyond Afghanistan'. SSRN policy paper.

Privy Council Office. 1991. *Citizens' Forum on Canada's Future: Report to the People and Government of Canada / Keith Spicer, chairman*. Available at https://publications.gc.ca/site/eng/9.699760/publication.html.

Pugh, Michael. 1996. 'Humanitarianism and Peacekeeping'. *Global Society: Journal of Interdisciplinary International Relations* 10 (3): 205–24.

Pugh, Michael. 2004. 'Peacekeeping and Critical Theory'. *International Peacekeeping.* 11 (1): 39–58.

Purich, Don. 1986. *Our Land: Native Rights in Canada.* Lorimer Press.

Rapaport, Anatol. 1992. *Peace: An Idea Whose Time Has Come.* Ann Arbor: University of Michigan Press.

Ravenhill, John. 1998. 'Cycles of Middle Power Activism: Constraint and Choice in Australian and Canadian Foreign Policies'. *Australian Journal of International Affairs* 52 (3): 309–27.

Razack, Sherene. 1996. 'The Perils of Story Telling for Refugee Women'. In *Development and Diaspora: Gender and the Refugee Experience,* edited by W. Giles, H. Moussa and P. V. Esterik. Dundas, ON: Artemis Enterprises.

Razack, Sherene. 2000. 'From the "Clean Snows of Petawawa": The Violence of Canadian Peacekeepers in Somalia'. *Cultural Anthropology* 15 (1): 127–63.

Razack, Sherene. 2004. *Dark Threats and White Knights: The Somalia Affair, Peacekeeping, and the New Imperialism.* Toronto: University of Toronto Press.

Razack, Sherene. 2007. 'Stealing the Pain of Others'. *The Review of Education, Pedagogy and Cultural Studies* 29 (4): 375–94.

Rech, M., D. Bos, K. N. Jenkings et al. 2015. 'Geography, Military Geography, and Critical Military Studies'. *Critical Military Studies* 1 (1): 47–60.

Reeves, Audrey. 2012. 'Feminist Knowledge and Emerging Governmentality in UN Peacekeeping'. *International Feminist Journal of Politics* 14 (3): 348–69.

Regan, Patrick. 2014. 'Bringing Peace Back In: Presidential Address to the Peace Science Society, 2013'. *Conflict Management and Peace Science* 31 (4): 345–56.

Regan, Paulette. 2011. *Unsettling the Settler Within: Indian Residential Schools, Truth Telling, and Reconciliation in Canada.* Vancouver: UBC Press.

Richardson, H. J. III. 1995. 'The Constitutive Fiction of Neutrality in UN Peacekeeping'. *Proc. African SICL* 63.

Richler, Noah. 2012. *What We Talk About When We Talk About War.* Toronto: Goose Lane Publishers.

Richmond, Oliver P. 2003. *Peace in International Relations.* London: Routledge.

Richmond, Oliver P. 2008. 'Reclaiming Peace in International Relations'. *Millennium: Journal of International Studies* 36 (3): 439–70.

Richmond, Oliver 2014. 'Jekyll or Hyde: What Is State building Creating? Evidence from the "Field"'. *Cambridge Review of International Affairs* 27 (1): 1–20.

Richmond, Oliver P. 2019. 'Peace and the Formation of Political Order'. *International Peacekeeping* 26 (1): 85–110.

Richter-Montpetit, Melanie. 2007. 'Empire, Desire and Violence: A Queer Transnational Feminist Reading of the Prisoner "Abuse" in Abu Ghraib and the Question of "Gender Equality"'. *International Feminist Journal of Politics* 9 (1): 38–59.

Rikhye, Indar Jit. 1984. *The Theory and Practice of Peacekeeping*. London: The International Peace Academy, C. Hurst & Co.

Roach, Kent. 2003. *September 11: Consequences for Canada*. Montreal, QC: McGill- Queens University Press.

Roehrig, Terence. 2013. 'South Korea, Foreign Aid, and UN Peacekeeping: Contributing to International Peace and Security as a Middle Power'. *Korea Observer* 44 (4): 623–45.

Rossdale Chris. 2019a. 'The Contemporary Politics of Anti-militarism'. In *The Routledge Handbook of Radical Politics*, edited by Uri Gordon and Ruth Kinna, 67–81. New York: Routledge.

Rossdale Chris. 2019b. *Resisting Militarism: Direct Action and the Politics of Subversion*. Edinburgh: Edinburgh University Press.

Royal Commission on Aboriginal Peoples (RCAP). 1996. 'Chapter 9: The Indian Act'. In *Report of the Royal Commission on Aboriginal Peoples: Looking Forward, Looking Back*, vol. 1, 235–308. Ottawa: the Royal Commission on Aboriginal Peoples.

Rubistein, Robert A. 2008. *Peacekeeping Under Fire: Culture and Intervention*. New York: Routledge.

Ruddick, Sara. 2003. *Maternal Thinking: Towards a Politics of Peace*. Boston, MA: Beacon Press.

Russet, Bruce, and John Oneal. 2001. *Triangulating Peace: Democracy, Interdependence, and International Organizations*. New York: W. W. Norton.

Sabaratnam, Meera. 2020. 'Is IR Theory White? Racialised Subject-Positioning in Three Canonical Texts'. *Millennium* 49 (1): 3–31. DOI: 10.1177/0305829820971687.

Said, Edward W. 1978. *Orientalism*. New York: Pantheon.

Sasson-Levy, Orna. 2003. 'Feminism and Military Gender Practices: Israeli Women Soldiers in "Masculine" Roles'. *Sociological Inquiry* 73 (3): 440–65.

Schellhaas, Constanze, and Annette Seegers. 2009. 'Peacebuilding: Imperialism's New Disguise?' *African Security Review* 18 (2): 1–15.

Schneider, Gerald, and Nils Petter Gleditsch. 2010. 'The Capitalist Peace: The Origins and Prospects of a Liberal Idea'. *International Interactions* 36 (2): 107–14. DOI: 10.1080/03050621003784689.

Schurman, Donald. 1990. 'Writing About War'. In *Writing About Canada: A Handbook for Modern Canadian History*, edited by John Schultz. Scarborough, ON: Prentice Hall.

Scott, David, 2013. 'Australia as a Middle Power: Ambiguities of Role and Identity'. *Seton Hall Journal of Diplomacy and International Relations* 14: 111.

Searle, John 1965. *Speech Acts*. Cambridge: Cambridge University Press.

See, Scott W. 2018. 'The Intellectual Construction of Canada's "Peaceable Kingdom" Ideal'. *Journal of Canadian Studies* 52 (2): 510–37.

Segal, David R. 1995. 'Five Phases of United Nations Peacekeeping: An Evolutionary Typology'. *Journal of Political & Military Sociology* 23 (1): 65–79.

Seyle, Connor. 2019. 'Operationalizing Positive Peace: Canadian Approaches to International Security Policy and Practice'. In *The Palgrave Handbook of Global Approaches to Peace*, edited by Aigul Kulnazarova and Vesselin Popovski, 193–213. Basingstoke: Palgrave Macmillan.

Shantz, Jeff. 2016. 'They Have Always Been Military: On So-called Militarized Policing in Canada'. *Journal of Social Justice* 6. Available at http://transformativestudies.org/wp-content/uploads/They-Have-Always-Been-Military.pdf (accessed 16 November 2022).

Shapiro, M. 1989. 'Textualizing Global Politics'. In *International/Intertextual Relations*, edited by J. Der Derian and M. Shapiro, 11–22. Lexington, MA: Lexington Books.

Shaw, Martin. 1991. *Post-military Society: Militarism, Demilitarization and War at the End of the Twentieth Century*. Cambridge: Polity Press.

Shear, Sarah B. 2019. 'The "Manifest Destiny" Narrative Routinely Ignores Voices of Indigenous Peoples in the Thanksgiving Story'. *The Conversation*, 28 November. Available at Available at http://www.milwaukeeindependent.com/syndicated/manifest-destiny-narrative-routinely-ignores-voices-indigenous-peoples-thanksgiving-story/ (accessed 14 October 2022).

Shepherd, Laura J. 2006. 'Veiled References: Constructions of Gender in the Bush Administration Discourse on the Attacks on Afghanistan Post-9/11'. *International Feminist Journal of Politics* 8 (1): 19–41.

Shepherd, Laura. 2008. *Gender, Violence and Security: Discourse as Practice*. London: Bloomsbury.

Shepherd, Laura. 2014. 'The Road to (and from) "Recovery": A Multidisciplinary Feminist Approach to Peacekeeping and Peacebuilding'. In *Rethinking Peacekeeping, Gender Equality, and Collective Security*, edited by Gina Heathcote and Dianne Otto. Basingstoke: Palgrave Macmillan.

Shepherd, Laura. 2018. 'Militarization'. In *Visual Global Politics*, edited by Roland Bleiker. London: Routledge.

Shepherd, Laura. (2022) 'White Feminism and the Governance of Violent Extremism'. *Critical Studies on Terrorism* 15 (3): 727–47.

Simpson, Audra. 2014. *Mohawk Interruptus: Political Life Across the Borders of Settler States*. Durham, NC: Duke University Press.

Simpson, Leanne Betasmosake. 2017. *As We Have Always Done: Indigenous Freedom through Radical Resistance*, 3rd edn. Minneapolis: University of Minnesota Press.

Singh, Schweta, and Diksha Poddar. 2021. 'Piecing-up Peace in Kashmir: Feminist Perspectives on Education for Peace'. In *Feminist Solutions for Ending War*, edited by Megan MacKenzie and Nicole Wegner. London: Pluto Press.

Sion, Liora. 2006. '"Too Sweet and Innocent for War"?: Dutch Peace-keepers and the Use of Violence'. *Armed Forces & Society* 32 (3): 454–74.

Sion, Liora. 2007. 'Reinterpreting Combat Masculinity: Dutch Peace-keeping in Bosnia and Kosovo'. *Sociologie* 3 (1): 95–110.

Sitkowski, Andrzej. 2007. *UN Peacekeeping: Myth and Reality*. Westport, CT: Praeger.

Sjoberg, Laura, and Sandra Via. 2010. *Gender, War, and Militarism: Feminist Perspectives*. Praeger.

Sjolander, Claire Turenne. 2007. 'Two Solitudes? Canadian Foreign Policy/Politique estrangere du Canada'. *Canadian Foreign Policy Journal* 14 (1): 101–8.

Sjolander, Claire Turrene. 2010. 'John W. Holmes and the Reconciliation of Immoderate Views'. *International Journal* (Spring): 321–29.

Skånland, Øystein Haga. 2010. '"Norway Is a Peace Nation": A Discourse Analytic Reading of the Norwegian Peace Engagement'. *Cooperation and Conflict* 45 (1): 34–54.

Smith, Rob. 2016. 'A Gustafsen Warrior in Exile: The Story of "OJ"'. *APTN News*, 8 April. Available at https://www.aptnnews.ca/investigates/a-gustafsen-warrior-in-exile-the-story-of-oj/ (accessed 14 October 2022).

Spivak, Gayatri Chakravorty. 1988. 'Can the Subaltern Speak? In *Marxism and the Interpretation of Culture*, edited by C. Nelson and L. Grossberg, 271–313. Urbana: University of Illinois Press.

Spivak, Gayatri C. 1994. 'Can the Subaltern Speak?' In *Colonial Discourse and Post-Colonial Theory: A Reader*, edited by Patrick Williams and Laura Chrisman. Hertfordshire: Harvester Wheatsheaf.

Stabile, Carol A., and Deepa Kumar. 2005. 'Unveiling Imperialism: Media, Gender and the War on Afghanistan'. *Media, Culture & Society* 27 (5): 765–82.

Stairs, Dennis. 1994. 'The Postwar Study of Canada's Foreign Policy'. *International Journal* 50: 12–19.

Stairs, Dennis. 2003. 'Myths, Morals, and Reality in Canadian Foreign Policy'. *International Journal* 58 (2): 239–56.

Standing Committee on National Defence. 2007. *Canadian Forces in Afghanistan: Report of the Standing Committee on National Defence.* Available at https://www.ourcommons.ca/Content/Committee/391/NDDN/Reports/RP3034719/nddnrp01/nddnrp01-e.pdf (accessed 16 November 2022).

Staples, Steven. 2006. 'Marching Orders: How Canada Abandoned Peacekeeping – and Why the UN Needs Us Now More Than Ever'. Report to the Council of Canadians. Ottawa, ON.

Statistics Canada. 2015. 'A Profile of the Canadian Forces'. 5 January.

Stavrianakis, Anna, and Jan Selby. 2012. 'Militarism and International Relations in the Twenty-first Century'. In *Militarism and International Relations: Political Economy, Security, Theory,* edited by Anna Stavrianakis and Jan Selby. London: Routledge.

Stinson, Kathy. 2010. *Highway of Heroes.* Fitzhenry & Whiteside.

Stompin' Tom Connors. 2020. 'Stompin' Tom Connors – Blue Berets (Official Music Video)'. YouTube. Available at https://www.youtube.com/watch?v=sYmQ-N2tLms (accessed 14 October 2022).

Storey, Kenton. 2022. 'The Pass System in Practice: Restricting Indigenous Mobility in the Canadian Northwest, 1885–1915'. *Ethnohistory* (1 April), 69 (2): 137–61. DOI: 10.1215/00141801-9522152.

Summerfield, Ian. 2018. 'The Canadian Peacekeeping Identity – Myth or Reality?" *Canadian Forces College* JCSP 44.

Tardy, Thierry. 2011. 'A Critique of Robust Peacekeeping in Contemporary Peace Operations'. *International Peacekeeping* 18 (2): 152–67.

Terry, Jennifer. 2009. 'Significant Injury: War, Medicine, and Empire in Claudia's Case'. *Women's Studies Quarterly* 37 (1/2): 200–25.

Tetley, D. 2007. 'Calgary's Hornburg Had "Warrior's Heart"'. *Calgary Herald,* 29 September, A3.

Thobani, Sunera. 2010. *Exalted Subjects: Studies in the Making of Race and Nation in Canada.* Toronto: University of Toronto Press.

Ticktin, Miriam. 2017. 'A World without Innocence'. *American Ethnologist* 44 (4): 577–90.

Toronto Star. 1988a. 'Canadian Troops Share Nobel Prize'. *Toronto Star,* 29 September, A1.

Toronto Star. 1988b. 'U.N. forces win Nobel Peace Prize, Canadians among soldiers cited for "hazardous" service'. *Toronto Star,* 30 September, A20.

Toronto Star. 1990. 'Kahnawake Tense as Police, Mounties Set to Replace Army'. *Toronto Star,* 16 October, A9.

Tronto, Joan. 2008. 'Is Peacekeeping Care Work?' In *Global Feminist Ethics,* edited by Rebecca Whisnant and Peggy DesAutels, 179–200. New York: Rowman & Littlefield.

Tsagourias, Nicholas. 2007. 'EU Peacekeeping Operations: Legal and Theoretical Issues'. In *European Security Law*, edited by Martin Trybus and Nigel D. White, 102–33. Oxford: Oxford University Press.

Tsagourias, Nicholas. 2014. 'Self-Defence, Protection of Humanitarian Values and the Doctrine of Impartiality and Neutrality in Enforcement Mandates'. *The Oxford Handbook of the Use of Force in International Law*, edited by Marc Weller, Alexia Solomou and Jake Rylatt. Oxford: Oxford University Press.

Truth and Reconciliation Commission. 2015. *Truth and Reconciliation Commission Final Report*. Available at http://www.trc.ca/index.html (accessed 14 October 2022).

Tuck, Even, and K. Wayne Yang. 2012. 'Decolonization Is Not a Metaphor'. *Decolonization: Indigeneity, Education & Society* 1 (91): 1–40.

Uguen-Csenge, Eva. 2019. '53% of Canadians Want Next Federal Government to Build Trans Mountain Pipeline Expansion, Poll Says'. *CBC News*, 13 September. Available at https://www.cbc.ca/news/canada/british-columbia/poll-trans-mountain-pipeline-support-angus-reid-1.5282430 (accessed 14 October 2022).

Ulery, E. 2005. 'The Uruguayan Armed Forces and the Challenge of 21st century Peacekeeping Operations'. Unpublished thesis, Naval Postgraduate College, Monterey, California.

Ungerer, Carl. 2007. 'The "Middle Power" Concept in Australian Foreign Policy'. *Australian Journal of Politics and History* 53 (4): 538–51.

UN DPKO/DFS. 2008. *United Nations Peacekeeping Operations. Principles and Guidelines*. New York.

United Nations. n.d. Charter of the United Nations. Available at https://www.un.org/en/about-us/un-charter (accessed 16 November 2022).

United Nations Peacekeeping, n.d.a. 'Mandates and the Legal Basis for Peacekeeping'. Available at https://peacekeeping.un.org/en/mandates-and-legal-basis-peacekeeping (accessed 16 November 2022).

United Nations Peacekeeping, n.d.b. 'Terminology'. Available at https://peacekeeping.un.org/en/terminology#:~:text=Peace%20enforcement,-Peace%20enforcement%20involves&text=It%20requires%20the%20explicit%20authorization,peace%20or%20act%20of%20aggression (accessed 16 November 2022).

United Nations Peacekeeping, n.d.c. Website. Available at https://peacekeeping.un.org/en (accessed 16 November 2022).

United Nations. 2000. Brahimi Report. Available at https://peacekeeping.un.org/en/brahimi-report-0 (accessed 16 November 2022).

United Nations Peacekeeping Operations. 2008. 'Principles and Guidelines'. Available at https://peacekeeping.un.org/sites/default/files/capstone_eng_0.pdf (accessed 14 October 2022).

Vaittinen, Tiina. 2019. 'Collective Discussion: Piecing-Up Feminist Peace Research'. *International Political Sociology* 13: 86–107.

Veterans Affairs Canada. 2014. 'Reconciliation: The Peacekeeping Monument'. Available at http://www.veterans.gc.ca (accessed 14 October 2022).

Veterans Affairs Canada. 2019. 'The Canadian Armed Forces in Afghanistan'. Veterans Affairs Canada, 14 February. Available at https://www.veterans. gc.ca/eng/remembrance/history/canadian-armed-forces/afghanistan (accessed 20 November 2020).

Wagner, Eric. 2006. 'The Peaceable Kingdom? The National Myth of Canadian Peacekeeping and the Cold War'. *Canadian Military Journal* (Winter): 45–54.

Waiser, Bill. 2011. 'The North-West Rebellion'. Unpublished manuscript. Available at https://www.d11.org/cms/lib/CO02201641/Centricity/ Domain/3295/north-west%20rebellion.pdf (accessed 16 November 2022).

Walker, R. B. J. 1993. *Inside/Outside: International Relations as Political Theory.* New York: Cambridge University Press.

Wallensteen, Peter. 2015. *Quality Peace: Peacebuilding, Victory and World Order.* Oxford: Oxford University Press.

Ware, V. 1992. *Beyond the Pale: White Women, Racism and History.* London: Verso.

Warrior Publications. 2014. 'Oka Crisis, 1990'. Unpublished manuscript. Available at https://warriorpublications.wordpress.com/2014/06/11/ oka-crisis-1990/ (accessed 16 November 2022).

Wattie, Chris. 2008. *Contact Charlie: The Canadian Army, The Taliban, and the Battle that Saved Afghanistan.* Key Porter Books.

Weber, Cynthia. 2014. *International Relations Theory: A critical introduction,* 4th edn. London: Routledge.

Wegner, Nicole. 2017. 'Discursive Battlefields: Support(ing) the Troops in Canada'. *International Journal* 72 (4): 444–62. DOI: 10.1177/ 0020702017741512.

Wegner, Nicole. 2020. 'Militarization in Canada: Myth-Breaking and Image-Making through Recruitment Campaigns'. *Critical Military Studies* 6 (1): 67–85. DOI: 10.1080/23337486.2018.1444727.

Wegner, Nicole. 2021a. 'Helpful Heroes and the Political Utility of Militarized Masculinities'. *International Feminist Journal of Politics* 23 (1): 5–26. DOI: 10.1080/14616742.2020.1855079.

Wegner, Nicole. 2021b. 'Ritual, Rhythms, and the Discomforting Endurance of Militarism: Affective Methodologies and Ethico-Political Challenges'. *Global Studies Quarterly* 1 (3).

Weinberg, Albert K. 1935. *Manifest Destiny: A Study of Nationalist Expansionism in American History*. Reprint Services Corp.

Weiner, R. O., and F. N. Aolain. 1996. 'Beyond the Laws of War: Peacekeeping in Search of a Legal Framework'. *Columbia Human Rights Law Review* (27): 293.

Wekker, Gloria. 2016. *White Innocence: Paradoxes of Colonialism and Race*. Durham, NC: Duke University Press.

Welland, Julia. 2015. 'Liberal Warriors and the Violent Colonial Logics of "Partnering and Advising"'. *International Feminist Journal of Politics* 17 (2): 289–307.

Welland, Julia. 2021. 'Feeling and Militarism at Ms Veteran America'. *International Feminist Journal of Politics* 23 (1): 58–79.

Wentges, Taylor. 1998. 'Force, Function and Phase: Three Dimensions of United Nations Peacekeeping'. *Peacekeeping & International Relations* 27 (2): 5.

Westendorf, Jasmine-Kim. 2020. *Violating Peace: Sex, Aid and Peacekeeping*. Ithaca, NY: Cornell University Press.

Whitworth, Sandra. 2004. *Men, Militarism, and UN Peacekeeping*. New York: Lynne Rienner.

Wibben, Annick, Catia Cecilia Confortini, Sanam Roohi, Sarai B. Aharoni, Leena Vastapuu and Tiina Vaittinen, 2019. 'Collective Discussion: Piecing-Up Feminist Peace Research'. *International Political Sociology* 13 (1): 86–107.

Wight, Martin. 1995. *Power Politics*. London: Continuum.

Woods, Allan. 2007. 'To Sell Canada on War, Try 'Hope' but Not 'Liberty'; Focus Groups Advised Harper to not Echo Bush'. *Toronto Star*, 17 February, A01.

Woodward, Rachel. 2000. 'Warrior Heroes and Little Green Men: Soldiers, Military Training, and the Construction of Rural Masculinities'. *Rural Sociology* 65 (4): 640– 57.

Woodward, Rachel, and Trish Winter. 2007. *Sexing the Soldier: The Politics of Gender and the Contemporary British Army*. London: Routledge.

Yanow, D. 1992. 'Silences in Public Policy Discourse: Organizational and Policy Myths'. *Journal of Public Administration Research and Theory* 2: 399–423.

York, Geoffrey, and Andre Picard. 1990. 'Skirmish Raises Tension at Oka: Mohawk Women Attack Soldiers'. *The Globe and Mail*, 5 September, A1.

Young, Marion Iris. 2003. 'The Logic of Masculinist Protection'. *Signs* 29 (1): 1–25.

Youngs, Gillian. 2006. 'Feminist International Relations in the Age of the War on Terror: Ideologies, Religions and Conflict'. *International Feminist Journal of Politics* 8 (1): 3–18.

Zine, Jasmin. 2006. 'Between Orientalism and Fundamentalism: Muslim Women and Feminist Engagement'. In *(En)gendering the War on Terror: War Stories and Camouflaged Politics*, edited by Krista Hunt and Kim Rygiel. Burlington, VT: Ashgate.

Zolo, Danilo. 2001. *Invoking Humanity: War, Law and Global Order*. London: Continuum.

INDEX

EU representative:
Easy Access System Europe
Mustamäe tee 50, 10621 Tallinn, Estonia
Gpsr.requests@easproject.com